HOW TO BREED DOGS

How To
Breed Dogs

by
LEON F. WHITNEY, D.V.M.

REVISED EDITION

Ninth Printing—1980

HOWELL BOOK HOUSE, INC.

230 Park Avenue, New York, N.Y. 10169

To the memory of

MR. AND MRS. O. B. GILMAN

Master breeders of one of the most popular breeds
—beloved by all who knew them—
this book is affectionately dedicated

Ch. Scioto Bluff Sinbad, Parti-Color Cocker Spaniel, sire of 100 show champions, the most recorded for any dog in American Kennel Club history.

Contents

On the cover:
The Great Danes handsomely picturing consistency of breeding are Champion Dinro Taboo Again, at left, and his son, Ch. Dinro Talisman, bred and owned by Rosemarie Robert, Dinro Dane Kennels, Carmel, N.Y.

Introduction

HOW TO BREED DOGS grew out of an earlier book called *The Basis of Breeding*, published in 1926. *The Basis of Breeding* covered the field of domestic animals. Dog breeders wanted a book explaining reproduction and heredity as these subjects apply only to dogs. To fill the need, *How to Breed Dogs* was written and published in 1937. It was revised in 1947. The present revision, the third, represents practically a new book.

Unfortunately, very little genetic work has been done with dogs since 1947, but many new findings in the field of reproduction have been published. In the former editions I published several studies of my own without waiting to publish them first in scientific magazines. I devoted entire chapters to these studies.

The most important study in canine genetics published between 1947 and 1971 was the excellent book by Dr. C. C. Little, *The Inheritance of Coat Color in Dogs*. With the help of a grant from the Rockefeller Foundation, Dr. Little and his associates sent out questionnaires via the American Kennel Club to breeders who reported the results of authentic matings. Previously Dr. Little had reported the results of a study he had made of Pointers. He is one of the world's top geneticists and we are privileged to have his great contribution to our knowledge of color inheritance in our dogs.

In this edition I have continued to use layman's language in explanations wherever possible.

Most of the work with dogs that I published in the past was financed by myself. Admittedly a large part of it dealt with the hunting breeds, because I was always greatly interested in hunting. The studies provided examples of dog and game animal psychology, and I could sell the puppies to help finance my work. Many of the observations were made on dogs used also in nutritional research. Over 12,000 puppies have been born in my kennels, mostly for nutritional research studies. One would have to be blind not to have made some useful observations.

My thanks to all who have assisted in the preparation of the book, to all who supplied pictures, to scientists whose work I have drawn from, to those who have helped me with my dogs, to my secretary, Mrs. Muriel Schonfeld, and to my wife, who patiently put up with my indulging a lifelong hobby—dogs.

Leon F. Whitney, D.V.M.

Orange, Conn.

Am. & Can. Ch. Favorite v. Marienlust (1945–1959), Smooth Dachshund, sire of 87 AKC champions.

Favorite's son, Ch. Falcon of Heying-Teckel, sire of 74 champions. As much as possible, breeders should select sires or dams from stock that has produced uniformly excellent dogs.

11

PART I

REPRODUCTION

Varied types of dogs, each the result of evolution under the guidance of man.

1

Life and the Cell

WHEN we study heredity we study certain properties of life. Life is in living matter which may be analyzed chemically. We call it protoplasm but we do not know what makes it live. The essential property of this matter is that it is able to reproduce itself.

The living matter is contained in units, which are called cells, and just what causes cells to have certain definite shapes is a secret contained within their innermost parts. Just what causes groups of cells to cling together and form the final product is also a secret contained within the cells themselves.

Most of the cells which compose a mature plant, or dog, or human being, are so small that they cannot be studied by the unassisted eye. Compared to the individual cells that compose the mature creature, the smallest bird or mammal is gigantic in size. So we must keep in mind when discussing heredity that we are dealing with units much smaller and a force much greater than we can rightly imagine. We are dealing with theories too.

Now theories are useful to us, especially when they produce results, but we must never forget that for the most part our ideas about breeding are still theories, although very well substantiated.

Every mature animal is the product of two cells which united and became one. This cell then became two, the two four, the four eight, and so on. The individual which we see is more than an individual; it is a composite of millions of descendants of the origin cell.

This makes heredity all the more wonderful to us when we consider the fact that the descendent cells are all so different from each other. There are some cells whose job is to manufacture other cells which, in turn, become the blood cells and carry nourishment about the body to supply the many cells of the body with food, and to take away their waste products. There are other cells which become the nervous system, some which become the brain. Brain cells end development and never increase after a certain point and thus account for memory, because if the cells had to be continually renewed the individual would not be able to remember. There are others which become muscle cells, others bone cells, and others disease destroyers. But the most important of all are those called germ cells, whose job it is to manufacture cells which pass along the heritage received from the parents, which, in turn, received theirs from their parents and so forth, back to the Adam cell of us all.

These cells which have the job of passing along the heritage are *the* important part of nature. The rest of the animal or plant is simply accessory to them. All the rest of the cells, with their many uses, are just tricks of nature to insure that the germ cells shall be passed along and not die out with the individual. He eats so that he is nourished, so he may grow, and so he may mate at the proper time and thus pass on the heritage. No matter what organism we consider, whether a single-celled animal, an apple tree, a dog or a man, we find that each is being constantly tested to see whether it is in harmony with its environment, and if it is, then it is allowed to increase up to a point where it can find a living and where the maximum number of its species may survive. After that, it is prevented from increasing by a constant struggle for existence, so that, forever, there is more and more perfect adaptation to the environment. The environment is the guide to the types of plants and animals which we know.

16

A typical cell in diagrammatic form.

What is a cell anyway? It appears under the microscope, as the illustration shows. This is a typical cell, but all cells do not look like this one. The business part is the globe within the center, which is called the nucleus. The body of the cell, or cytoplasm, is thought to have but little effect upon the heredity of the individual.

During a resting period, the contents of the nucleus appear to be composed of a network. During the period of division, they look very different. The network assembles into lines, or bodies. Some are bent and some are mere globes, while some are fairly straight. When a scientist wants to look at cells and study them, he has a difficult time unless he stains them. Without stain, they appear to be transparent bits of jelly. The parts are visible, but not as they are when stained. Some parts of the cell take up stain more readily than others, and the bodies in the nucleus absorb so much that they become very distinct. They are called, therefore, color bodies, or chromosomes.

Every complete cell has a pair of each chromosome, except that there is one which sometimes has no partner or an unequal partner, which, as we shall see, is the key to sex.

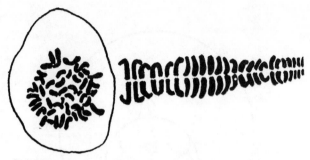

Left: How the chromosomes appear in the nucleus of a cell.
Right: The pairs arranged to show partnership. These
represent human chromosomes.

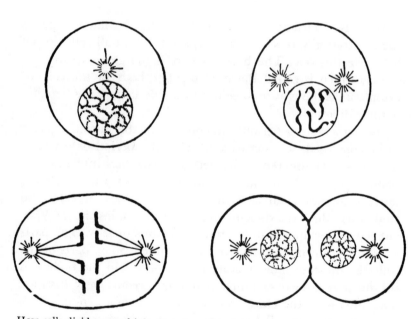

How cells divide to multiply. Note how the chromosomes each double and then
one of each pair goes into one of the daughter cells.

2

Reproduction

CELLS multiply by dividing. How can that be? One cell divides and becomes two; two divide and become four; four divide and become eight. That is the process. But there is vastly more to it than appears on the surface. A study of this question with a microscope reveals some astonishing and beautiful processes.

Suppose we go back to that original cell with which we started. Let us now examine the nucleus and see what goes on within it. It would be very easy for us to understand how a division could come about in a piece of jelly, and this individual piece of jelly become two, but that is only the external appearance. Let us forget about every other part of the cell except the nucleus and see what happens. The network of chromatin, as we have already seen, is slowly drawn into chromosomes, and that, of course, is when the cell is getting ready to divide. Each chromosome has a partner. As soon as the chromosomes have all become visible, then one notices that each chromosome is in the process of becoming two.

Take, for example, the fruit fly, which has four chromosomes. The four chromosomes become eight chromosomes, and one of

19

each of the new pairs goes into each of the two daughter cells that result from the division of the parent cell. Now this has a tremendous bearing on the subject of heredity and it is exceedingly important that we understand it. Always keep in mind the *pairs* of chromosomes and remember that each chromosome is constituted of many, many little units called genes.

Life in a Test Tube

In 1967, newspapers announced that life had been created in a test tube. In 1971, the new knowledge about the chemistry of the genes is taught in every high school and college biology course. High school graduates converse in the new terms, which to even the college graduate of ten years ago are a new language. Actually, with the manufacture of RNA, the simplest form of life had been created. But what has it to do with dogs? The same as it has with every form of life.

If the following seems too complicated, skip over it. It is possible to understand enough about the fundamental basis of breeding without this knowledge, just as it is possible to understand the mode of inheritance of coat color without knowing about the color granules in the hair of dogs. But knowing at least a little about the very fundamentals does heighten our interest in nature.

The amazing thing is that it is all done on a scale so minute that it is almost unimaginable that anything could be known about it. A chromosome with all its component genes must be magnified 1000 times to be readily visible, and even then the separate genes are only indistinctly visible. Yet the structure of these ultramicroscopic things is now known—one of the miracles of modern science. To have learned the facts, scientists of many nations—Japanese, American, English and others—shared their findings until the whole structure was explained.

Some of the work was done with viruses, much with bacteria, and the principles which apply to their inheritance apply also to dogs.

It has long been believed that heredity was based on chemical reactions, but now we know a good deal about how the genes

20

are organized chemically and what transpires in their internal mechanism. It is no longer just theory; the theory has been tested and found to conform to nature.

The process of the division of the chromosomes and the genes which compose them is now called *replication,* because each makes a replica of itself.

DNA and RNA

The genes consist of DNA (deoxyribonucleic acid, or ribonucleic acid without oxygen). The *ribo* stands for ribose sugar, which also is found in the essential vitamin riboflavin.

One must have some knowledge of chemistry to appreciate the following: The DNA molecule is built up from four different nucleotides, each of which is made up of sugar plus phosphate plus one of four different bases: *adenine, guanine, thymine* or *cytosine.* The molecule is based on two sugar phosphate strands wound around each other in a double helix. Imagine a small rubber ladder which you twist top and bottom in different directions. The up and down strands are held together by rungs, each made up of a pair of the bases.

Hydrogen bonds hold the base pairs together. The hydrogen connection is very weak, so the strands separate easily in duplicating the genes. It is handy to call the bases A, G, T, C. The rungs are not made up of pairs of AA, GG, etc., but AT, TA, GC and CG, held together, as we have seen, by hydrogen. As adenine is opposite thymine and only guanine opposite cytosine, the structure is internally complementary.

When replication occurs, the two strands separate and a sister strand is laid down alongside each strand. Since only A will pair with T and C with G, the new strand is exactly complementary to the old one and the two double helixes (twisted ladders) formed are identical. In this way, the "genetic information" coded by the sequences of the bases is preserved.

This structure of the genetic material is common to all living things, even bacteria. The only exceptions are some viruses, which have only one strand instead of two.

It is interesting to see how the information which the DNA

possesses is made available. This is done by a transcription process involving RNA synthesis on the DNA template. RNA is an abbreviation for ribonucleic acid. Besides differing in its sugar, RNA differs from DNA because it contains the base *uracil* instead of *cytosine*. An RNA messenger is formed which explains transcription. The messenger molecule is complementary to part of a DNA strand in the same way that sister DNA strands are complementary to each other. The difference is that the uracil in the RNA pairs with guanine in the DNA. Each strand of RNA forms the message which can move away from the DNA, out through the nuclear wall into the cytoplasm.

Once in the cell body rather than within the nucleus, this message controls the manufacture of protein in the form of its building blocks, amino acids.

In all living creatures which have cells with nucleic acid within them, the DNA generates a triplet code of nucleotides which is first "read" and then transcribed as the RNA is synthesized. The DNA remains within the nucleus. In the cytoplasm of the cell, in the proteins which were brought by the blood to the cell body, are the amino acids. The blood has obtained them from food. The RNA, working as both boss and laborer, makes protein from the amino acids.

When the messenger RNA with its code passes through the membrane of the nucleus, it becomes associated with clusters of ribosomes. Each RNA triplet codes for a specific soluble RNA, to which is attracted a specific amino acid. These amino acids attach themselves in sequence to the messenger RNA template on the polyribisome, becoming linked into a combination of two or more amino acids to form a peptide chain. When the peptide chain is released from the polyribosome, it finally assumes its characteristic form by associating with other chains.

We hear about "the translation of the language of heredity." This means that the code in which the composition of the proteins is recorded in the DNA was discovered. When the composition of the proteins is known, then the character of the organism is known. Scientists learned how "code words," as they called them, are put together in the DNA and, since words make sen-

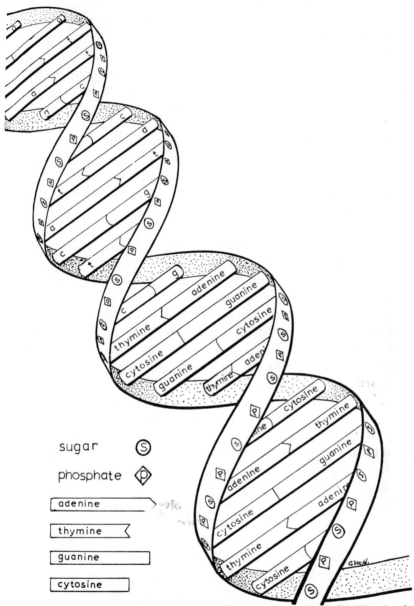

sugar   ⓢ

phosphate ◈

adenine	⟩
thymine	⟨
guanine	
cytosine	

The theoretical construction of a gene showing the double helix.—*Reprinted by permission of Coward-McCann, Inc. from LIFE'S KEY—DNA by Carleen Maley Hutchins. Copyright © 1961 by The National Foundation.*

tences, how the DNA sentences are "read." The sequences of the amino acids and their chemical structure are now known for many proteins.

DNA contains varying sequences of adenine, thymine, guanine and cytosine. The problem was this: How could the sequences of these bases specify the 20 different amino acids which cells use to build protein? The 20 amino acids can be put together in various combinations to make an immense variety, just as the 26 letters in our alphabet can be put together in such variety that we have huge dictionaries. The four bases are the code letters and there are 64 different words in which these letters can be combined, three at a time, yet all we need are 20. It was learned that some amino acids can be specified by more than one three-letter word.

How do we explain mutations—those sudden changes in heredity which we shall consider in Part II? What happens when they occur? Chemicals and X-rays have caused mutations. Some are changes in chromosomes, some in genes. Sometimes genes get left out or pieces of chromosomes become joined to other chromosomes of which they are not normally a constituent. Sometimes the genes are in a new order. One of the four bases may replace another, such as adenine replacing guanine, or one of the four bases may become lost.

Now that the immensely complicated riddle of gene chemistry is so well understood, we are on the threshold of even greater progress in genetics.

The end result of any quality or trait of the individual, which we are studying, is affected, probably, by all of the chromosomes working in unison. It was at one time believed that there was one gene for each characteristic of the body. For example, one for eye color, one for hair color, one for skin color, etc. Now we believe that it is the difference in one or more pairs that causes the difference in the end result. Actually, all of the genes are concerned in the production of every trait and the difference in one pair is what causes the end result. This may seem to you like splitting hairs, but actually it is not.

If these cells were formed after all the rest of the animal had been formed, as an afterthought, as it were, we would then be correct in referring to the germ plasm second and the animal first, for it assuredly would seem secondary. But since it was one of the very first matters to be attended to by the divisions of the original cell, we must think of it as coming before the animal.

The Continuity of the Germ Plasm

This germ plasm goes along creating one animal after another, each time combining with other germ plasm, so that every new generation consists of half from the germ plasm which created one parent and half from that which created the other. The dog is only the product of the germ plasm which he is carrying, as custodian. He had nothing to do with its creation. As we get further into the subject you will see that to be a good dog breeder you must constantly keep in mind this fact, and regard each dog as just the fruit of the germ plasm, the exemplification of what a certain strain of germ plasm is capable of creating. We may love the dog, but if we are dog breeders interested in doing the best we can for the breed, we must not rationalize, but must look the problem squarely in the face, realizing that it pays to learn this way of approach. From now on, dogs are just fulfillments and the germ plasm is the prophecy.

We may understand that all of the genes are concerned in each end result, but it is easier to understand some of the facts we need to learn if we will forget it for the moment and think of the genes as being the determiners or factors which control different traits in the body, so long as we know that each trait we are considering is determined by just one pair of genes.

In the following two chapters we are going to see what happens, from a more or less mechanical point of view, when dogs mate. We have seen how animals grow, namely by cell division, and have seen how each of the chromosomes first become two and have seen how one of each of these goes into a new cell, so that every cell has the proper number. This goes on and on until the mature animal is as large as he will become. Then certain of the cells stop growing. Others never stop—the nails and the hair, for example. Then too, think of the myriads of cells which have to be continually replacing others. Think of the cells which exist in the mammary glands, whose task it is to build up and then break down to furnish nutrition.

But the most important fact of all to remember is that during the early growth of the animal, at about the sixth division after the original cell divided, one pair of cells is put aside. These go their own way, dividing and increasing in a different way from the rest, and this group which stays together, constitutes the germ cells. They are set aside for the purpose of creating the animal's contribution to the next generation, and will be part of the gonads when the animal is grown. Gonads are testicles in males and ovaries in females.

Alleles and Chromosome Maps

Other terms to remember are *homozygote* and *heterozygote*. A pair of genes work together in producing a characteristic, such as coat color. Both genes may be the same or different. When they are the same we speak of them as being *homozygous,* when different as *heterozygous: homo*—the same; *hetero*—different. Zygote means "yoke." So two of the same genes yoked together are a homozygote; two different (one dominant, one recessive) are a heterozygote.

Yet another genetic term one must know is *locus.* This simply refers to the position on the pair of chromosomes we are considering. Another term is *allelomorph,* which means "another form of." The full term is seldom used, but the abbreviation is —*allele.* Sometimes genes have mutated and occupy the same loci. The different genes which occupy the same loci are called alleles. When more than two alleles have been found situated at a certain locus, they are called multiple alleles. When still more genes belong at the same locus they are called an *allelomorphic series.*

What puzzles fanciers when they see a series mentioned is how so many can be at a certain locus at one time. The point is, they can't. There is space for only one at a time. We say that some are *epistatic,* which we can think of as stronger. The weaker alleles in the series are *hypostatic.*

It may be difficult to understand how several sets of alleles belong at the same loci. When this is so, some get left out. Example: two kinds of albinism. In Pekingese dogs we sometimes find a kind called *cornaz*. It is the commonest kind found in wild animals. A white raccoon which has the cornaz type of albinism shows faint yellow rings on its tail. In dogs a slight yellowish cast is observable. A true albino is clear white with no yellowish cast. Both types pass for albinos. Both have pink eyes. Both colors are determined by a pair of genes. The genes for both belong at the same locus, yet they produce different colors.

When chromosomes replicate there are often instances where genes "cross over" from one to another. There are genes which seem to be inherited in blocks, or groups, indicating that they must lie closely together on a chromosome. In this case we find certain traits being inherited in groups. From such knowledge geneticists have been able to make maps of chromosomes showing accurately where genes for given characteristics lie on each.

As yet we know very little about where different genes are positioned on the many chromosomes of our dogs. But we do know about some loci and what genes lie there, even if we don't know on which chromosome the loci are found. We will consider this more fully in the chapter on coat color inheritance, for there is good evidence that a number of color-producing genes lie at the same loci.

3

The Male Organs
of Reproduction

SOME animals are not dual sexed, but the mammals are. The sexual organs, which are another device of nature to insure perpetuation of the species, are fairly well known to all observers of natural history. It will be worthwhile to mention only the essentials here, as they apply to dogs.

Taking the male organs first, we find the all-important testicles, the sanctum sanctorum of the male germ cells. If we could take a very thin section across the center of a testicle and single out one or two tubules we should find that they were constituted much as they are seen in the illustration. Each would be a mass of cells, of course, but most of the cells would be sex cells, which are descendants of the origin cell without all the differentiations which have occurred to the rest of the cells of the body. Throughout the testicle we would find cells in all the phases of the complicated process called cell division. These would be of no use in themselves as fertilizing agencies, because they are complete. Before they can fertilize a female cell they must become dispossessed of half of their constituent parts.

28

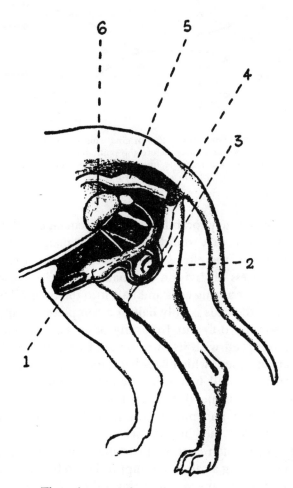

The male organs of reproduction in the dog:
1—penis in sheath
2—testicle
3—scrotum
4—anus
5—rectum
6—bladder

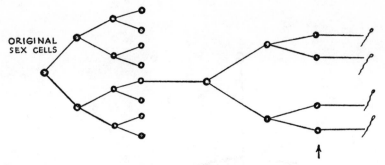

ORIGINAL
SEX CELLS

How sperm are descended from the original male sex cells. Several cell generations or divisions take place before the point marked by the arrow, when each cell contains half the requisite number of chromosomes, and from which sperm are directly formed.

Otherwise, when they combined with the female cell they would make another cell that would have twice as many parts as were needed. In order, therefore, to take care of this matter, they go through a process of division and half of the chromosomes go into one of the resulting cells and half into the other. Then each of these resulting cells is only half of a complete cell in a sense. Each is also very different from any other cell in that it is a free swimming cell with its own mode of propulsion. This is a tail-like arrangement which flaps back and forth and propels the body part of the cell forward. The cell is called a sperm cell (spermatozoon). Generally we use the word sperm to designate both the singular and plural meanings. In size each sperm is about 1/2500 of an inch in diameter.

These sperm congregate in little ducts, where they live for some time awaiting a call to attempt to be useful. The ducts, or storage receptacles, are long twisting tubes, one on the side of each testicle. It used to be thought that the sperm were stored with the semen, but now this belief is no longer held. Instead, they are stored in the epididymis, as the twisting tube is called.

When an emission occurs semen is discharged from the prostate gland. This creates a suction which draws the sperm quickly along the sperm tubes and mixes them with the semen. Likewise there is likely some propulsion due to rhythmical contractions of the vas.

Sperm cell, B, as compared with a red blood cell A.

It might appear that this would only insure a small number of sperm being drawn up the tubes. However, because of the extremely small size of the sperm, a very large number can fill a very small space. In the storage space they are packed like sardines in a box. One drop would contain a very great number. The tube that conveys them looks only about as large as a thick thread, but handles so many in a short time that it is almost incomprehensible to us who think in terms of much larger units. It has been variously estimated that at one emission a dog discharges many million sperm. Any one of these may be capable of uniting with a female cell and only one does unite to fertilize the egg. But at best, only an infinitesimal part of the whole number are utilized, the rest all being wasted.

As everybody knows, the testicles are located outside of the abdomen. There is a definite purpose in this. It is necessary that

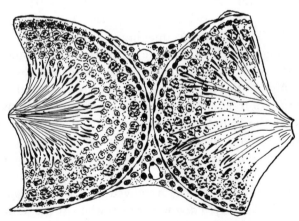

Cross section of parts of two tubules of testicle showing the original sex cells developing by stages until they become sperm.

the sperm be manufactured at a much cooler temperature than body heat. Animals whose testicles have been retained in the abdomen are always sterile so far as I know, although an operation which moves them down will sometimes induce a reduced fertility. If the testicles are reimplanted in the abdomen, then the animal becomes sterile again.

Sperm can stand more cold than heat. Many species have been studied. The first dog study was the author's in 1927, in which it was found that sperm examined did not live over two or three days in the female reproductive tract. Dead sperm could be found four days after mating. In 1938, Griffiths and Amorasol found live sperm in Greyhounds 72 and 96 hours after mating. This is longer than has been found for other species and makes the dog more or less unique in this respect.

Cryptorchidism

A dog with one testicle is called a monorchid; one with none is referred to as a cryptorchid, provided they were not removed surgically or accidentally. The term actually means "hidden testicle," so it is necessary to distinguish between the various kinds of cryptorchids. The testicles may be hidden in the abdomen, causing sterility; they may be somewhere along the passage through the layers of abdominal muscles, or may be in the position outside of the muscles and under the skin, so they may be felt readily. There are two openings in the muscles known as rings, through which the testicle descends. These rings do not seal tightly but keep open enough to allow for the various parts which compose the cord to pass without pressure, and for a certain amount of freedom for a muscle (cremaster) to move freely in drawing the testicle close to the body in cold weather and allowing it to relax in warm. This helps adjust the temperature of the testicles because they function best in a cool environment.

A dog with both testicles removed is a castrate and not a cryptorchid. Actually, a dog with one testicle in the scrotum and one hidden is a cryptorchid. A dog with one testicle is a monorchid.

Cryptorchids should be castrated, in my estimation, because the condition makes for unreliable dispositions, and because of the high percentage of such testicles which become affected with neoplasms (tumors and cancers). But often these dogs are sold by their owners for breeding purposes unknowingly. Then the question arises whether the owners should have known and whether they guaranteed the dog to be a breeder. It would seem, in fairness to every buyer, that any dog sold, for breeding or not, should be sound in this regard. By sound, I mean, possessing both testicles in the scrotum, not one in the abdomen and one in the scrotum. This of course brings up the question of when the testicles of a puppy descend. Male puppies are born with their testicles already descended, but are not easily palpated. In feeling very young puppies it will be noticed that the testicles appear to slide forward beside the penis, but when the pups are held upright the testicles move down into the proper position. This fluidity is doubtless an aid in protecting them because the puppies lie on their bellies, and with the testicles against the soft abdomen there is much less chance of damage.

Surgery for cryptorchids is often suggested, but those who suggest it often do not realize how difficult, or even impossble, it is in many cases. I have removed dozens of testicles from the abdomens of dogs and have been surprised to find that the testicles are often attached to tissue in the position of an ovary, had the dog been a bitch. To cut this loose, to stretch the fine blood supply without breaking it, and to bring it outside of the abdomen, enclosed in the peritoneum, is a delicate job often impossible to attain. Moving a testicle down to the scrotum after it has come through the abdominal rings is much more easily accomplished.

This raises a further question: is it worthwhile to move a testicle down into the scrotum in order to prevent cancer and to make the dog more likely to be fertile? Is it not better to remove it altogether? It would seem better to remove it. One testicle is ample both for fertility, if that is desirable, in view of the fact that cryptorchidism runs so strongly in families (see chap. 6 Part III), and for maintenance of male characteristics. Moving it down for show purposes is dishonest; removing it would label the dog as he truly is, and be less expensive and much easier on the dog. That he should have hidden testicles removed is hardly open to question.

Kraus tried to learn the number of cryptorchid dogs born in the dog population and found that the number was somewhere between .05 percent and .10 percent. The right testicle, he says, is the one most often hidden. He also noted a distinct tendency toward malignancy in cryptorchids.

That the testicle exerts a great influence on the behavior and youthfulness of a dog can hardly be doubted. But doubters will be interested in the work of V. R. Phadke, who grafted sections of testicles from a young dog into a sterile Great Dane and rejuvenated him. There was no attempt to render the recipient fertile, nor does the paper state how long the rejuvenation remained. In most such transplants the effect lasts but a few months or years at best.

Studies on the inheritance of cryptorchidism are difficult because the bitch has no testicles. It is necessary to find bitches which have produced cryptorchids when bred to normal dogs and to breed these bitches to cryptorchids. That many bitches produce cryptorchid pups when bred to normal dogs is well known to every dog breeder with wide experience.

Some breeds are ridden with this defect. It has been suggested that short-headed breeds are most afflicted. Hätt in Germany found that in 57 litters of Boxers, 23 percent of the 168 males were cryptorchids.

Cryptorchidism definitely does not follow single gene Mendelian inheritance. If this were so, where it is found in a litter, 50 percent of the puppies would be expected to show it. In many litters only one puppy does.

Another reason why this problem is difficult to study is that many very young cryptorchids are injected with hormone to cause testicles to descend. And another: the surgical implantation of glass testicles in the scrotum of show dogs. If the number which I have been asked to do (and of course refused) is any indication, there must be a good many cryptorchids which appear normal.

34

4

The Female Organs
of Reproduction

IN THE female, the cells within the ovaries are the essential
part. They, too, increase by division and growth. They do not
become free swimming cells, but are more or less passive. No
one knows how passive the ripened ova really are, what part
they play in the selection of sperm, or whether there is any
choice. These cells are produced in a different way. They do
not become two daughter cells, each having half of the chromosomes, as the male sex cells do, but go through several
divisions, finally ridding themselves of their surplus chromosomes by excreting them in a little body called the polar cell.
Thus, the chromosome number is maintained at half when the
ova are ready for fertilization. The last half are cast off just at
the time fertilization occurs.

The ovaries ripen a great many ova. Each is contained within
a little sac or follicle growing toward the surface of the ovary.
The process continues as a sort of race until one has reached the
surface, and then the sac bursts. In the bitch the ovum is discharged into the capsule surrounding the ovary. There it is fertilized by one of the many sperm which will be waiting, if the

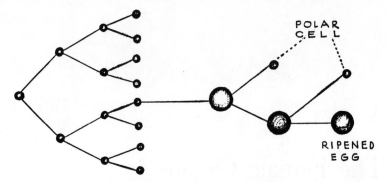

POLAR CELL

RIPENED EGG

How dog cells (ova) are descended from the original female sex cells. Note the way in which half the chromosomes are discarded in polar cells, so the ripened egg will not have more than the male sperm.

bitch has been mated. If not, the ovum may have to wait, and if it does, it is believed that it may move down the tube. The tube moves in a zigzag path around the outside of the capsule and finally terminates at the upper end of the horn of the uterus. There are two ovaries and hence two tubes, each of which go into one horn of the uterus.

But let us see what happens to the ovary during this process of ripening the ova. Around each ovum, there is a little drop of fluid which was manufactured by the ovary. This contains a hormone which we call the follicular hormone, because it was manufactured in the follicle. It is the hormone or chemical which is directly connected with the physiologic activities of the bitch which indicates a readiness to mate. As soon as a follicle has burst and emitted the ovum, then that follicle begins to fill up with a mass of cells which grow with very great rapidity. They form little bodies which are called luteal bodies (or *corpora lutea,* pl.; *corpus luteum,* sing.). These newly formed bodies also secrete a hormone, and it is this hormone which puts an end to the mating cycle. When a sufficient amount has been secreted the bitch is no longer willing to mate.

The whole mating period in the bitch transpires within the space of so few days that it is easily seen that these hormones are exceedingly potent and exert a great effect upon the behavior of the animal.

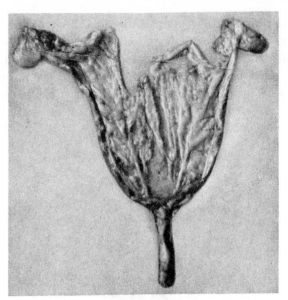

The reproductive system of a bitch. Note the sacs surrounding the ovaries at the upper ends of the horns of the uterus. This was removed from a bitch pregnant two weeks, hence the congestion of the horns.

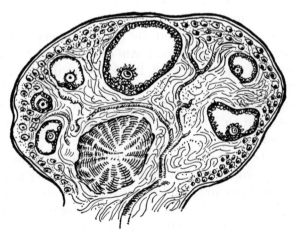

Cross section of an ovary showing follicles.

37

So much for a brief review of the physiology of reproduction insofar as it concerns the development and discharge of the all-important sex cells. Now let us look at the cells themselves to discover what happens during the process of fertilization, because it has a bearing on a knowledge of heredity and sex.

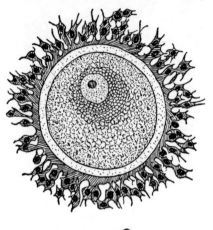

Sperm cell (*below*) as compared with
a ripened egg cell or ovum.

When we say fertilization, we mean the uniting of the sperm and ovum. The word has several meanings based upon inaccurate observation. The Babylonians saw that sprinkling pollen from a male date palm upon the female flowers increased the yield. They also saw that enrichment of the soil with certain substances also increased the yield. But while we use the same word to describe two different operations, we understand the difference. Some people think of the process of fertilization as the mating act, but that is very different from the intricate process which transpires when sperm and ova unite.

In comparison, the sperm is very much smaller than the ovum. Around any ovum probably hundreds of sperm are required for one to be able to enter. Students of sex speak about the "sperm swarm." It is probable that the sperm secrete enzymes which weaken the ovum's cell wall and permit the entrance of at least one sperm. Male dogs whose semen has a scarcity of sperm

38

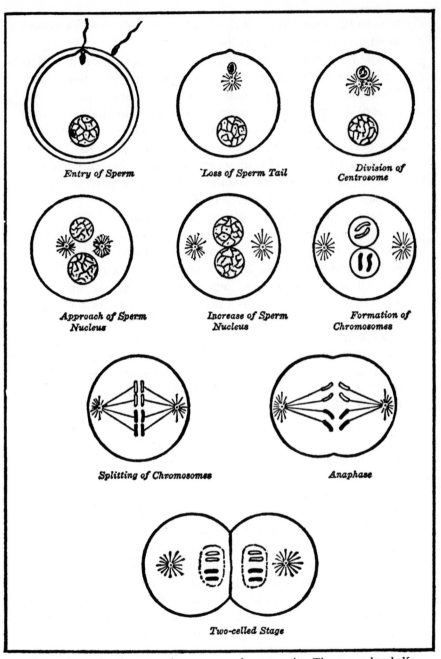

Entry of Sperm

Loss of Sperm Tail

Division of Centrosome

Approach of Sperm Nucleus

Increase of Sperm Nucleus

Formation of Chromosomes

Splitting of Chromosomes

Anaphase

Two-celled Stage

Here we see what happens when sperm and ovum unite. The sperm has half the requisite number of chromosomes, but the ovum exudes half of its chromosomes before the remaining half combine with those of the sperm. In this way some characteristics are lost forever to the germ plasm. (*From Walter.*)

seem to be as infertile as if they had none at all. It takes a good sperm swarm to insure fertility.

When a sperm has gained entrance, the ovum's cell wall is made thicker and impervious to the entrance of other sperm. Then the ovum casts off half of its chromosomes, and the nucleus of the sperm begins to grow from the nourishment it finds in the body of the ovum. When it has grown to a size equal to that of the nucleus of the ovum the two join. Each has half the requisite number of chromosomes, and thus when the two have come together each chromosome finds its right partner and we can say that a new life has been created.

Here in this tiny speck of protoplasm are all the architectural plans for the mature animal. Here *is* an animal. It needs food and a place of protection in which to develop. But aside from what it gets from food, it does not receive from its mother— its incubator—any nervous impressions, any actual blood, any more than it does after it is a suckling. The intermediate agent between the pup and its mother is the *placenta*. The mother's blood runs through it and manufactures nourishment just as the mammary glands do for it after birth. The placenta is a foetal mammary gland, although I have never heard it referred to as that. Now you would not say that the pup could receive nervous influences from the bitch after birth and neither should we say it can before.

Effect of Poisons

It can receive effects of malnutrition such as iodine deficiency, which causes it to be a cretin, or receive poisons which cause it to be stunted. What all the poisons are we do not yet know, but among natural things it is reasonable to think that evolution has created resistance to anything that might affect the fetus. Lead, alcohol, nicotine and other chemicals taken in large enough doses certainly affect animals and their germ plasm. But in the case of alcohol, it was found that animals have become immune to any ordinary doses. Experiments to produce effects from it were negative when the alcohol was fed through the stomach. You can give enough to almost kill an animal and still it won't affect his germ plasm appreciably. But by administering it through the lungs, you can cause some effect. Lead has caused dire results in humans. Radium and X-rays have produced effects when used upon a fetus and in one study they were found to have been the cause of shrunken brain cases in human infants. But what influences are there in dogs at all comparable with these? Is artificial diet a cause which might influence the germ plasm? Is high protein feeding a cause? Well, we have no evidence to show that the germ plasm has been affected adversely by high feeding. Unbalanced rations have often wrecked an animal, but so far as we know they have produced no effect upon its germ plasm. Nature has seen to it that this "arc of the covenant" is isolated from external influences, is kept sacredly protected, for it is actually the most important part of the animal.

For years there was disagreement on the number of chromosomes in dog cells. Malone said 22, Nogouchi said 40, Minouchi said 78, Painter 52. Little accepts 78 as the number.

Anton Schoterer made some very interesting observations along this line. By examining the ovaries of many bitches at different age periods, he found that, among the breeds studied, at birth the ovaries contained about 700,000 follicles. By the time the bitch reached puberty (the onset of the first mating cycle) the number was reduced to half, or about 355,000. At the age of five years there were only 33,840; at ten years only 518.

From this one might suspect that the ovaries just played out, but there are others who hold the belief that they are immortal, and that, if they could be transplanted from one custodian to another, they might go on reproducing almost indefinitely.

The author has attempted to learn the answer to this and related questions. He has successfully transplanted ovaries from twelve aged bitches into twelve young ones. Two produced puppies but most rejected the ovaries. Several were spayed to study the effects of the youthful body on the old ovaries. It was found that instead of continuing their slow-degeneration, they had become rejuvenated. Great numbers of active follicles can be seen. The ovaries have every appearance of those of young animals.

41

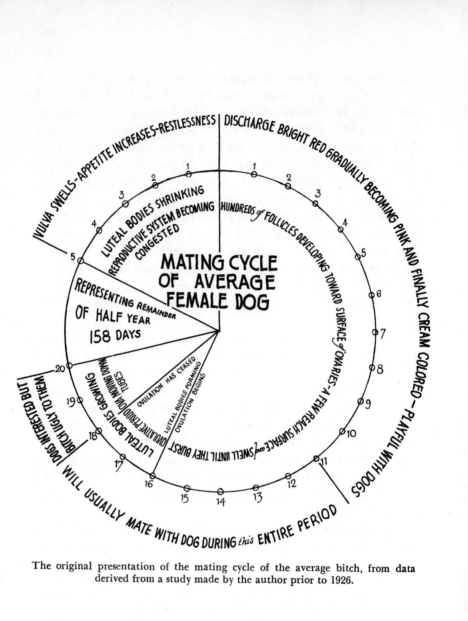

The original presentation of the mating cycle of the average bitch, from data derived from a study made by the author prior to 1926.

5

The Mating Cycle

W E HAVE considered the male and female reproductive organs and we have seen what might be termed the mechanics of their functioning. Now it is time to consider the female sex cycle from its beginning to its ending. It must be understood at the very start that this cycle is exceedingly variable depending upon certain factors such as age, the time of the year, and possibly upon the food.

It has been the author's experience, based upon much data, that summertime tends to shorten the mating cycle, especially in its early stages. However, we shall consider the mating cycle as being the average length of duration, which is, by outward appearances about 19 to 20 days. It is represented in the diagram. This way of representing the mating cycle is original with the author and has now been used to apply to many species by other students.

The whole cycle is divided naturally into four stages. These are as follows:

1. A stage which we may designate as the preparatory stage. The bitch appears to attract the dogs, or at least those dogs

43

which approach her are not repelled. The vulva begins to swell from congestion of blood, and generally the bitch is inclined to urinate more frequently.

Inside, the same congestion is going on all through the reproductive tract. There is a thickening of the horns of the uterus and of the vagina, and in the uterus the luteal bodies have gone from the ovaries.

2. The second stage begins with the first showing of blood or of the bloody discharge from the vulva. In the case of some dogs this is very profuse and in others it is scarcely noticeable. Occasionally no evidence of blood whatever will be found. The dogs will still be interested in the bitch but she will not be willing to mate with them. Many bitches will be in a very frolicsome and playful mood with the dogs all during this period, which ends naturally when the bitch is first willing to accept the dog. During the first part of this period the vagina is also exceedingly tender and even if the dog's penis enters slightly the bitch will usually recoil from the sensitivity. The bitch continues to urinate frequently.

Inside, the congestion has reached a high peak. In the ovaries the ova are developing within the follicles. If one looks at a vaginal smear of the mucous taken during this period, one sees mostly red blood cells, and the outer layer of cells from the uterine wall are shed and appear to be long and narrow much like muscle cells. As the period progresses, the shapes of the cells which are seen appear more square or diamond shaped with sharp corners. The total duration of the period is generally about ten days, but this is subject to the greatest variability. Among my records there are many cases of bitches which were willing to accept the dog after only four and five days from the first signs of bleeding. These were not bitches which appeared swollen in the vulva for a long time either. One foxhound never was swollen for more than three days before she began to bleed and then would accept the dog five days after that. I am not at all sure that my previous statement is true, that the average duration of the pre-acceptance period is ten days. I am not at all sure that the average bitch first accepts the dog at the eleventh day. I am sure that there are a great many which do so, and know that it is the common consensus of opinion among breeders that such is the case. But I am today more inclined to believe that the *average* time before a bitch will accept a dog after she begins to bleed is seven days.

When I made the study of these phenomena many years ago I said that the duration was ten to eleven days, and it certainly was in the case of the bitches which I used in the study. But when I consider all of the old bitches and assemble the records of hundreds of meticulously observed cycles, I think the estimate of eleven days will have to be reduced by three at least. It may well be that there are types of bitches which can be classed according to longer or shorter cycles.

3. The acceptance period follows the first two. At this time the bitch will mate with the dog. Sometimes he will have to tease for hours but she will finally give in. The sensitivity may or may not have gone from the vagina. Some bitches will be willing to stand and let the dog attempt to copulate but as soon as the penis touches the lining of the vagina, they will jump away as though in pain. It is difficult to say just when the first day of the acceptance period is. Shall we call it the day when she shows by her actions that she is willing to stand? I have called it the first day she is willing to stand. This is generally several days before the congestion has left the vagina. But not all bitches will allow the dog to copulate completely until about two or three days before the congestion has started to leave the vulva, or the external part of the reproductive tract, the part that is visible. Some of them will allow it four or five days before that time.

I am accumulating data in various ways and all of this points quite conclusively to the fact that the time when the congestion or firmness leaves the vulva, and starts to become flabby, synchronizes exactly with the time of ovulation. In fact, it may be that the development of the luteal hormone, which puts a brake on further ovulation and accounts for certain changes in the reproductive tract, is responsible for the changed vulva. But the time when congestion starts to leave the vulva is usually not coincident with the first day of acceptance in bitches, but rather several days later. When mating takes place on the first day of the acceptance period, it is the exception when a bitch conceives. The illustration on page 219 shows one of the puppies from a litter of ten, all of which were uncommonly alike. These puppies were from a purebred Pointer bitch. She was bred on the afternoon of the first day she would accept a dog, to a large Bloodhound, black-and-tan in color. The solid color is dominant over the white, and if the pups had been by this sire, they would have been solid colored. But they were not, despite the fact that he was a proved sire. The next day that the bitch would stand she was mated late in the evening to the big black, tan and white hound shown with her. All of her puppies were black and white. If ovulation took place early in the acceptance period, and the sperm lived a day in the reproductive tract of the bitch, surely some of the pups would have been sired by the Bloodhound. But none were. She was mated every other day to the tri-colored hound and he was the father of all the progeny.

As a next step in testing this theory I mated a fine English Foxhound bitch to a Bloodhound, the second day she would stand naturally. On the third day I mated her to the same black, white and tan hound mentioned above. She also produced ten puppies, all by the tri-colored dog, and none by the solid colored dog. This adds further evidence to the theory that ovulation takes place late in the acceptance period and that early breeding, more often than not, results in failure.

Cases of mixed paternity are numerous in dogs. Not a little of this is because copulation took place just before ovulation and the sperm lived a short time, but in the interim, the bitch was bred to another dog and the sperm of the two dogs mixed and both became fathers of the litter. Sometimes more than two dogs are fathers of the same litter.

When the dog is connected with the bitch he continues to force semen along the horns of the uterus and even up through the Fallopian tubes. I have shot a bitch the moment she and the dog separated, made an incision and tied the horns of the uterus at intervals, and found the semen already around the ovaries. This was just twenty minutes after copulation began. Probably as much as twenty centimeters of semen is discharged from a good sized dog during one mating. One investigator studied this and found this large quantity. It would be less in smaller dogs. But we must remember that the reproductive tract could not hold such an amount and therefore much of it must of necessity be forced right through the Fallopian tubes into the capsule surrounding the ovaries and out of the opening in the side of the capsule directly into the peritoneum (abdominal cavity). It is sterile and probably passes into the blood of the bitch. When the pair separate there is always a considerable amount of semen which is flushed out with the withdrawal, but only a small part of what is actually discharged.

Now to understand what happens inside the bitch, and how and why she behaves as she does, it is necessary to know that the ovarian follicles with the ova in them are growing and after about four or five days these have swelled to such an extent that some of them burst. This, or any time after this that the bitch will naturally stand for the dog, is the ideal time to mate dogs for maximum sized litters.

Different investigators have set somewhat different days as the time of ovulation.

The author concluded in 1927 that there was variation but the day was about the 15th day of the ascertainable period. This was followed by Evans and Cole's two papers in 1927 in which they said ovulation transpired within a day of the first acceptance. In 1938, Griffiths and Amorosal studied six Greyhounds and found ovulation occurring from the first to the fourth day of the acceptance period. In 1940 I published a larger report on 73 complete mating cycles and found the sixth day of the acceptance period to show the greatest number of ovulations, but some ovulated on the first and two on the fourteenth. Besides these I published a list of dual matings—where the same bitch was bred to two dogs at different times of the same cycle. These data showed that ovulation in general was near the middle of the acceptance period. Experience and these data indicate that the most opportune day to mate dogs is after the 14th day, provided they have normal-length mating cycles.

Dr. Carl Hartman helped solve the problem. He moved a

Dr. George N. Papanicolaou, discoverer
of the new science of Exfoliative Cy-
tology, author of the "Pap Smear."

bitch's ovary out through the abdominal muscles to a position
just under the skin which he kept shaved. There he could feel
the ovary. Ovulation in that bitch occurred on the 14th day.

This acceptance period stops when the bitch resists all advances of males to mate. The division time comes sometimes
rather suddenly and it is caused by the growth in the ovaries of
very rapidly growing bodies, known as luteal bodies. These
are believed to secrete a hormone which terminates the desire for
mating. But this desire does not always end at the time of
ovulation. Sometimes, however, an experienced dog obtains an
odor from the bitch very soon after this which causes him to
refrain from attempting to mate.

The vaginal smear picture corresponds closely to the ovarian
cycle. Soon after ovulation occurs, one finds the smear flooded

with cells which help to prevent infection, leucocytes. There are usually fewer red blood cells present and the cells from the lining of the vagina are rounded at the ends, and more or less egg shaped. They come from deeper layers. I said "fewer red cells" advisedly. We often read that one of the ways to determine the proper time to breed a bitch is when the color discharge changes from red to straw color. In the case of some bitches this is a reliable method, but all too many bitches continue to bleed quite profusely as long as they will accept a dog to make it universally applicable.

4. The last period follows. The bitch will be pregnant if she has mated with a dog at the proper time, and other conditions are right. If not, the luteal bodies persist until the start of another cycle. Now the curious thing is that another cycle actually follows immediately upon the heels of the first, but only internally. There is a periodic change in the ovaries if the bitch is not pregnant or nursing puppies. But this change is not noticeable outwardly. Precisely what causes the cycle to come to full fruition we do not know. Experiments are under way to determine the cause. Glandular secretions exert a powerful effect. Light, possibly acting on the pituitary gland, which is very close to the optic nerve, has a great deal to do with the mating cycle. At least it would seem to be the predisposing cause for so many bitches coming in season at certain times of the year.

The Effect of Light

When we attempt to place the frequency of the mating cycle of individual bitches within the six-months cycle, we can come to false conclusions. The results of my own study on 1,000 bitches shows that the average is not six months but between seven and eight. There can be no doubt that the length of the day or night tends to swing bitches into what we may call the normal cycle with peaks at August and February. Many bitches, when kept indoors, have a less reliable cycle because they are not kept indoors all of the time. Their day length is made more or less uniform by turning on the electric light at night. But this does not entirely compensate for the fact that the natural light does not remain constant.

A friend of mine who breeds and races Whippets was charged with bringing 80 racing dogs from the vicinity of Philadelphia, to Cuba. It was specifically stated that 40 were to be bitches which had just finished their mating cycles. He rounded up the number and took them down. Within six weeks every single bitch had come in season. Surely, here we have one of the best possible illustrations of the effect of light. I took 11 Cocker Spaniels which had been in season over a wide span of time, and which had spent a large part of each day indoors, and just at the time when the days were longest, put them in runs in the open where the sun shone. From July 10th to August 12th, nine of them had come in season and been bred. The uniform light conditions and longer periods of light probably brought them in season irrespective of when their last periods had been.

Many studies have been made using ferrets, raccoons and other animals, mink and foxes for example, to determine what, if any, effect the numbers of hours of light, natural and artificial, had on their mating cycles and the priming of their fur. Bissonette was the pioneer in this important work. By hanging an ordinary 25-watt electric light bulb where its light would have to be seen by the animals, he found that he could accelerate the start of the mating cycle. In the case of raccoons, by giving them one hour of light in addition to the regular daylight each day for the first week, two for the second, three for the third, and four for the fourth, he could have them in heat naturally, and they would mate and ovulate and raise their young. Using many of the raccoons which the State of Connecticut was breeding to produce coons to liberate, he was able to force them to mate and raise young two months in advance of the ordinary breeding season. They were whelping their young when the others were just copulating.

I have already reported above what happened to Whippets which were moved southward. While I was studying at Auburn, Alabama, I was running my kennels at Orange, Connecticut. I had many bitches shipped to me, and it was most interesting

50

to note that they would come in season from one to two months in advance of the expected times. Bitches are often found which come in season four months following the last period. In going over my records, I find that I have seen it occur eight times, and in seven of the eight they came in season in August, when the days were noticeably getting shorter. The other came in in September.

Now it is highly interesting to see what the effects of light may be. The graph below shows that there is definitely a peak.

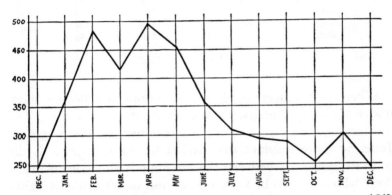

Seasonal variation of incidence of mating cycles in bitches. Curve covers 4,242 cycles as determined by birth registrations in American Kennel Club and Chase Publishing Company reportings. No peak is shown in Fall months because fewer bitches are bred then.

This curve was made up of two breeds. German Shepherd Dogs from all over the United States made up 2,242; American Foxhounds from the southern states constituted the remainder, 2,000. It is interesting to compare these two groups. We may take the German Shepherd Dogs as standard for the rank and file of dogs for the whole country. The southern Foxhounds show a very different kind of curve as will be seen. Climate or light are doing something to them. Now if we compare another approximate group, the Pekingese, we find much less monthly fluctuation. The figures were collected from the birthdays of litters and then, by figuring back two months, the birthdays were computed. The following table shows the birth months of these three groups:

Month	Pekingese	German Shepherds	Southern Foxhounds
Jan.	166	180	170
Feb.	180	230	249
Mar.	195	181	243
Apr.	173	228	262
May	161	216	240
June	178	192	165
July	163	167	144
Aug.	154	201	96
Sept.	133	171	117
Oct.	153	169	84
Nov.	182	163	134
Dec.	172	145	98
	2010	2242	2000

When these figures are plotted on graphs they become more understandable. The first six months are most interesting. The shortest day of the year comes in December and the longest in June. So if we consider that period we see how great is the contrast, especially between the Foxhounds and the Pekingese dogs, which tend to be kept indoors and under artificial lights, like human beings, so that the length of their days is much more uniform than those of the Foxhounds, which are usually kept out of doors the year round.

The last six-month period is of interest but not so significant because of the fact that fewer litters are wanted through the winter months, and because the American Foxhound breeders want their bitches to hunt with and thus skip the matings at that season.

From all these facts it would seem that bitches are subject to the length of the day as are other species. When the days get longer and when they get shorter are the times when most bitches come in season. Artificial light seems to help to bring them in, if the day can be materially lengthened in this way.

In 1943 Peterson and Mayne published a paper showing that the temperature at the time of conception has a marked influence on the proportion of sexes born. Overall the ratio is 100 males to 106 females. They showed that there were a greater proportion of males "as we deviate from normal temperatures, especially with temperatures above normal." In dogs, as we have seen, there are more males conceived in the colder months.

First Season Matings

"Should a bitch be bred during her first mating cycle?" This is a question which perturbs many new breeders and a few old. The answer is more or less tied up in what answer we make to another question, "Does mating a bitch before she is full grown stunt her growth?" If you asked that question of breeders of cattle, they most likely would say it does. But so far we have no evidence that it does with dogs. We have but little evidence that a bitch will come in season before she has grown to her natural size. Every dog breeder knows that although she may be full grown at this time she has not always filled out, and no one whom I know would deny that she would fill out after she had whelped her first litter.

Whenever the question comes up in a group discussion someone says, "Well, it wouldn't be right for a 13-year-old girl to have a baby." This is a case of anthropomorphizing the dog. There is no basis for comparison; the 13-year-old child is nowhere near grown when she first menstruates, and a bitch is almost always full grown when she first comes in heat.

Many a man who wanted little dogs has bred his bitches the first season hoping that this would prevent their growing, only to learn that they filled out and were not stunted as the owners had hoped for.

There seems to be no reason for not breeding a bitch the first time she is ready, and often many good reasons for doing so. Some breed enthusiasts believe that developing a litter of puppies tends to give their bitches better spring of rib, and since their standard calls for rib spring, they hold the practice of early breeding desirable. Others want puppies in the spring and not in the fall, so that if they allow the first season to go by it is the same as skipping a whole year.

I have made very many of these first-season matings and have

53

never seen a bitch harmed in any way by it. One noted Boston Terrier breeder contends that if Boston bitches are bred at their first season, it tends to make their pelvises more pliable and that they are thereafter better able to whelp litters without cesarean operations. I question this point, however, as it applies to the first few mating cycles. Very possibly if a bitch which had this difficulty in whelping were not bred until she was six or seven years old, she might then have greater difficulty because of greater rigidity of her pelvis. But again, do we know that in the case of the dog there is the same elasticity in the pelvis that there is in human beings, from which all such lessons seem to be too often drawn when actually there frequently are no grounds for comparison? Personally, I think there are grounds for doubt.

Most bitches will not come in season until they are quite well developed physically and in fair condition. Some will be too thin to recommend breeding, and some too fat, but it is possible, by feeding some fat during pregnancy and through lactation, to increase the weight of a bitch quite materially while at the same time permitting her to develop and nourish a litter. It is also very easy to reduce the weight of a fat bitch by giving her an adequate diet and an increasing amount of exercise. This will not injure her. Many are the Foxhound bitches which will run all night or all day on a fox track while they are carrying litters of pups. There is even one instance, seen and sworn to by many prominent people, in which a bitch joined in a chase and while she was running on the trail, stopped to whelp, and as soon as she had dropped a puppy, picked it up in her mouth and gave chase again, until stopped and taken back to her home to complete delivery. There is a lesson there for those who feel their bitches are delicate at that time, and should be coddled. Exercise will do them good if they are accustomed to it gradually. Violent exercise to which they are not accustomed will quite often mean that the bitch will lose her litter. But enough to gradually thin a fat bitch down is certainly not disadvantageous or harmful.

6

Pregnancy

WHEN the bitch has been bred the next question is, how can we tell when she is in whelp? This is not at all difficult and any dog breeder can learn to do it. For practical as well as scientific purposes it is often very much worthwhile to be able to determine whether a bitch is pregnant before she shows it by the distention of the abdomen. It is worthwhile for the veterinarian who is consulted and valuable to the dog breeder. It is almost a necessity in the case of certain studies of reproductive phenomena.

Almost anyone with experience can say five or six weeks after breeding whether or not a bitch is going to whelp, especially if she is going to have a large litter. But not everyone can tell at the third week, and few are able to tell until whelping time when a bitch is carrying only one or two puppies.

In the case of phantom pregnancies, so common in bitches, when the abdomen enlarges and the mammary glands increase in size, oftentimes the diagnosis is to the effect that the bitch is pregnant. The increased appetite causes the bitch to eat a great deal and very frequently the dog breeder is misled. On the contrary, many pregnancies which are thought to be phantom

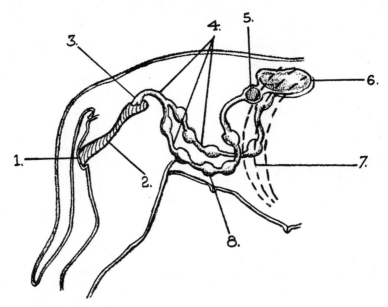

How the fetuses are carried in the bitch in the fourth to fifth week of gestation.
  1—Vulva
  2—Vagina
  3—Cervix
  4—Main body and horns of uterus
  5—Capsule surrounding ovary
  6—Kidney
  7—Ribs
  8—Lumps containing embryos easily palpable through abdominal walls

pregnancies are not so at all, but are genuine pregnancies which terminate in the resorption of the fetuses. Indeed, so common is this phenomenon that I have been able to determine that it may be the expected behavior of very old bitches. One bitch which lived to be almost 15 years old became pregnant at her last three matings and developed the puppies up to about 28 days after which time they were gradually resorbed. I have noted this in many very old bitches.

It was during the time when I was accumulating data for my paper, *The Mating Cycle of the Dog,* and following that time, that I learned how to diagnose pregnancy by palpation. After having dissected the reproductive tracts of 40 bitches, in all stages of pregnancy, I learned just how and where the uterus lays in the abdomen with relation to the intestines and other organs. Ever since that time I have been carefully recording the size of the developing fetuses, as they felt to my fingers. These impressions were recorded only in the cases where the exact time of copulation was known.

What is felt even by trained fingers is obviously not really the fetus at all. Rather it is the sum total of the fetus, the amniotic fluid surrounding it, the placental membranes and the thickened walls of the uterus. Hereafter I shall refer to what is felt by the word "lump," for this describes it accurately. At first the fetus is very much smaller than the total lump. As it grows the proportions change so that the fetus constitutes the greater part of what one may feel.

When the lump that one feels is about the size of a large pea, the embryo is slightly smaller than a grain of wheat and jelly-like to the touch. But during the last week of pregnancy the fetuses themselves may be felt distinctly, provided there are only a few in the bitch. This is because the sacs are soft, and the fluid moves aside at the touch of the fingers so that the contour of the fetuses is easily traceable. If there are many fetuses, the abdomen is generally so much distended that it is impossible to get one between the fingers in order to feel it.

It is generally possible to determine pregnancy in the bitch at about 22 days after fertilization. Skilled fingers are required at this time. From the 24th day on until the 35th day it is quite an easy matter. But after the 35th day the increasing flabbiness of the fetal sac, the greater amount of amniotic fluid and the general increase in the size of the abdomen make it a very difficult matter. It is no longer necessary because one does not have to palpate then to detect the fetuses. The general appearance of the bitch is enough.

It will be well to recall the general construction of the bitch's reproductive tract, in order to better understand where and how to feel for the lumps, if one is interested in determining pregnancy. In the non-pregnant bitch of average size the length of each horn of the uterus is about seven inches. The vagina is about three inches long. The Fallopian tubes in the bitch are very small, and run from the tips of the horns of the uterus in tortuous paths around the capsules which surround the ovaries.

They terminate at small inconspicuous slits in the sides of the capsules. When copulation has ceased, the semen from the dog will have passed up the entire length of the uterus through the Fallopian tubes and entered the capsules around the ovaries. If the bitch is killed or spayed at this time and the reproductive tract removed, if one inserts a medicine dropper through this slit, some fluid can be withdrawn and it will be found to contain spermatozoa.

Very likely fertilization occurs within this capsule, and the fertilized ova are moved through the Fallopian tubes and into the horns of the uterus, where they develop. As they grow, the walls of the uterus also grow and the horns of the uterus lengthen. As pregnancy progresses the uterus may be 3½ feet long in a bitch of the size of a German Shepherd Dog or a large Setter. This length depends largely upon the number of puppies developing. The fetuses are not always placed evenly in the uterus. How much migration there is before attachment we do not know. In a dissected bitch I have found six fetuses in one of the horns and only three in the other. Quite often one finds lumps well up in the uterus so that one has to feel just behind the ribs to find anything at all. At other times it is possible to feel a lump almost down at the cervix. From the cervix the two parts of the uterus may sometimes run forward among the folds of intestines. Occasionally they lie on the abdominal floor. In the former case, as pregnancy advances, the lumps may be felt almost always under the intestines.

Palpation to Determine Pregnancy

As the uterine horns elongate they gradually twist and turn, making the contortions very difficult to follow. It is therefore only necessary to put the fingers on the far side of the abdomen, the thumb on the near side and gently press until a lump is felt. Then by moving the fingers forward or backward others can generally be felt. And as I have said, in the early stages, it is only necessary to feel just above the floor of the abdomen. A great difference will be noted in the size of the lumps felt in the uterus from one day to the next. The growth is very rapid and if a three-day interval elapses between palpations, the difference will be most marked.

I find palpation easiest to accomplish when the bitch is in a standing position. With one hand I hold her by the head, generally pinching the base of one ear to draw her attention and cause her to relax. In the case of large breeds, it requires an assistant to hold the bitch's head, and then both hands may be used. Without an assistant, I find it best to lay a large bitch on her side, and by placing one hand under the side and the other on top, the lumps may be felt.

Some bitches are exceedingly difficult to palpate, because of their tendency to keep their abdominal walls tense. Rubbing the ears and other movements often do not avail, but a steady pressure on the abdomen will usually cause the bitch, in time, to relax enough to determine whether or not she is pregnant. In my experience dogs of the Bull Terrier type are most difficult, while those of the hound or setter type are easiest to palpate.

There is one opportunity for error in this detection of pregnancy by palpation; namely, feeling lumps of feces in the large intestine, and mistaking them for fetuses. When a bitch is constipated, she may have many small hard lumps in the intestine. If a possibility of such confusion exists, it is advisable to give a mild laxative and put her on a diet of laxative food for a day or two, and then palpate again.

From the records which I have made of the different sizes of the lumps as gestation progressed, I have been able to construct the diagrams on Pages 61 and 62. In accumulating these data I have palpated the bitches at every possible opportunity.

There will be found to be individual variation in different bitches. I find from my records that one bitch in five matings has never carried her puppies over 60 days. Others doubtless carry theirs for 63, but my own experience leads me to believe that the 61st day after ovulation is more likely than not to be the date of parturition rather than the 63rd day given in most of the whelping tables.

To predict the probable whelping date from the day when the lumps in any bitch feels as shown at 28 days on the diagram, it is well to know something of the past history of the bitch. When one has a past history of a short gestation period, it is possible to predict very closely when to expect the pups. I have collected a great many data pertinent to the subject. It was noted that the longest time (after the lumps felt as they generally do at 28 days) was 36 days to whelping. The shortest was 32. This was the bitch referred to above. Three times her gestation period was 59 days and twice, 60 days. Two other bitches show a figure of 36 days. In their cases their gestation periods were a full 63 days.

The following charts show the relative sizes of the lumps which one feels by palpation through the abdominal walls. By comparing the feeling of the lumps in any bitch with those shown here, a close approximation of the number of days that the bitch has been pregnant can be made.

In observing the various points in the chart showing the sizes of the lumps, one will notice that in the early stages there is not the difference one might expect between the various breeds. For instance, in a Schipperke weighing eight pounds, the size of the lumps at 21 days is about half the diameter of the lumps of the St. Bernard at the same day, or about one-eighth the cubical contents. But note that the St. Bernard is $17\frac{1}{2}$ times as heavy. This same dog in better flesh would have weighed 20 times as much, easily. The development in the latter weeks is more along the lines to be expected by the difference in breed size. But

60

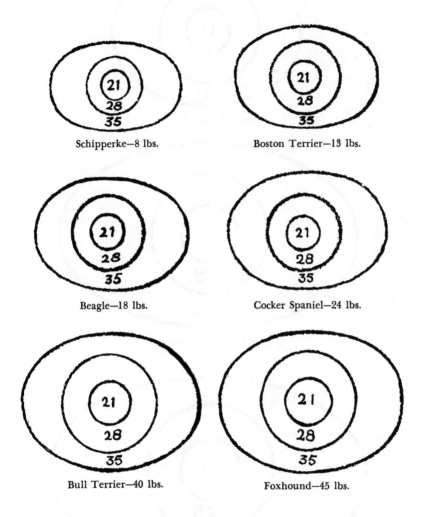

Schipperke—8 lbs.

Boston Terrier—13 lbs.

Beagle—18 lbs.

Cocker Spaniel—24 lbs.

Bull Terrier—40 lbs.

Foxhound—45 lbs.

How the lumps feel in pregnant bitches of various breeds at periods of 21, 28, and 35 days after mating.

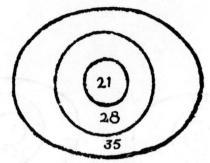

Basset Hound—50 lbs.

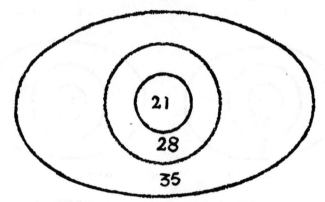

Irish Wolfhound—120 lbs.

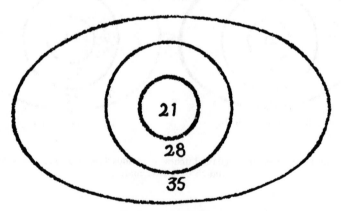

St. Bernard—140 lbs.

How the lumps feel in pregnant bitches of various larger breeds at periods of 21, 28, and 35 days after mating.

even so there is not the difference at whelping that one would expect. Thus a Beagle weighing 15 pounds whelped a litter weighing an average of close to four ounces each. The puppies of a Great Dane weighed 17 ounces each at birth. If the puppies of the bigger dog had been proportional to its greater weight they would each have weighed 28 ounces. One litter of puppies from a 28-pound Beagle weighed 10 ounces each, and there were six in the litter.

The chart was made not from palpating one dog of each of the breeds shown, but in some cases many. Dozens of mongrels of varying sizes were palpated. None of these is included but it is surprising how closely the size of their lumps checks with those of purebred bitches of similar sizes. I have had the opportunity of examining so many Bloodhounds that I ceased recording the size of their lumps. And they are an exceptionally easy breed to palpate because they are flat sided, thin skinned and very yielding to the touch.

Worms

Once pregnancy is assured, it is well to be certain that the bitch is not infected with worms. One of the most difficult tasks in the raising of young puppies is overcoming the results of hookworm infestations. We often hear it said that it is dangerous to worm pregnant bitches. This is not so. Your veterinarian can do it or show you how to do it safely.

It is essential to try to prevent the infestation of pregnant bitches with worm eggs of any species. Hookworm larvae, as well as those of roundworms, are carried in the mother's blood and many bore through the placenta and enter the puppy. They remain dormant until whelping, after which they develop and live in the intestine. In the event that the pregnant mother is passing worm eggs in her stool, it is practically certain that her puppies will need to be dewormed at the age of two to three weeks of age. Hookworm larvae living on blood soon deplete the puppy's red cells and they become anemic. By any of several methods it is safe to deworm them early.

63

The terms "phantom" and "pseudo" pregnancy are somewhat misleading. Actually, on the basis of all we know about the processes in the ovaries, such a phenomenon is not rare, but normal and to be expected in fertile bitches whether they are bred and miss (because of sterility in the male, or because of having been mated too early or too late) or whether they are not bred. If they ovulate they should be expected to have a phantom pregnancy. My own observation points emphatically to the conclusion that bitches which do not develop a phantom or pseudo pregnancy were sterile, at least at that particular mating cycle.

Period of Gestation

More thought has been given recently to the gestation period in dogs. Pearson and Pearson in England studied the gestation periods of Pomeranians and Pekingese, as well as crosses of the two, and concluded that the gestation in these small breeds was 60 days with a variation of three days one way or the other. They suggest that the larger litters had shorter gestation periods than the smaller, and that the size of the litter hastens the end of gestation. They ask, "Can it be that this duration is individual and possibly an inherited characteristic? If so it would be of evolutionary importance."

That there are some bitches which carry their litters much longer than others can hardly be doubted. One Boxer bitch which I have attended for two litters in succession worried the owner because she carried the puppies 67 days and 68, counting from the 16th day of the mating cycle. Possibly she would have carried them longer had I not injected pituitrin at the owner's insistence.

In 1940 I published a study in which the data show the gestation period to be 61 days rather than the 63 usually considered as correct. But since so many bitches are bred before ovulation, perhaps 63 is safe to figure on because the sperm live several days. Even then the true gestation period is from the day of conception (not the day of mating) to the day of birth.

It is interesting to know how much weight a bitch loses

when she gives birth. I have weighed many. Here is a typical large litter from a bitch which weighed 72 lbs. 7 ozs.:

14 puppies weighed as soon as dry	8 lbs. 15 ozs.
Placenta and amniotic fluid	9 lbs. 1 oz.
	18 lbs.

The bitch weighed 54 lbs. 8 ozs. Therefore the fluid which dried from the puppies must have weighed about 3 ozs.

Resorption of Fetuses

As we have seen, it is natural and normal for aged bitches which come in heat and conceive, to resorb their fetuses. The precise mechanism of this phenomenon is not completely clear. It is thought that with the death of the fetus, due perhaps to some interference with the placental attachment to the wall of the uterus, all of the solid contents of the uterus is digested by enzymes and the liquified material goes into the circulation of the mother.

In 1959 and 1960 this author published two papers detailing his studies on the effects of a yeast extract called Malucidin which, injected into the vein of a pregnant bitch, produced complete resorption of the fetuses within 48 hours. All told over 200 pregnant bitches were resorbed by this method, after which the extract was sent to many veterinarians to use on clients' dogs. They too reported success.

In the first 40 days of pregnancy, resorption occurs; during the last third, the treatment results in abortion. Subsequent pregnancies are not effected. When the use of Malucidin has been approved by the Food and Drug Administration, it should be a great boon to dog owners and breeders.

Dr. George D. Whitney first used it to cure a common ailment of bitches called pyometra (pus in the uterus). To save an infected bitch it had been necessary to remove the enormous pus-filled organ, but one injection caused the cervix to open and the uterus to drain. Many bitches completely recovered and subsequently raised healthy litters. In the future it should be possible to save valuable infected bitches for breeding by this simple procedure.

Birth (Parturition)

At the conclusion of the gestation period—61 days—the bitch feels new sensations which impel her to prepare a bed in which to whelp. The precise time when this feeling strikes her has never been determined, but it is about three days before normal whelping. In my research with Malucidin, I found that when bitches were aborted by its use, if the abortion occurred more than three days before the normal expectancy, the bitches were not interested in the fetuses but dropped them about the kennel and took no care of them. During the last three days, the bitches became motherly and even though the pups were dead, they did mother them, cleaned them, ate the placenta and fetal membranes. Probably it was Prolactin which engineered this behavior.

It is assumed that she feels the motivation three days before she is due to whelp. Therefore, she should be provided with a place to whelp so she may become used to it and contented. If one finds the bitch trying to find a place to whelp, it does not mean that she is due shortly. However, if an appropriate place is not furnished she may have her pups in some outlandish place, perhaps in the corner of the run, or if in a home, she may push all the shoes on the closet floor into a pile and use that as a bed.

The whelping bed should be saucer-shaped so the pups will stay in a pile in the center. When the bitch lies down she will usually nose the pups together and lie down around them with her teats where the pups can find them. We read about whelping beds on flat floors with rails around the edge so puppies will roll under the rail and not be crushed by the mother. We also read that cloths make a satisfactory whelping bed. Cloths do absorb the discharge from the vulva but they also become tangled around the pups and the dam lies on her pups because they can't struggle from under her weight.

In kennel conditions, a deep straw bed, shaped like a saucer is all any bitch wants, provided the whelping box is about six inches longer and wider than the bitch is long. The sides should be a foot high. For pet dogs kept in homes, straw will litter the premises. A piece of carpet on a closet floor will suffice, provided one has the time to watch the litter carefully and frequently to be sure the bitch does not crush the pups.

One point to be sure of is not to permit the bitch to whelp on rough boards or concrete. When the puppies nurse they lie on their bellies and scrub the raw navels on the rough surface. If the navels become infected, the pups usually die.

A contented bitch will lie on her whelping bed for many hours before she begins to whelp. For the benefit of those who have never witnessed whelping or assisted with the process, this is what you may expect. The bitch may stiffen out and some may grunt, straining and relaxing many times before any puppy appears at the vulva. Sometimes one sees a bubble there filled with pink fluid. With each straining the bubble increases in size until it bursts. Sometimes the bubble bursts inside the uterus, in which event the head or the tail end of the pup shows. Each straining pushes it out until the pup flops out onto the straw bed, wiggling and gasping.

The dam, impelled by the odor, reaches around and licks the pup. She finds the umbilical cord, tugs on it gently, cuts it off with her incisor teeth and pulls the placenta out and swallows it. Anywhere from a quarter of an inch to two inches will remain with the pup. Sometimes when two pups come close together she has time to take care of only one and the cord and placenta will drag around in the bedding, drying up into a string which should be cut off by the owner. In the event you may have read about how one must sterilize scissors and tie off the cord with sterile thread, simply smile at such advice. The whelping bed will be a bacteriological flower garden. The dam's lips are full of many kinds of bacteria. People who give such nonsensical advice are thinking of human births.

The bitch will consume all the afterbirth, lick the pups almost dry and push them together. She keeps the whelping bed clean of puppy feces and urine by consuming all of it. In fact, puppies will hold their excrement until they feel the rough tongue of the mother licking them, and this serves as a signal to relax the sphincter muscles. Only then will the pups urinate and defecate normally. If puppies are left orphans, the owner, raising them, must rub some cloth or cotton over the vulva, penis and anus to stimulate the pup to void. If this is not done the bed becomes filthy and wet.

Some normal whelpings encompass 24 hours, some 45 minutes. Slow whelpers can be helped by dosing with Pitocin. One thing that can be done without drugs to hasten birth is to insert two fingers into the vulva of the whelping bitch, bend them and pull hard. Keep a steady strain and the bitch responds by straining.

One can tell when the whelping is over by feeling through the abdomen. Place one hand under and one over the abdomen. If there are more puppies to be born, they are clearly palpable. Or you may feel a lump that is placenta. The bitch will be restless until the uterus is empty. Then she will get up, defecate and urinate, move away from her pups but keep an eye on them. She will leave them for longer and longer periods.

When they are about three weeks old, she will eat her meals and return to the nest and vomit the food. The pups, smelling the acid regurgitated, partially digested food, usually wallow in it, eating all they can hold, whereupon the dam eats what's left and licks the puppies clean. This is the normal expectancy; it is abnormal not to do it. However, the kind of feed which the bitch eats has an effect on this vomiting. Dogs fed a meat diet vomit much more than dogs fed a diet of mostly cereals and dehydrated protein.

All prepared for the big event to start.

The photo above, and those on the five pages that follow, are from a pictorial feature, "A LITTER DELIVERED," which appeared in the Spring 1955 issue of Gaines Dog Research Progress, published periodically as a service to veterinarians and breeders by the Gaines Dog Research Center. They are reproduced here by special permission.

The photos are by Ed Bakal, and were taken in an animal hospital. The Boxer bitch pictured is Royal Maya, owned by Mary Alice Ipedjian of Scarsdale, N.Y.

A remarkable aspect of these pictures is the bitch's apparent indifference to the invasion of her privacy.

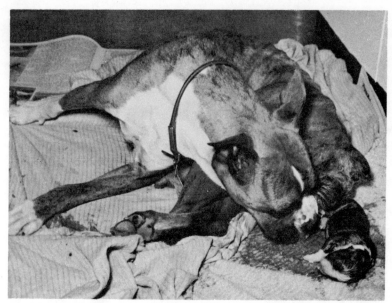

Firstcomers are served, licked clean and dry.

A rest between deliveries.

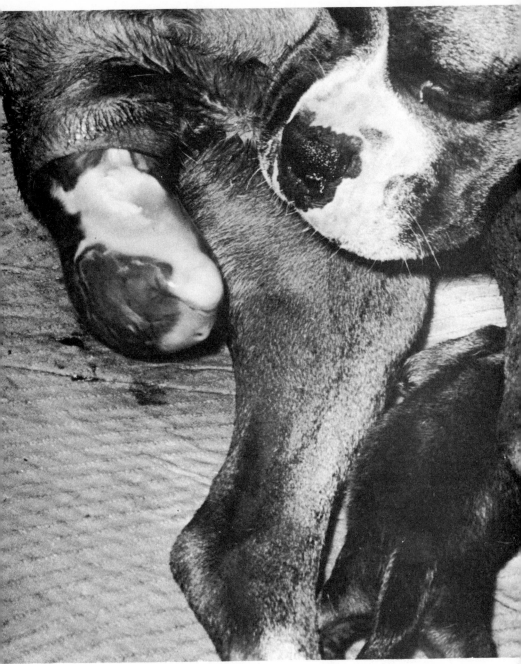

A puppy emerges, halfway out of the vagina.

Same puppy, three-quarters of the way out.

Maya bites umbilical cord.

Time for inspection . . . and a cleaning.

Her work well done, Maya settles down to feed her family.

7

The Sex Hormones

HORMONES are regulators which are secreted by glands. These chemicals are carried about the body by the circulating fluids, blood and lymph. Mention of sex hormones sometimes conveys the erroneous impression that they, in particular, are produced only by the ovaries and testicles—gonads. But such is not the case. There is considerable interaction of most of the ductless glands in the body, but in the regulation of sex and sex behavior, the pituitary—a small thing with two lobes and located beneath the brain—and the testicles and ovaries are the principal controlling glands.

Testosterone is produced by the testicles, which begin to function at puberty, producing what are known as the secondary sex characteristics.

Testosterone produces the sexual drive and causes the appearance of maleness which so markedly differentiates the male from the female or from the early castrated male. It has been synthesized chemically and is generally used as testosterone proprionate.

It has been found that the pituitary hormone controls the functioning of the testicles. Remove it, and production of sperm slows to a stop. One of the ways of accomplishing the lessening of pituitary stimulation on the testicle is to inject testosterone. Dr. Clyde Deming and the author undertook an experiment along this line. We removed a testicle from each of four dogs. We treated them with testosterone proprionate for a month. Then the other testicles were removed. Thus, each dog was his own control. We found testicular degeneration from this substitution therapy. This compares with other studies with mice and rats. The injection of the testosterone may cause the animal to exhibit strong signs of maleness but he may become infertile.

The pituitary hormone causes the descent of the testicles into the scrotum. Most male puppies are born with the testicles already outside the abdomen. A synthetic hormone called A.P.L. (anterior pituitary like) sometimes assists in causing the descent of the retained gland, if injected early enough. In humans it has been reported to be successful. In dogs, it has not met with so much success, possibly because of the time difference in testicular descent.

On the female side we find a greater variety of hormones. There are pituitary and ovarian as the primary consideration, but there are also hormones secreted by the placenta, and those found in the urine of pregnant animals. Some of the manufacturers of biologics maintain stables of mares, so as to be able to obtain large amounts of urine from which they extract hormones. Then too there are synthetic hormones of which stilbestrol and A.P.L. are examples.

The follicles in the ovary produce a hormone, *estrone,* and the luteal bodies produce two—*progesterone* and *relaxin.*

The word *gonadotrope* means having a special affinity for, or influence on the gonads; whereas an *estrogen* is any substance which has the power of producing the mating cycle, which is manifested by growth in the vagina, uterus and mammary glands.

Gonadotropes are produced commercially from the pituitary gland, from the placenta, from the blood serum and the urine of pregnant animals. They are also made synthetically and sold under many trade names.

The ovaries produce the follicular hormone, which when

injected starts the development of the heat period, and the luteal hormone, progesterone, which puts a brake on the changes initiated by the follicular hormone by acting in an antagonistic manner and prepares the lining of the uterus to receive and develop the fertilized ova.

Emmenin, a hormone obtained from the placenta, may be given by mouth, as can *stilbestrol,* which is produced synthetically and is one of the most commonly used of all sex hormones. The latter is similar to ovarian hormone.

Of the ovarian hormones, estrone is found in pregnant urine, and estriol is found in the placenta.

The corpora lutea produce a hormone called relaxin, whose function it is to relax the pelvis before birth. This is found in the blood and urine during the latter part of pregnancy. But the corpora lutea are in turn maintained on the ovaries, where they prevent follicles from developing by pregnancy, pseudo or false pregnancy and lactation. So long as these persist, the corpora also persist and the mating cycle does not transpire. But if the corpora lutea are removed, it is only a short time before the mating cycle starts.

At the time of birth the pituitary secretes another hormone—*prolactin*—which causes the bitch to develop maternal instincts and to secrete milk.

From a practical point of view it is quite a simple matter to bring a bitch into heat, and produce ovulation. By giving stilbestrol alone the heat period seems normal, the bitch shows the desire for mating, but she does not conceive. Her natural mating cycle will start when it is due next just as though she had not had her artificial heat period. I worked this out carefully with controls. If, however, A.P.L. is injected about the 11th or 12th day of her heat, she will usually ovulate, and—if bred —produce puppies.

Other practical considerations in the knowledge of the use of sex hormones is their use in preventing conception, or in producing abortions or postponement of mating cycles.

If a mating has been made, let us say, by the escape of a bitch, how may we prevent her having puppies? One way is a high douche under pressure given immediately after mating, which can be dangerous. Another is the injection of some estrogen in large enough doses. This will prevent the reception of the ova by the uterus. Dr. G. L. Kelly and the author found this was feasible by giving 2000 to 4000 international units of *Theelin* or *Amniotin* to dogs weighing 15 to 60 pounds. Six doses, one a day, starting as soon as the mating took place, sufficed.

Using testosterone and other hormones often causes abortion, and mating cycles may be postponed by continued injections of progesterone. When they are stopped the bitch soon comes in heat. This is especially important to hunters who are afraid their bitches will come in heat during the hunting season, which is too short at best.

Testosterone injected into female puppies if continued through their growing period will produce penises of considerable size. The penis is a development of the clitoris and protrudes from the vagina. In a study in which I gave the injections to part of the females in a litter, the development was considerable. The penis was three or four inches long.

Breeders often ask if the human tests for pregnancy cannot be applied to dogs. Lesbouyries and Berthelon tried the usual rabbit test and found they could not accomplish it, but when they waited until after the eighteenth day of pregnancy and injected urine from bitches into rats whose ovaries had been removed, the rats developed mating cycles, provided the bitches were pregnant. They suggest that this would be useful in the case of bitches which were too nervous to allow palpation. I would think that it might be useful after the 35th day of pregnancy in the event a bitch is going to have a small litter, because during the sixth and seventh week it is almost impossible to detect the foetus by palpation; and the surrounding membranes are so soft.

Another practical application of a sex hormone is in prolonging the reproductive life of old bitches. Stilbestrol appears to be of considerable service here. I first tried it on four old Cocker Spaniels, each of which had become pregnant at their last mating cycles, but had resorbed the foetuses. I have been palpating bred bitches to determine pregnancy for many years. It seems that old bitches generally become pregnant but resorb their puppies. By giving these bitches small doses of stilbestrol every three days (2 milligrams for a Cocker Spaniel) they carried their pregnancies full term. One old Border Collie had twice resorbed her litter. Giving her 2 mgs. of stilbestrol every three days enabled her to carry two puppies full term. The injections have apparently saved so many of these puppies that it seems beyond the realm of mere coincidence. Stilbestrol may be given orally but somewhat larger amounts need to be given than when it is injected.

While we are on the subject of hormones it is pertinent to ask how important they are to weight regulation. Many dog owners wonder whether removing the testicles or ovaries will be responsible for weight gain. Considerable research has gone into the answer to this question. Quinlan and Steyn even studied the effect of spaying on the performance of 36 female Greyhounds, spayed when they were 6–12 months of age. They learned that their performances on the race track were equal to that of unspayed sisters. Only two showed any tendency to overweight and it is quite probable that two out of 36 unspayed bitches would also have showed such an inclination.

Common observation with all species of animals shows that removal of testicles in males or ovaries in females at an early age does affect the appearance, producing animals which look neither male nor female.

Composition of Bitch's Milk

A number of studies on the fat content of bitch's milk have been studied, but in none have I found the breed of the dogs from which milk was taken specified. These studies state that bitch's milk ran from 7.8 to 12.5 butterfat.

A study never published was one I conducted when I was working on a formula to closely approximate the milk of bitches. Using a Babcock test, I found a great variation in the percentage of fat. The amount varied from one with 8.7 percent up to one producing 13.0 percent of fat. The stage of the lactation period seemed to cause considerable variation. One Bloodhound bitch at the start of the lactation period—the fourth day—had 9.2

percent and at the fifth week showed 12.1 percent. The percentage among Cocker Spaniel milk was quite uniform, running between 10.00 and 11.6 when compared during the third week of lactation. However, the Spaniels were the old Idahurst dogs, a linebred family for several generations.

The bitch with highest fat content was an American farm shepherd bitch whose milk never ran below 12.0.

Milk production is under the control of hormones, one of which is *prolactin* (made by the pituitary gland). This is called the "Mother love" hormone because it engenders the mothering instinct in animals. Injected into even a spayed bitch it will cause her to steal puppies to mother. In a natural birth, it begins to be manufactured close to the time of birth. If a bitch aborts even as close to normal time of birth as three days, she may refuse any interest in the puppies. Two days before, she usually will mother them.

8

The Role of the Vitamins
in Reproduction

W HATEVER affects health affects reproduction, and food
is one of the basic sustainers or destroyers of health. The consideration of all of the other factors is outside of the province
of this book, but some elements are so basic as to be an in-
tegral part.

It is becoming increasingly clear that vitamins are only one
group of the essential elements of food. Animo acids, fatty acids
and other factors as yet only dimly understood are of great
importance and in that sense in the same category as the
vitamins. However, certain vitamins are essential in very specific
ways so it behooves every dog breeder to understand something
about this subject in order that he may be assured his dogs'
diets are complete in these all-important factors, and also that
he may have some explanation for failures in reproduction and
take steps to correct faulty diets and thus guard against failures.

Proper diets for the nursing matron and for growing puppies
will not be considered in this book, as important as they are. The
author has written extensively on these subjects elsewhere.

Unfortunately, little actual experimental data have been
accumulated, using the dog as the subject, to study reproduction.

Most of the existing data are derived from studies of other species, and the assumption is that the same facts hold for dogs. Such data are all we have and such assumptions are risky. Still, in no instance can the feeding of vitamins known to be essential to reproduction in other species do any harm to dogs, provided they are not fed in too great amounts, so the studies made on other species are of great value.

The terms vitamin B_3 or fat soluble E, and so forth, are fast going out of favor with chemists, and the real names becoming the common designation. Dog breeders are not chemists and so we shall use both names.

Vitamin A

Possibly the most important vitamin from the standpoint of reproduction is vitamin A, found abundantly in carrots, alfalfa, many green and yellow vegetables, fish liver oils, egg yolk, animal livers and fatty deposits. It is always found tied up with fat.

Absence of vitamin A from the diet causes a degeneration in the testicles of males even before the outward evidences like "sore eyes" are apparent. Males soon lose the power to produce sperm cells and are therefore sterile.

The female is much more resistant to A deficiency. The chief effect is upon the lining of the reproductive organs, and fertility is diminished, possibly due to this effect.

In some species vitamin A deficiency has been shown to give rise to still births, to resorption of foetuses, to production of weak offspring, to failure to conceive and even to infections of the uterus. Long continued deliveries and possibly failure to pass the placenta are also attributed to a deficiency or absence of this essential.

Abnormal offspring sometimes appear. In pigs, whose mothers were deprived of vitamin A, many cleft palates and harelips were found as well as other deformities.

Milk secretion is lessened and it is apparent that when puppies are deprived of this vitamin in their mother's milk, they cannot develop normally.

Vitamin B₁ (Thiamin chloride)

This vitamin, so common in the diet of well fed dogs, is an important one, because dogs are not always well fed. Many baked-biscuit type of dog foods are very low in this factor, and also low in many of the vitamins so commonly found associated, which are destroyed to a large extent in the baking processes, or by long boiling.

But these vitamins are commonly found in natural grain foods and some in meat, so that they need not give much trouble in dog diets. In foxes and dogs, feeding of raw fish causes a paralysis (Chastek) due to a substance which destroys vitamin B₁. Cooking destroys the destroyer before the vitamin, so in this way fish is made safe to use.

In males, a lack of the vitamin causes inanition, loss of sex interest and inability to copulate. Even before external symptoms appear, the prostate gland atrophies.

Females similarly deprived do not develop normally in the sex organs, nor do they come in heat. The ovaries degenerate but possibly because of an indirect effect. The principal effect is on the pituitary gland and its secretions which, as we have seen, in turn affects the ovarian thiamin function.

In pregnant animals, the effects of thiamin starvation are similar to vitamin A starvation: resorption, delivery of stillborn or weak offspring, difficult birth, retention of placenta. There is also delayed shrinking of the uterus.

In lactation, thiamin is essential, and from three to five times the usual intake are required or offspring die, and without it milk flow ceases. Appetite diminishes, so milk flow naturally slackens. A lack of the vitamin in milk reacts on the puppies which show loss of appetite and often bend backward and cry.

Thiamin is found in abundance in whole cereal grains, meat (especially pork), liver, heart, kidneys, milk, eggs. It is soluble in water so that cooking leaches it out into the water in which food is cooked, and it is destroyed by heat, so the less cooking the better. Thiamin can be bought as hydrochloride and ½ milligram per day is probably sufficient for the average dog. It would be difficult to find any ordinary dog diet which would not contain that much. Generally nothing is gained by its addition.

Vitamin B₂ (Riboflavin)

Evidence is accumulating that this vitamin, found in milk, liver, eggs, alfalfa and commonly distributed in small amounts throughout many foodstuffs, is concerned with foetal development. Veal is one of the richest natural substances and it is reasoned that inadequate supplies to the mother will be reflected in improper development. As in the case of Vitamin A, cleft palates and harelips, in this case in puppies, have been definitely traced to a lack in the diet of the bitch. It is one of the B-complex members which will stand considerable boiling.

Vitamin B₆ (Pyridoxine hydrochloride)

Because it is generally known that injection of this vitamin is valuable in reducing the common morning sickness of human pregnancy, dog breeders sometimes use it thinking it is essential to dogs. But as yet no direct evidence has been presented showing benefits derived from it.

Vitamin C (Ascorbic Acid)

So far as we know, this is not required by adult dogs. But without it small puppies fail to thrive, so it would be well to feed some to lactating bitches. The amount found in commercial dog foods is usually sufficient.

Vitamin D

Because vitamin D and calcium and phosphorus are so intimately associated with growth it has been suggested that indirectly, at any rate, there is some connection between the vitamin and reproduction. Critical research has shown that there is no direct connection between D and the organs of reproduction or the production of hormones.

However, there is a direct connection between the ability of a bitch to whelp normally and lactate properly in two ways. If she is rachitic, her pelvis may be so ill-formed that she cannot deliver puppies. Secondly, lack of the vitamin which we know is so intimately connected with calcium metabolism will affect the calcium in the milk and, being low itself in the milk, will produce early rickets in the puppies.

A dog manufactures its own vitamin D if it is exposed to the sun, which irradiates the ergosterol in the tissues and changes it to the vitamin. In summer, provided calcium and phosphorus are present in adequate amounts in the diet, no vitamin D is needed. For dogs in shaded outdoor runs or those kept indoors, it should be supplied. Most dog foods have more than adequate amounts.

Vitamin E (Tocopherol)

So far, we have no data showing the requirements of dogs for this vitamin. Many species have been found not to require it. Rats definitely must have it. Most of the evidence depended upon by dog breeders is "testimonial" evidence, the silliest kind known. If dogs are like rats in this regard they need a small amount of this fat soluble substance. It is found abundantly in nature, usually tied up with the oily germs of seeds. But there is some in the fat of meat.

Rancidity quickly destroys this vitamin. Sometimes dog breeders feed wheat germ oil and cod liver oil which may be rancid and destroy the E activity. Some feed huge amounts of E thinking it will increase fertility. It probably won't. But in small puppies it is essential, so it is wise to be sure the diet of the lactating bitch has an adequate amount.

Beside these, there are other vitamins concerned with general health, but those considered above are the only ones which, to date, have been found to be directly concerned with reproduction.

Vitamin F

Three of the unsaturated fatty acids, Linoleic, Linolenic acid and Arachedonic acid, are often referred to as vitamin F. Only a minute amount of Linoleic acid is required but the absence of these acids will produce dire results: growth slows, the skin thickens and hair falls out, starting in the feet and legs and

85

spreading along the sides. The ears become pussy and an obnoxious odor is given off.

Several weeks of deficiency are all that are needed for symptoms to show in puppies, but several months are needed in the case of older dogs. Corn and other vegetable oils, even in small amounts, meet the requirements.

Speaking practically, reviewing all of the canine requirements for vitamins, it is possible to feed dogs two substances and furnish an ample amount of all. Alfalfa leaf meal, made by drying and grinding tender alfalfa, is in the author's opinion the most worthwhile single diet item to be had for dogs. I believe I was the first person to advocate its use. Very few breeders have fed it conscientiously but many have fed it in the better grades of dog food. Some breeders may even have refused to feed certain dog foods because they looked green. It must be remembered that wild dogs and dog-like animals eat a great deal of intestinal contents of the animals they kill and in this way obtain a large quantity of nutritional essentials. Alfalfa is the best way yet discovered of supplying these.

It is highly important that the meal be ground uniformly and quite fine. It must be fresh, as stale alfalfa leaf meal has lost much of its vitamin A. It must be of good quality—20 percent protein. Cheap grades run below 17 percent and are too woody to be fed dogs for best results. The addition of 7 percent to 10 percent alfalfa leaf meal is enough and if the ration is properly adjusted, is not too laxative. But this is one of the objections to it and it must be fed judiciously with an eye to laxation.

The second substance is irradiated yeast. One manufacturer is now producing yeast with 4,000,000 units of vitamin D per pound or 9000 to a gram. The D requirement for a dog is about 300 units, when he is kept out of the sun. So his daily requirement would be one-thirtieth of a gram—a very small amount—just a pinch.

9

Influences Affecting Sterility

HAVING seen how the organs of reproduction in both the dog and bitch function, let us turn our attention to the very practical problem of sterility. Let us inquire into the causes and remedies for this most vexing question to every dog breeder. I shall treat it quite fully because I know just how often the spectre appears in otherwise well regulated kennels. I know too how very frequently the man who ships his bitch away to be bred has her returned bred, yes, but not pregnant. I know likewise how our hopes are often dashed, and how paper promises of profits are swept away.

During the summer of 1936 I bred many bitches to my stud dogs. Of these every single bitch whelped a litter. At the same time I shipped thirteen Cocker Spaniels, three Beagles, one Schipperke, two Bloodhounds and one Samoyed to be bred. Of these, three of the Spaniels, one of the Bloodhounds, one of the Beagles and the Schipperke did not conceive. Instead of 100 percent success I had just 60 percent in the number shipped away to be bred. I am convinced that all of the bitches were fertile and, as a matter of fact, each one of them developed an udder and had all the symptoms of phantom pregnancy, thus showing that each actually ovulated. Some other fact or facts were the cause. What was it? What were they? This record is uncommonly good in this respect.

From hundreds of letters in my files asking questions about sterility I know that there is a much less chance of pregnancy being insured when dogs are shipped away to be bred than when they are bred under the watchful eye of the owner. The causes for this constitute another very important consideration. I think the journey has very little to do with it and that this should be practically ruled out from the start, with one important exception.

First let us review just what are the principal conditions, all of which have to be right for conception.

Here are ten points to be remembered, presented a little too dogmatically perhaps, but we shall consider them one by one later on:

1. *Feed the bitch properly.*
2. *Feed the dog properly.*
3. *Exercise the bitch sufficiently.*
4. *Exercise the dog sufficiently.*
5. *Be sure the bitch has no obstruction.*
6. *Be sure the dog has an abundance of sperm.*
7. *Mate them after the congestion has left the vulva.*
8. *Be sure the dog has no prostate disease.*
9. *Be sure the pair are tied for several minutes.*
10. *When possible use a dog larger than the bitch.*

Now we can consider the above points. Let us take the first two together. The food makes some difference, to be sure, but considerably less difference than certain manufacturers would have us believe. A bitch generally will not come in season at all unless her diet contains just about all her nutritional requirements.

Remove any vitamin and the dog will suffer. Insist on proof that whatever you feed your dogs is a complete diet and one which has, all by itself, nourished several generations of dogs.

Long and varied scientific papers have been written on this one subject, but since the average dog breeder relies on some manufacturer to provide his dogs with their food, he can soon learn which of these foods are complete and which are not.

An improperly fed bitch may not come in season at all, and a dog which has long been improperly fed will not have the vitality to properly breed a bitch.

Exercise is not altogether vital to either dog or bitch because they will often get all the exercise they need in their own yards. In fact, some dogs of both sexes have been notoriously fertile when they have been exercised scarcely at all. But there are so many cases on record where very fat dogs have been made fertile by reducing them via the path of hard exercise, that this is a precaution worth taking. Almost every dog breeder knows of cases where dogs which were very fat repeatedly failed to conceive and these same dogs when they were thinned down have been fertile. But it is usually true too that a fat dog that keeps fat during plenty of exercise is fertile. Some dogs, on ample rations will be able to do very strenuous work and keep up, and these are most generally fertile dogs.

Some may wonder why I have not mentioned, as a precaution, to be sure that the bitch has both her ovaries. But studies on other species show that there must be something in the blood which provides for the number of ova secreted rather than the number of ovaries or the ovaries themselves. It has been shown that when a rabbit, for instance, has had one ovary removed, she will have just as many young as she did before the ovary was removed. That is why it is not so very important that we worry about obstructions in the female reproductive tract. They are exceptions, and even though one horn of the uterus is obstructed, the bitch can still be fertile, but she will not produce as many puppies as though both horns were unimpaired. In the case of bitches which have had repeated Caesarian operations, occasionally one horn becomes damaged and closed off, and still the bitch continues to have puppies.

Probably one of the most common causes of sterility is not that the dog has no sperm in his semen, but that he does not have enough. If a good service produces 10,000,000 sperm there is a good concentration, and thus in any microscopic field one will see a large number. In fact, if only a small proportion of that number is discharged, one will see a great many. But normal dog semen should appear faintly milky white. It is watery in consistency, but only the first fluid discharged should be color-less. The very great number of sperm give the semen its color.

Frequency of Mating

Now, if a dog is bred too often it does not mean that the concentration will be diminished because the quantity of semen is less as well as the number of sperm. Therefore, the danger in over-doing the breeding for any single dog is that there is likely to be too little semen and sperm and not necessarily too weak a sperm swarm.

There have been records of a dog being bred daily with fairly good results. Some of the great stud dogs whose progeny became famous and who were therefore in great demand as studs, have been used daily, but some only every other day. My own experience is that once every other day is not too often to insure an excellent service every time. In fact, one of my dogs was bred to the same or different bitches every other day for nearly two months. He was never tied less than 25 minutes and once during that time was tied for one hour and ten minutes, which is the longest I have personally ever seen a pair of dogs tied.

Dogs have no rutting season as have some other species, despite the fact that, as we have seen, there are two seasons when many more bitches are in season than at other times. It is really unfair, therefore, to compare them, as many have done, to rams, which do have a rutting season, and which will successfully breed 60 ewes within perhaps two days. Dogs are ready to mate at any season of the year and are as successful in their services at one time as another, if they are in good physical condition.

The bitch must not only be in season to be bred, but must be in the proper stage of that season. She must be so well advanced in the acceptance stage of the mating cycle that the ovaries have had time to discharge the ova, or within a day or a little over that time, and this, as we have seen, means that the average time should be after the 13th day of the mating cycle. We cannot judge this time by the color of the discharge, but we can judge it fairly well by the decided loss of congestion in the vulva. I said "average time" because we have seen there is a great variation in the total duration of the cycle in different bitches.

The vulva should be examined every day and the time when the relative rigidity begins to recede is, so far as I can determine, the most opportune time to make the first mating. From then until the last day that the bitch will accept the dog has proved in my experience to be the proper time to mate, and usually, if not always, one service during that time is as good as many. I have had to hold bitches after they had apparently gone by, in order to effect a service. The dog was ready but the bitch not, and these services have resulted in pregnancies. As I think back over my experience along this line, it occurs to me that, from what I know today, some of those bitches which I thought I had to hold because they appeared ugly toward the dog might have been coaxed by the dog to mate, had they been given time. The play and teasing which frequently precedes the actual copulation often facilitates matters.

The same thing applies to old stud dogs. A dog that has bred many bitches soon comes to know when a bitch has gone by. He will often take one smell and walk away. I have seen them do this when the bitch was very eager to stand. Then when the bitch does the playing, she can often tease him into apparently forgetting the inhibitory response he received from the odor.

For a good service a dog must remain tied to the bitch for several minutes. If he stays tied only a short time the chances are very good that he is not fertile, although there are exceptions to this. As we have seen, the first fluid which the dog secretes is largely a colorless sterile fluid which is highly alkaline. This neutralizes the male and female tract to a limited extent, and not until this fluid has been secreted do the sperm begin to come in the semen. The first sperm which come are diluted in this fluid and as anyone can determine by a simple microscopic examination, there must be considerable semen and sperm secreted to raise the sperm swarm to a point where the concentration is very great. There is generally at least a cubic centimeter of this clear fluid discharged. In short, the best service is the long service.

When dogs fail to produce, one often examines the semen and finds many sperm, and concludes that the dog must be fertile. This may be so even when there seem to be an abundance of sperm. After years of experience, when I examine the semen of a dog I look for pus cells every time. It is not at all rare to find a quantity of these roundish rough cells in the semen of a dog that is perfectly fertile. They are about the size of a red blood cell, but instead of being disk-like, they are spherical and their exterior is very irregular and rough. A few in a microscope field may mean nothing, but when they are profuse, the chances are good that the dog will prove sterile. I do not know why they should indicate sterility unless it is that their presence also indicates that there is a toxic substance in the semen which picked it up either as it came through the genital tract, or when the prostatic secretion was contaminated due to disease. Certain it is that with two dogs which were sterile, despite the fact that they had plenty of sperm in the semen, but also showed great numbers of pus cells, vigorous exercise in time cleared up the trouble. The only change in their régime was that they were exercised very hard. They lost weight but soon picked it up and from that time on were completely satisfactory as stud dogs.

So often do we hear dog breeders advised that the reasons their bitches fail to conceive is that they are "too acid." So they douche the bitch with bicarbonate of soda, and the next time the bitch produces a litter. But there again they did not use a check bitch which had not been douched. So far as I have been able to learn, there is no scientific evidence that the acid condition so often referred to really exists. The large quantity of alkaline fluid from the dog will take care of it, and there is danger of over-doing the introduction of the chemical. People forget that the douche under pressure can reach completely up to the ovaries and the water alone may act as a deterrent to fertility.

Fatal Resorption from Disease

There is one more cause of misses in bitches. This had passed entirely unsuspected until recently, yet it is a very potent cause and more often a cause than one would suspect. When I was collecting the data for my paper on *The Diagnosis of Pregnancy by Palpation,* I felt the lumps of pregnant bitches and noted their growth. In some cases it became apparent that certain bitches were resorbing their fetuses. The lumps would grow to be as large as a good sized English walnut and then shrink away to nothing. This occurred through distemper epidemics and I learned that when a pregnant bitch contracts distemper, she resorbs her developing puppies; and yet one would hardly know that she had any illness whatever. The disease affects her very lightly indeed and passes unnoticed in the great majority of cases. I believe that this is the explanation of why old bitches seem immune to the disease. Actually what has happened in their cases is that they have had a light case of the disease and the owners didn't realize it. They simply thought the bitch missed when bred.

When I say "distemper" I refer to the genuine Carré's Disease, not to Hardpad or other diseases whose symptoms are similar to, but lighter than, those of what was the horror of dog breeders before the introduction of effective vaccines.

Today, with the widespread vaccinating of dogs, shipping a bitch away to be bred is much safer than it was some years ago.

These then are the main points to be remembered so far as fertility in our dogs is concerned. Now I want to consider two other questions of great importance to breeders. These are: What should be done to prevent so many misses when dogs are shipped away to be bred? What hints can be given about accomplishing a service when dogs are difficult to breed? We shall consider these points in order.

10

Special Breeding Problems

THE failure of bitches to conceive when they are shipped a distance to be bred is one of the most exasperating things that besets the breeder, especially the newcomer in the field. With the following precautions in mind, it may be possible to overcome some of the failures, especially if they are borne in mind by the owner of the bitch and the owner of the dog as well.

Let us suppose that you own a fine Pointer bitch. You have done fairly well with her in your local field trial. She comes of excellent stock and you want to raise a litter of pups from her. So you read the foremost magazine which deals primarily with gun dogs and there you see advertised at stud "the great Yankee Demon." You have read of his exploits in winning many field trials and feel it would be a good combination if you bred your bitch to him. His stud fee is advertised at $150. You write and are told to ship the bitch when she comes in season. When she comes in season, away she goes to be bred to Yankee Demon. Back she comes, almost by return express. Your hopes are sailing on the clouds. You vision a grand litter and begin to tell your friends about the fine pups you are going to have to show them some day. You even picture yourself handling one of them in your local field trial and making the other men sit up and take notice.

The bitch begins to develop a better appetite and now you are almost certain she is pregnant. Then you are quite sure that when she stands up against the wire of her pen as she comes out to greet you that you can see a little development in her belly. After a few more weeks, you become slightly dismayed because that belly does not become any more distended, but look, you see for yourself, her udder is developing. Hooray! She is going to have a small litter and, good rationalizer that you are, you begin to think "that's better than a big litter anyway, because she can take better care of a few than a lot." And before long you are telling your friends that you think it is best for a bitch to have a small litter.

But woe to you, the time comes and she does not whelp. The time goes by. You even decide that she ought to have a cesarean operation to remove the one that simply must be there and so you take her to the veterinarian who tells you that many bitches develop phantom pregnancies, and then you are ready to cuss.

Now, this is no exaggeration. It is the story of what happens to thousands of breeders year after year, and something should and can be done about it. I think that while neither the owner of the bitch nor the owner of the stud is entirely to blame, nevertheless at least 70 percent of the fault of such failures lies with the owners of the studs. I say this advisedly because, of all the bitches which have been shipped to be bred to stud dogs of which I have had charge, not one was returned without being pregnant. Bitches have come from as far away as Colorado, when they were five days on the road.

Now let us put ourselves in the place of the owner of some stud dog of great renown. He receives letters from dozens of people every week asking about servicing their bitches. He accepts those which he thinks his dog can handle adequately and the temptation is to accept far more because every stud fee which he has to turn down, means a lot to him. He has never found an easier way to earn $150. Few of us have. Therefore, he accepts many more bitches to breed than he should and uses the dog once on each bitch, which should be enough. He has a good many of his own bitches to service too and knows that if he can advertise pups with his great stud as sire, he can get a big price for them. His own bitches must come first.

His kennel is arranged so that he has room for several bitches and it is generally filled with a few others besides his own. The run or runs for bitches in heat is well-planned so that no dogs can get in nor any get out. But like everyone else he does not care to keep dogs any longer than necessary. When a bitch comes to the station he gets her and brings her home. If she is ready to breed he breeds her and generally crates her up and returns her. If she is not ready he keeps her until she will stand for the dog and then returns her as soon as she has been bred, that is if he does not have another to be bred that same day.

He has no way of knowing exactly when was the first day that the bitch would accept the dog or when she first began to exhibit her mating cycle. About all he knows is what he can judge from the bitch as he sees her. So perhaps it is not fair to lay at his door as much as 70 percent of the fault, but I think it is.

Let us see what he should do and you should do in order to make such breedings more successful.

Your Part—Be sure that you keep track of your bitch so that you know the very first day that she begins to show red. You determine that you want her bred sometime between the 13th and 17th days. Therefore you should calculate how far she will have to go and by making allowances for the train trip see to it that she arrives as near the 13th to 14th days as possible. You should write to the owner of the stud dog as soon as you know the bitch is in season and ask him not to plan to accept any other bitches for his dog at about the time yours will be ready to breed and give him that date. There is not much that you can do beside furnishing a roomy comfortable crate, which isn't absolutely necessary to insure pregnancy, but is humane.

The Stud Dog Owner's Part—He should insist upon knowing the day when the mating cycle began. He should be willing to board the bitch until she has been willing to accept a dog for three days and then breed her. He should try her to his dog to make sure of this, on the first day she arrives. If he knows from a letter that she would already accept a dog before she was shipped, then he should cooperate by breeding her to his dog as soon as she arrives and has made herself at home. There is no good reason why she should not be returned directly after a little exercise, if the journey is not too long, and if the crate has been cleaned and aired.

Some people who own stud dogs insist on keeping bitches until the mating cycle is entirely over and then there is no danger that a bitch will have missed by his dog, arrive home, be bred to an inferior dog and raise a lot of poor puppies which are heralded as pups from the great champion. This indeed is a bad advertisement for him and for his owner, for if there is anything that is good for a dog's reputation, it is to be known as the sire of fine puppies. Such a sire is worth immeasurably more than the dog who is good himself but sires no outstanding progeny.

It is for that reason that the stud dog owner should always offer his dog at stud only to acceptable bitches, otherwise he may have to breed him to inferior bitches and these will hurt his reputation. Such precautions are wise indeed. Personally I prefer to have a bitch at the kennels just as long during her mating cycle as I can and do not begrudge the time spent in caring for her. Then I breed her every other day after the thirteenth, as long as she will stand, unless I have to use the dog on some other bitch. In order to determine the thirteenth, I try her with the dog and watch her actions, as well as feel of the vulva to determine when the congestion has left. I breed her first, two days after the first signs of definite acceptance.

Now for that other problem of how to mate dogs when it is difficult to accomplish. It is nearly always possible when one has the time and patience. I have never failed when the matter has been turned over to me and the dogs were in good condition, and near the same size.

The question of size is quite easily overcome in a variety

of ways. A small pile of straw is about the best thing I know to place behind the bitch to assist the mating. If the bitch is too tall, it is easy to put her hind feet on the ground and make the dog stand on the straw. If the bitch is too low, the straw may be bunched in a hard lump under her and her hind feet placed on the lump. I have tried breeding racks made of raised platforms with holes in them for the bitch's legs to stick through, but they continually pull their feet through and stand on the platform. They are too unnatural. Sacks filled with sand are good too, as are holes dug in the ground, but in the long run I have never had as good luck with anything as with straw or hay.

Artificial Insemination

It is hardly likely that many breeders will attempt such very diversified crosses as a Bloodhound and a Bassett Hound, where the bitch has to be stood on a box, but when and if they do, they will be able to work out a plan. If not, then artificial insemination is in order. With the proper equipment this is not at all difficult to accomplish.

According to any available scientific reports, I was probably the first person ever to have performed a successful artificial insemination on a bitch. This was back in 1916 when I crossed a St. Bernard with a French Bulldog. Ever since that time I've tried to develop better means. Discarding speculums, lights and other equipment, I now use only a 10 c.c. syringe equipped with a 6 inch long flexible silver needle with a blunt tip.

I reach my middle finger into the vagina and feel the cervix at the upper end. I insert the needle beside my finger and feel the tip enter the cervix, pushing it up perhaps an inch. When a dog and bitch are "hung," they turn and pull in opposite directions. If you feel the bitch, touching just above the anus, you will feel a rhythmic pulsation. This is the start of peristalsis, a wave-like motion which travels along the horn of the uterus and moves the semen along, aided by the pressure from the ejaculations of the dog. To make artificial inseminations successful, I learned long ago to try to simulate the pull of the dog's penis. So, after the syringe needle is in place, I place two fingers in the vagina and, bending them, pull so hard I almost move the bitch backward. At once the pulsations start and continue as long as I pull. With my left hand I press the syringe plunger. Ten minutes is sufficient to insure success.

The simplest way to obtain semen from a dog is to masturbate him by holding the thumb and first finger tightly behind the bulb of the penis, so that as the bulb swells, the hand may grasp it, and some squeezing is beneficial. There is a sensitive area directly behind the bulb which when pressed between the thumb and forefinger will cause the dog to push forward as in the act of copulation. The penis should be clear of the sheath and the pressure should be maintained until one can feel the congestion start to leave the penis. Even then it is well to hold the container under the tip so that as many drops of semen can be caught as possible. As the penis shrinks, sometimes an additional cubic centimeter will be discharged. I have tried holding the penis backward between the dog's legs just as it would be if he were tied to a bitch, but this is not any more satisfactory than holding it directly downward under the dog.

Some dogs will not ejaculate unless they receive the stimulation of having a bitch in season nearby or directly in front of them. I had one dog which would not react as I wanted unless he was in the act of breeding a bitch. I would let the penis slip out to one side and catch hold of it as though he were tied to the bitch. He would throw his leg over and would furnish a large quantity of semen. But I never was able to get any satisfactory results from him in any other way.

If it is desired to use the semen later, instead of injecting it at once, it must be stored in a relatively cool place. About fifty-five degrees has been found best, and at that temperature it may be stored several days, some claiming results when it has been kept a week, but it would seem risky to use it more than a day or two old and it should of course have been stored in sterile receptacles.

Preservation of Dog Semen

There is no good reason why dog semen should not be preserved and used over several years to impregnate bitches. Semen of other species is preserved and also shipped great distances in Thermos containers.

In 1971, this is as yet so new to some breeders' associations that they have not endorsed it, but in time it will doubtless be approved by all. Of course, everything in the procedure relies upon the honesty of those taking part in it.

W. J. Saeger was probably the first man to successfully inseminate a bitch with stored semen. He used some nine months old. He followed the usual procedure of diluting the semen with lactose, glycerine and egg yolk used in preserving cattle semen. Whether this is necessary except to dilute or extend the semen in the case of dogs is not clear but Saeger had success with the diluted product.

It is necessary to make a sperm count in order to know how much to dilute, if success is to be achieved. If there is a good sperm swarm the dilution is less than where there are fewer sperm. The mixture is dropped into hollows in a piece of dry ice where it is instantly frozen and becomes pellets. These pellets are then stored in liquid nitrogen at a temperature of −320F. One would expect that the cold would destroy the delicate sperm but not so; heat destroys them.

In thawing out the pellets, they are placed in a container which is immersed in 3% sodium citrate solution at room temperature.

It is obvious that the procedure is not for the average dog breeder who is unlikely to own the proper equipment. It does open the possibilities for an association or cooperative with an expert in charge.

There is one little trick which is worth knowing when one is confronted with difficulty in getting a dog interested in a certain bitch. I refer to attempting to breed only after a meal. Time and again I have seen dogs that refused to breed, be fed a medium sized meal and within a few minutes after it was eaten, start to mate and generally accomplish it. You will have much better results too if you try it. Sometimes dogs will become nauseated during copulation but it does no harm. Seldom do old accustomed stud dogs vomit but young ones often do. They will be sick no matter when they last ate, so that letting the dogs mate after a meal is not the cause of the nausea.

Psychological Problem

There are some dogs that refuse to copulate while a person is close to them. Even these may become willing and indeed eager to copulate when a person they know is in attendance. If a dog is shy it sometimes is very difficult to effect a mating with a bitch which may not be his size. I find it best to feed the dog and then turn the bitch loose in the run with him. This is better than bringing a shy dog to the bitch's run. After he has tried enough to become thoroughly excited, I gently step in and remain at a little distance. Then I approach and hold the bitch by the collar. If he is willing to attempt copulation I gradually come a little closer to the side of the bitch still holding on by the collar. Finally I am able to adjust the bitch and the dog does not object. When he has once connected and become tied, it is a good idea to stay very close to the pair for some time, petting the dog so that he will see there is no harm in having you about. After a few lessons like this he will welcome your presence and never again resent it.

There are bitches which are so small in the vaginal opening that even a small dog cannot insert his penis with hard pressing. This often happens with the sight hounds like the Greyhound, the Saluki and the Borzoi. The penis of the male dog of these breeds is quite small but even then they find it impossible to press the bulb of the penis past the opening. It is easier for them after the vulva has become thoroughly relaxed late in the mating cycle, but not always possible. In such cases it is wise to insert one finger into the opening and then stretch hard. The

101

muscle fiber is very tough, but it is possible to stretch it considerably. I have had to do this with bitches of several breeds.

Another difficulty in breeding is a web of tough flesh which occasionally one may feel in virgin bitches which is like a tough string vertically across the vagina. Sometimes this will cause pain to the dog when he forces his penis against it. It probably corresponds to the human hymen but is not round with an opening in the middle. This canine web has to be broken with the finger or sometimes with a pair of blunt pointed scissors. I have found one so tough that I could not break it even by hooking the end of my finger around it and pulling. For that reason it is well to insert the finger in the bitch's vagina if the stud seems unable to insert the penis, as though there were some obstruction. If the dog's penis can get past it on either side, the swelling of the penis will doubtless rupture it.

There are those who say that it is necessary for dogs to play together for a while in order to accomplish a good service. This is not necessary. Some hold the opinion that one service is not sufficient, and that the first only paves the way for the second, which is the successful one. This is not so. Others think that breeding a stud dog only once to a bitch makes him nervous and that he should be allowed to mate as often as he would if the pair were living naturally together.

The time for dogs to mate naturally is toward the very end of the acceptance period. For the argument to carry most weight, that is, if we want to treat the dogs as naturally as possible, we should put them together only toward the very end of the period. I have known of many pairs of dogs that have been reared together which showed not the slightest interest in copulation until almost the last day and then bred and had puppies. I have often speculated on the reason for this. The most opportune time for fertilization is earlier than this. The most reasonable explanation of it is that it may be a provision of evolution to prevent too close inbreeding. A bitch will naturally start roaming toward the end of her bleeding period. She will cover miles and miles of ground sometimes. She attracts all the dogs within a wide area and thus mates much earlier than she does when she is left alone with one.

Darwin noted there was some selectivity on the part of females for males even among polygamous animals. I am sure he was right but I am not sure that the dog is entirely polygamous. One time I took two bitches and two dogs of the same breed and let them each play together and copulate in separate pens. Then I put all four into one big run and they stayed in pairs as distinctly as pairs of pigeons, never paying any attention to the others' mates. After four days of this I took the males out and after keeping them out a day turned both back into the run with the bitches and both went to their proper mates.

I have observed many times, as have other students, that when a bitch is loose in the city she generally does show a preference for dogs of the Shepherd or Collie type, the longhaired sable or tri-colored dogs. There are well substantiated stories of certain dogs of this type being the fathers of most of the mongrels in many small towns. I have known of such dogs and one in particular. Many bitches, as soon as they could escape from their homes, would dash to the home of his owner and frequently the owner came outside to find his dog tied to a bitch. This dog seldom sought out the bitches but they sought him in preference to any other dog in town.

Many people think that the bulk of the male dog's penis must enter the vagina and that tieing must occur in order for conception to take place. But this is not so. Difficult matings are frequently brought to our hospital. In the cases of dozens where the males could not push the bulb in far enough to become tied, I have held it against the vulva for at least five minutes, allowed the dog to dismount, and pull, and all have resulted in conceptions. These have been with many breeds. Success is higher than in artificial insemination.

Sometimes the male's bulb swells within the sheath, and sometimes outside of the sheath when he fails to maintain contact with the vagina, or becomes too excited. When this happens most owners keep the dogs apart, waiting for the penis to lose its congestion. The best and quickest way to reduce the swelling is to allow the male to mount and to make copulatory motions. This will reduce it promptly, when preventing the mounting may mean an hour's delay.

Age at Eye Opening

By observing the time at which puppies open their eyes, one can tell whether they were premature, late or on time. For many years I kept a record of the eye opening times. By consulting these data it is obvious that the great majority of puppies begin to open their eyes at ten days. This is approximately correct because the eyes, on the tenth day of a normal gestation period, do appear to be open. Close inspection shows some eyes with the lids still stuck together along the outer edge (they start to open from the inside) and this last bit has cleared by the end of the eleventh day.

Among my record are eleven litters in which there were two distinct times of eye opening. Of a Bloodhound litter, three puppies were larger than the other seven, and the seven were three days later in opening their eyes.

It is quite possible that dual conceptions may account for this phenomenon, and possibly in it we have one explanation for runts in the litter. Two of my litters each had one puppy which was smallest and several days late in opening the eyes. Almost always, those which open the eyes late are more backward than the normal eye openers.

Sex to Order

There is a book which shows that producing the desired sex in a litter is merely a matter of douching the vagina of a bitch with bicarbonate of soda or with lactic acid. Hundreds of dog breeders, including the author, tried it. Some succeeded, most failed. A statistical evaluation shows that in the natural course of events a certain percentage would succeed. These would be those who testified to the efficacy; the rest kept quiet. A study with rabbits by Quisenberry showed that the procedure was not only useless but dangerous.

Spaying and Castration

Much could be said on the question of castration and spaying dogs and bitches. It is a prime consideration of the dog breeder. Castration is often advisable in keeping dogs from running away from home, and in preventing dogs which might become ugly from developing such a character, provided the owner is uninterested in breeding. Spaying effectively eliminates undesirable bitches from a breed, and has much to recommend it. Much has been written on the subject with, until recently, no scientific studies to back up the opinions. Some advise early spaying, saying that it tends to prevent bitches from becoming too fat. But if we study any experiments with other species, then surely one could not arrive at such a conclusion.

Chickens are caponized early in order to make them overgrown fatty creatures, pigs are castrated young in order that they may grow rapidly and with the most efficient use of food. If the operation is done when the pig is a grown boar, there is little change in the appearance. A spayed bitch looks and acts more like a normal bitch if she is allowed to become almost fully matured before she is spayed.

Studies with rats show this very well, as do those with other animals. It seems best to allow the sex glands to grow along with all the rest as long as possible before they are removed. While the operation is much easier for the veterinary surgeon when the dog is smaller, it would seem best for the dog to wait.

Quinlan and Steyn have added to our knowledge in this field. They studied the performance records of 36 female Greyhounds which had been spayed when they were from six to twelve months of age. Only two showed any tendency toward overweight. Their track records compared equally with those of the unspayed litter sisters. Spaying did them no harm. I wonder if, among 36 bitches unspayed, we could not find at least two which had a tendency to overweight? Surely we could.

Anderson used three dogs to study the effects of castration. He castrated a male puppy and compared it with a dog he castrated when it was mature. Then he spayed a mature bitch. So far as their general responsiveness is concerned, all three showed some degree of deterioration but the two operated on during maturity showed less than the one castrated while young.

Students of this subject will find further data in the work of Arenas and Sammartino, who studied the effects on the uterus of removal of the ovaries of bitches as well as removal of the pituitary.

Mary and Bill, from a cross between a Bloodhound and Bull Terrier.

Unusual Prolificacy in Bitches

I have been keeping records of bitches which produce large litters of puppies. Very often someone will have a bitch that produces 12 puppies, or 15, for that matter, and think "here is a record." The picture of the bitch is usually sent to the local newspaper and published. I have many such pictures. There are four showing Irish Setters with 17 puppies. Each claims a record.

Irish Setters are a very prolific breed indeed and it is probable that they may be the most prolific of the Setters. I have two records of Italian Bulldogs each with 22 puppies. I went to see one of these in Port Chester. N.Y., when the puppies were two days old and counted them. There was no mistake.

Usually, however these big litters are but flashes in the pan. The mothers produce a big litter and ever after, normal-sized ones. A St. Bernard bitch produced 22 puppies in one litter and 19 the next, making a total of 41 in two litters.

But there is no record anywhere that I can find of a bitch being as prolific over a period of time as Mary, one of my Bull-hounds. Here is her record:

In one of my genetic experiments I crossed a pure-bred English Bloodhound with a purebred English Bull Terrier on May

7, 1934. On July 7th a litter of seven pups was whelped. All were black-and-tan with white trimmings. On July 3rd I bred another similar pair of purebred dogs of the same breeds and they produced another litter of seven black-and-tan pups on August 3, 1934. Several puppies from each of these two litters were raised to maturity. A female from the former litter and a male from the latter litter were retained. Both dogs looked remarkably alike, as the illustrations on pages 196 and 197 show.

On June 16, 1935, Mary, a bitch from the first mentioned litter, came in heat just after going out of a false heat that started May 1st, and was bred to William, a dog from the second, on June 29, and several times thereafter. On August 30th, Mary whelped 12 puppies, six males and six females.

From April 6, 1936, until April 20th Mary was again bred to William several different times. On June 5th she whelped 17 puppies, nine males and eight females.

In October, 1936, she started a short false heat. The day was not recorded. From November 14th to the 28th she was bred several times to a different dog, this time a hybrid resulting from a cross between a Bloodhound and a Basset Hound. On January 23, 1937, she whelped 15 puppies, nine males and six females.

On June 9, 1937, Mary started a false heat which was over in five days. From July 10th to the 17th, Mary was bred to William on several occasions. On September 11th she whelped 18 puppies, ten of which were males and eight females.

On March 18, 1938, she started a false heat of short duration. Then, from April 13 until April 25, 1938, Mary was bred to William five times. On 23rd she produced another litter of 18 puppies, nine of which were males and nine females.

On October 17, 1938, she was again mated to William and on December 15th, she produced 16 puppies of which ten were males and six females. I was away and no false heat was recorded by my assistant. Only six of these puppies were allowed to live.

On April 13, 1939, she was bred again to William and allowed to stay with him through her heat period. They copulated many times. On June 21st she had 17 puppies, ten males and seven females. Only six of these were allowed to live.

Fourteen puppies raised out of a litter of fifteen born to Mary *(see page 106)*, and raised by her alone—without human help.

She didn't come in heat again until March, 1940. The date was not recorded. But on May 21, 1940, she whelped 16 more pups, nine males, seven females with William their father.

Then something happened to Mary. She ceased being prolific and had no more false heats. Her vulva did not swell to quite such large proportions and she came in heat in October and was bred to William but the date was not recorded. She whelped five puppies on December 17, 1940, and raised them all, one male, four females.

In April, 1941, she came in again, was bred to William and whelped four puppies on June 10, 1941, two males, two females. On October 9th, she was bred to William again and every other day until the 15th when her acceptance period ended. On December 12, 1941, she had her last puppies, five in all, two males and three females. It became necessary for me to reduce greatly the number of dogs I owned and she was put to sleep with no little grief on my part. Her reproductive tract was removed and sent to Dr. Carl Hartman at the University of Illinois for study. It was found that she had a large cyst on each ovary, which doubtless accounted for her sudden drop in prolificacy.

In her first eight litters, Mary whelped 129 puppies, or an average of 16 to the litter. They were whelped from August 30, 1935, to May 21, 1940. One hundred and twenty-nine puppies in eight litters within five years is a record which may stand for many years. Her average for all 11 litters was 13 puppies per litter. Only two puppies were born dead of that whole number and they were in the fifth litter which she whelped on a very warm day. The longest time required to whelp was five hours on the seventh litter. The first five litters were whelped

108

in under three hours each, and on no occasion did she ever retain a placenta or show sickness due to whelping. And incidentally, during the entire reproductive years she never tasted meat, except in dehydrated form in the prepared dog food she consumed. Her puppies were allowed to nurse and usually by the time they were two and one-half weeks old were lapping milk from a pan.

It was interesting to note that the time between litters when she was allowed to raise as many puppies as possible by herself was much longer than when she was only allowed to raise six or where she had only four or five. After raising those large litters she became emaciated, but would recover quickly and put on weight exceedingly fast. She produced a great volume of milk at the expense of her own body, and lactated about ten weeks.

One of the litters of 18 was entirely raised by putting them on three shifts and exchanging them every two hours. The litter of 15 was left with her and she raised 14 herself. I never again expect to see such a wonderful mother. I never knew her to lie on a puppy. She would root her offspring into a pile with her nose and make sure she had them all there before she curled up around them.

Her pseudo-heat periods were interesting. In none of them did she swell nearly as much as she did in the genuine ones. She was not interested in copulation and the periods were not nearly as long as the genuine periods. About 25 days elapsed between the start of the false heat and the start of the real one.

In the first eight litters there were 72 male and 55 female puppies born; in the last three there were five males and nine females.

Newbold Ely of Ambler, Pennsylvania, has done what no one else has done, so far as records show: his Welsh Foxhound bitch, Lena, bred to a Walker Foxhound, produced 23 puppies and all were raised to maturity. This, indeed, is an achievement. The picture of the mother and puppies is shown on page 110. Her next litter consisted only of nine.

Lena, with her 23 puppies—all raised—a great achievement.

Here are some authentic large litters by breeds:

St. Bernard	23, 22, 19
Bloodhound	15, 16, 17, 17
Springer	18
Irish Setter	17
American Cocker	12
Bull Terrier	22, 17
Foxhound	23
Newfoundland	16

PART II
PRINCIPLES OF HEREDITY

Charles Darwin, father of the theory of evolution. He believed that changes in heredity come about through use and disuse, rather than by mutations—sudden changes. (*From a photo by his son, Leonard Darwin, who presented it to the author.*)

1

How Heredity Changes

WHAT puzzles the average breeder about as much as any other one detail is an explanation of how our great dogs of today could have come from the ancient progenitor, which was so very unlike the dogs we know. It just doesn't seem reasonable. Now right here, in the explanation of how these great changes have come about, is one possible help to dog breeders. Everyone has heard of a sport. I do not like the term sport, because it might mean any one of several different things. The modern word is mutation, and a mutation is the sudden change from the inheritance of the ancestors. Evolution built up dogs to have tails, but if a dog suddenly lost its ability to produce a tail, that would be a mutation. Suppose he were born with half a tail. That too would be a mutation. Suppose he were born with legs only half the natural length, that would be a mutation. Or suppose a shorthaired dog were born with long shaggy hair which made it a better animal in some respects for a northern climate: another mutation. Now, in a natural state of environment, that is the way evolution has come about. These sudden changes, which were selected by the environment, where they were useful to the animal to help it to be perpetuated, were really the stepping-stones upward. Some of them that are going on around us today are reported frequently, and some are quite dramatic. I think, for instance, it is dramatic when a thirty-pound dog appears in a stock which has never been known to produce individuals that weigh more than twenty pounds. That is a mutation. It more than likely breeds true. These mutations are upward and downward. They represent the acquisition of a certain ability, and the loss of some other ability, or characteristic. Everyone should everlastingly be on the lookout for just such changes in his stock. One never knows when one will appear. And if it is valuable, it should be taken advantage of.

Of course not all of the sudden changes or mutations are hereditary. A large proportion of them are simply body (somatic) mutations, changes in cells and their descendants which did not occur in the germ plasm. Such are not passed on to

An inherited short-legged mutation from normal Cocker Spaniels. A new breed could easily be developed from such a dog if there were any advantage in doing it.

114

The short legs of the Pembroke Welsh Corgi are the result of a mutation, which bred true.

progeny because what happens in the body is not hereditary, only the germinal changes which occur in the creator of the body—the germ plasm—are passed on.

Nor should one be confused by appearances of recessives which have been long masked. We shall consider these when we take up Mendelism. Too many have been called "sports" or "rogues," and that is another reason for the distinction in the use of these terms. A mutation is not the reappearance of a masked trait which used to be tolerated in a breed, but something hitherto unknown to the breed.

Suppose that there is one mutation for every hundred thousand dogs born. That seems like very few, to be sure, but it may be that there are as many or more mutations than that taking place. It means that there is always an opportunity for improvement in our breeds.

It is at times possible to induce mutations by the use of X-rays but all of these, as far as I know, have been downward in the scale of evolution instead of upward. They all represent some losses which are detrimental to the animal. If only someone could invent a way of causing mutations which would be helpful to the animal and to mankind, what a blessing he might confer upon us.

Hunting foxhounds does not of itself make their puppies any better. What it does do is to show up the most desirable hunters, which are used to produce the next generation. (From painting, *Through the Hedgerow*, by Thos. Blinks, 1886. Courtesy, The Sporting Gallery, Middleburg, Va.)

How Changes Do NOT Come About

There are several ways in which one can spend a lot of time making mistakes in the breeding of dogs. Yes, and money too. There have been many dog breeders using methods of improvement which were in reality not methods of improvement at all. It is necessary for us to consider some of these, not alone to learn what they were, and thus be prepared, but because each of them helps us better to understand the true principles which have been demonstrated as fact.

Science has shown us that we cannot improve our dogs by reliance upon (1) the inheritance of acquired characters, (2) maternal impressions, (3) birthmarks, (4) telegony. Perhaps this seems like a dogmatic statement, but I do not intend to let it go at that. We shall consider each of these points and see.

Acquired Characters

The inheritance of acquired characters! As to the history of this idea, we do not know. One finds a few statements in literature of two thousand years ago, that men more or less thought well of it. But it got its biggest boost in the days of Erasmus Darwin, of Lamarck, of Charles Darwin, and has been tooted ever since by well-meaning but not very scientifically grounded people. I believe that if Charles Darwin had not assumed it was correct that it would have died a quicker death than it is dying.

Lamarck, a Frenchman, believed in evolution but he rejected the commonly held opinion that it had come about through special creation. He thought that the effects of use and disuse were inherited. No one can say that the theory was not ingenious, or that it was not logical in the light of the knowledge of the day. As a matter of fact, if it had not had the elements of reasonableness, it would not be believed as widely as it is even today. Casper Redfield, a Chicago attorney, did more than any other man in America about 1915 to popularize the conception. There are two ways of attacking a problem, the scientific and the legalistic way. Mr. Redfield was an attorney. He set out to prove his point and he made a good job of it.

He proved that the older a man was before he became the father of a child, the better the child would be, provided the father and the mother had always striven hard to improve themselves. This, he said, accounted for the fact that the men and women listed in the Hall of Fame were more often the younger children in their families. He gave especial attention to trotting horses and showed that the longer a horse raced, the better were his colts. The same applied to dogs. Hunt a dog hard and long and he will have better pups than as though he were not hunted, declared Mr. Redfield in effect.

Lamarck had written profusely along the same lines, but had not used great quantities of figures to back up his assertions as Redfield had done. Moreover, Redfield attributed the influence upon the germ plasm to energy, which was generated. He knew that was the way in which the effects could make their impression. It was pretty hard to say he was wrong because he would ask for proofs. It was like assuming there are ghosts. Nobody can prove there are not ghosts but neither can one prove there are. But that doesn't warrant such an assumption. We can say it isn't reasonable and ask for proofs of the theory.

Just as today it takes courage to be a free thinker and experimenter, so it took courage for August Weismann to undertake his experiment with mice. He took a pair of mice at birth and cut off their tails. When they were grown, he mated them and cut off the tails of their young. He kept mating mice that had their tails removed for 20 generations and when he was through there was not a mouse born with a tail any shorter than the original, nor was any born tailless. Think of all the generations that men have been dehorning cattle, and still calves are born which grow regular horns. Dogs have had their tails docked for goodness knows how long, and we still have to dock them. The same applies to sheep and other animals.

As we have seen, the germ plasm of an animal is isolated from the rest of the body. There is no known natural way of reaching it to cause any effect. There would have to be some method whereby nervous energy would be transmitted, and mechanical structure of the genes and chromosomes would have to be altered. But there is no such connection. The proper conception

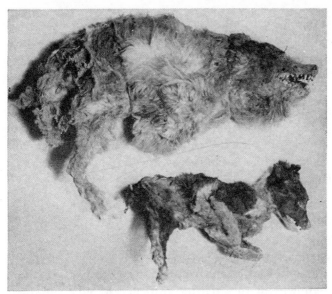

Here are dogs of 3,000 years ago, inhabitants of North America. They differ in many respects from our modern dogs and the differences probably came about by mutations. They were found among the remains of the Basket Maker Indians in Arizona.

of the basis of heredity shows us that it is quite impossible to change the germ plasm by the animal's behavior, and that is mighty fortunate indeed, for if, as the proponents of the theory of the inheritance of acquired characters hold, lack of action will cause disintegration, then heaven help the race! Most men and women are lazy. They do not do even a small part of which they are capable. If this lack of expenditure of energy were inherited, then the human race would soon be so badly off that there would be nothing left. Possibly this is one of the reasons why the germ plasm has been so well isolated.

If acquired characters are not inherited, how then is it that they seem to be? The answer is easy; they seem to be because we breed from animals which have been tested.

But aside from the theory being somewhat unreasonable, we now have excellent evidence that the germ plasm is immune to the effects of natural external influences. Dr. Charles B. Davenport, in studying records of cattle, found that there was no difference in favor of last calves over first calves of the same

119

cow, where large numbers were dealt with. Dr. Harry H. Laughlin found that the length of time that a horse has raced makes no difference in the speed that his colts can run. Many a dog breeder has disproved the theory, by breeding hunting dogs for show purposes for many generations, and then perhaps after five generations hunting the offspring of such dogs only to find that the fact their parents had not hunted made no difference. We must leave with the thought that it doesn't pay to breed dogs or any other animals, relying upon the hope that their acquirements will be inherited.

Birthmarking

Maternal impressions have been relied upon to upbuild animals and man for 30 centuries and more, and yet, there is not a single known bit of scientific evidence to substantiate it as a theory. Pregnant women have sat and listened to symphonies week after week so they might impress their children to be great musicians. Others have listened to great sermons so their children might be great preachers. Others have sat in museums day after day so their children might be great artists. It was even believed that a woman could influence the sex of her developing child if she thought sufficiently about it. Certain of our people still believe that this can be done.

Bible students will remember how Jacob cheated his old father-in-law, Laban, out of a good herd of cattle by the use of this device. He started out with a herd of Laban's cattle which were all solid colored. When they conceived, he laid before their eyes rods of alternate stripes. As I understand it, some were peeled and some not, to give this effect. The impression was passed on to the calves, and lo, they brought forth calves that were "ringstraked, speckled and spotted." He kept this up for a few years and soon crafty Jacob had a prime flock of speckled cattle, and these were his, according to the arrangement with Laban.

We can say from our knowledge of genetics that these bi-colored cattle would breed true because we know the solid color is dominant over the bicolor. In fact, that was how Jacob so easily obtained the bicolored cattle from the solid colored—they appeared as recessives. The rods had nothing to do with the process.

Here are four instances that are all authentic in modern times that have come to my personal attention. First, in Kentucky they have great field trials for Foxhounds every year. In one of these trials a lemon and white colored bitch was run that had an identification number 14 painted on her side. After the race she was bred and whelped some pups. One of these was born with a nicely colored 14 on her side.

Second, a biologist at Harvard University kept a cat in his rabbit laboratory to catch mice. The janitor warned him that if he didn't look out the cat would see the rabbits hopping around so much that when she had kittens they would hop too. The scientists jollied the janitor along, until the day came when the cat did have kittens and they hopped like rabbits.

Third, a Bloodhound bitch was used in France to chase the fallow deer. These dogs always come without white above the chest. But this one gave birth to a litter of pups and one of the pups was marked with white dots all over it like the fallow deer.

Fourth, a child was born with a defective arm. X-ray pictures were taken of it, which I saw. The reason for the arm was attributed to a fright the mother had. One day she had been suddenly surprised by the hired man who had a deformed arm very much like the baby's.

The truth of these instances probably lies in the fact that they are all coincidences, and coincidence is often mistaken for scientific proof. From a mathematical viewpoint it would be unlikely that such coincidences would not occur. But they are the ones that are noticed, and the news spreads very rapidly.

Considering the present enlightenment which genetics has given to the world, it is somewhat shocking that thousands of people have taken so seriously the appearance of that Foxhound with a number 14 on her side. Two generations back there was some reason for people in England to have taken the case of Lord Morton's mare seriously (see Page 126). Today there is no reason for these people in the central west to have drawn conclusions from this present instance.

121

At a Genetics Congress I showed a picture of this Foxhound bitch which I labeled, "an authentic coincidence," thinking that this would explain that although the facts back of this case were true the explanation was not sound, and that it was solely and simply a case of coincidence. This seems to have hurt the feelings of many who heard of it, and they seemingly felt that I was doubting their word. Even in the range of probability it would seem an impossibility that this could even have been a coincidence, but let us see.

On a trip to Kentucky, I went to the bottom of the case so far as I was able, and these are the facts as I found them. Anyone else is more than welcome to do the same and I feel sure that he will find no evidence of chicanery, no attempt to commercialize the dog, nothing but a straightforward recital of what happened. The mother and the pup are both dead, but pictures remain and the word of reliable people who are not interested in proving anything, and indeed were more interested in trying to see if there could not be some explanation, such as painting or dyeing. I think the facts are against these assumptions and so do all the others who have looked into it.

A fox hunter named Frank Hall of West Irvine, Kentucky, owned a bitch named Fashion. She was lemon and white in color. She was entered in a field trial and a number 14 was painted on her side as an identification mark. All the fox hunters in that section knew her. Her breeding was excellent, and Frank thought she stood a good chance of doing well in the trial. Several months later she was bred to a dog named Pat Stotts. Nine weeks later she whelped a litter of puppies. When they were little fellows Frank snapped a picture of them. He never noticed anything odd about any of them, and at weaning time he gave three of these pups to Dave Black. As they grew older Dave noticed the number 14 on the side of the one bitch pup. At first it was more or less indistinct, but as the pup grew it became more distinct. On the other side there was a straight line like a figure 1. He called the pup to the attention of Frank and when it was about half grown they took some pictures of it, one of which is shown. Frank told me that he wondered if it could have been the same pup and so he remembered that he had

122

Three puppy pictures of Number 14 taken at different ages. His mother ran in a field trial with a Number 14 painted on her side for identification. Too many people believe this was cause and effect—prenatal influence.

Did the heart on this puppy's side appear
because his mother had a love affair before
he was born?

snapped a picture of the pups when they were small and he got it out and there he could see the spot on the side. This spot is quite distinct in the original photo and there seems to be no doubt from the markings that this is the dog. I also have one of those pictures.

Frank had no other pups on his place at the time and Dave kept the pup around as a curiosity expecting to run it in fox chases. It grew to be a year old and died, but not until a great many people had gone to see it and had spread the word that Dave had another sure proof of the inheritance of maternal impressions. Frank Hall, the original owner, could not see much sense in the idea and told me that it was a coincidence, that was all, but others have used the case to bolster their beliefs in the moss covered and well disproved idea.

As soon as Number 14 was discovered I received letters and pictures from several of my friends in Kentucky. They had all examined the dog for dyes and chicanery and each felt it was genuine. Eight fox hunters who had known all the ancestors, who knew the cicumstances well, saw the dog for me and signed a typewritten affidavit, which I have. Mrs. Lucus Combs, daughter of General Roger Williams, went to see the dog and even pulled out hair to see if there was any white below the yellow, which would indicate the dog had been dyed in any place.

There is one interesting fact which should be mentioned. The dog was such a light lemon color as to be almost white to the eye. It was not until the puppy was several months old that Dave Black noticed it at all. But the camera records it was much darker than it appeared to the eye. The 14 was very inconspicuous on the live dog. It is too bad it was not marked in black, and too bad also that it was not a number 13 because that would seem to give the story just a little more authenticity. As a wit remarked, "Who taught the bitch to read? She must have known how to have marked that pup."

I have given the facts as I learned them, and I have no reason to doubt the word of any of the witnesses. The important thing is that this coincidence should not be allowed to add weight to the theory of maternal impressions.

When actual correlations have been made to test the truth of birthmarking, they have been practically nil. Take any one you wish. The figure 14 on the dog is the best of all that I have heard. This is a highly improbable thing to have happened, and yet it did, but is there a single person who thinks that the dog could read the 14 and so impress her pup?

In the case of birthmarking there is just one correlation that I have discovered. I have found that women who have sat and gazed on undraped statuary in museums always give birth to children who are naked at birth. That is the only 100 percent correlation along this line of which I have ever heard.

Birthmarks are usually considered as patches of mouse skin on humans, discolorations on the body, club feet, etc. They, too, can be classed as maternal impressions but of a physical manifestation. I need hardly go into an explanation of causes. They too are either inherited deformities or the result of injuries, or sometimes mutations which have come to be linked up with some event, such as fright experienced by the mother. In the case of these, too, it is coincidental in nearly all instances. Scientific attempts to find a connection have failed. A woman may have eaten strawberries and had a child with a red patch of skin the shape of a strawberry on its face. But that does not prove that the fruit caused the discoloration on the child's face. The fact is that many children are born with such marks whose mothers have never tasted strawberries. And children are born with club feet whose mothers were never beaten, as the silly old

125

superstition holds, and many children are born with moles covered with mouse skin whose mothers never saw a mouse during pregnancy. No, there is no proof that some physical formation was occasioned by a mental disturbance of the mother.

Telegony

Telegony is the supposed effect of the influence of a previous mating on the offspring of a subsequent. If a Cocker Spaniel is mated to a Wirehaired Terrier bitch, the puppies will be hybrids and then the next year if the same bitch is mated with a pure Cocker Spaniel, will her puppies in any way be influenced by the Wirehaired Terrier? There have been many instances to show that it would, and yet the best scientific evidence says that there isn't the slightest possibility that it will.

The idea was also held hundreds of years ago. It was even applied to perennial plants. If a plant just once produced a hybrid lot of seeds, it was pulled up and thrown away. Millions of wonderful animals were killed because of it. It was a two-edged sword in that it did both good and harm. It certainly gave men of the past a deeper respect for breed purity and a better reason for keeping breeds pure. It did harm because it was not truth and thereby occasioned the loss of money and fine animals to thousands of animal breeders through generations of the past.

The best scientific proof of its validity was Lord Morton's thoroughbred mare which I have mentioned. He bred her to a quagga. She had a foal with stripes. Next time he bred her to a horse of her own kind and the foal again had stripes. What better proof could one ask? But it was again a coincidence and not proof. The fact has since developed that many colts are born with stripes that fade out, just as the thoroughbred colt's stripes also disappeared.

I would not say that there are not occurrences which most assuredly look like this phenomenon. I have seen it happen several times among animals which I have been breeding. But I knew the true explanation. Suppose that you had a solid colored white Bull Terrier. He was mated to a brindle Bull. Then, next

126

A cross of a quagga with a thoroughbred mare
resulted in an erroneous conclusion.

time he was mated to another white dog. The first mating would
produce pups that had brindle and no solid whites. The second
might be expected to produce only white dogs, but instead the
bitch had two of her six pups with some brindle spots on them.
At once you might accuse the first stud of causing this effect.
But as a matter of fact, if you were impartial you would remember that quite frequently Bull Terriers have pups with
some brindle spots on them, and you would know the truth.

Four items are among the most cherished misnomers of animal breeders—inheritance of acquired characters, birthmarking, telegony and maternal impressions. Put no trust in them
whatever. We will improve our breeds more rapidly if we just
forget all about them.

Gregor Mendel, discoverer of the principle of alternate inheritance.

2

Gregor Mendel: His Theory of Alternate Inheritance

HAVE you ever looked through a microscope and seen what the red blood cells look like? Each of them is a little larger than a sperm cell. It is impossible for anyone to inherit the blood of another and for that reason we should never say that an animal is pure-blooded, or blooded, or blue-blooded, or use such expressions. These are simply antique and should be forgotten once and for all. They lead to very disastrous conclusions on the part of persons who have not thought much about this matter. In the years that I was Executive Secretary of the American Eugenics Society I had quite a number of letters from women who had had blood transfusions and men too, for that matter, and they wrote to ask whether their children were likely to be anything like the person who furnished the blood for the transfusion. That is not, however, the worst difficulty.

When one talks about blood, one naturally thinks of dilution, but heredity is not a question of dilution, but rather one of presence or absence.

Mendel's garden.

The man who threw the last shovelful of earth on the grave of the blood theory was Johann Gregor Mendel, a Moravian monk who did his work by studying inheritance in garden peas. I do not mean to imply that he necessarily ever gave a thought to the idea of the blood theory of inheritance, but so far as we are concerned, what he did for us was to remove it. For several hundred years before Mendel, men in Europe had been experimenting and had come to certain definite conclusions about inheritance. We find some words used by them which were later used by Mendel, old words which were given new meanings. We find many references in the studies of these old-timers, to the fact that certain traits seemed to skip a generation. An Englishman, named Knight, bred garden peas and drew certain very interesting conclusions which were in some respects not unlike those of Gregor Mendel, who did his work considerably later. And there was a Frenchman who mated cantaloupes and muskmelons. He noticed that they differed in certain respects and he wrote down in parallel columns the differences that he noticed. In other words, he tried to factor them out into the smallest possible common denominators.

About the same time that Mendel was doing his work, another Englishman, Sir Francis Galton, was studying color inheritance in the Basset Hound. He, too, found that heredity was not a case of dilution.

Unfortunately, Mendel's work was lost to the world until the year 1900. In 1866 he had read a paper before his little Historical Society and the Society later published this paper in all its detail, but because it was such an obscure journal and because Mendel was years ahead of the times, no one took any notice of it.

Dr. Liberty Hyde Bailey of Cornell, however, had made a listing, along with his other references, of this paper, although I understand he had not read it himself. A Dutchman named DeVries happened to see the reference among Dr. Bailey's listings. He read the paper and, in 1900, rediscovered Mendel's law of inheritance.

Mendel did not have the benefit of the knowledge about the genes and the chromosomes. Otherwise, his work would have been very much easier for him. However, what he did was to count and that was what his predecessors had failed to do, otherwise one of them would doubtless have discovered the theory instead of Mendel. Mendel showed us that where we reduced the individual down to its smallest inherited component traits, where there is a difference between two individuals in regard to one of these unit traits, and these two individuals are mated, then one trait will appear in the offspring, while the other will not. He called the trait which appeared the dominant and the trait which did not appear or receded, he called the recessive.

Each of these traits having been in the end determined by pair of genes in a pair of chromosomes, therefore, one half of the inheritance came from one parent and one half from the other. This is because one gene came from the germ plasm of one parent and its partner from the germ plasm of the other parent. Now suppose that we consider the character of ticking as an example. This is a simple matter in heredity. Every dog breeder knows what a blue belton English Setter looks like. The tiny black spots through the white give the appearance of a bluish cast. Hounds which carry this color modifier are referred to as being blue-ticked. We see the color in several breeds. Now this ticking is a simple uncomplicated Mendelian character. If we mate a ticked Setter which is pure for the trait, that is, a dog which has a pair of determiners or genes in his germ plasm, each of which determine the ticked color pattern, with a dog which is white, we should have a litter of puppies all of which are ticked. Experiments have shown that the ticking factor is dominant, and that is how we can predict in advance.

The germ plasm of the puppies will not be pure for the ticking, because each pup must have received one gene from one parent and its partner from the other, thus having one for ticking and one for the lack of ticking. If we mated a pair of white dogs we couldn't possibly have any ticked puppies because the whites do not carry the ticking. If they did we would see it and since we do not see it, we know that it is not there. That is why we say that a pair of dogs which carry recessive genes can never produce a dominant. In breeding, if a pair of recessives come from parents which appear dominant, we know

132

A pair of blue ticked hounds. The ticking factor is dominant.

that the parents were not pure for that trait. We know, too, that once a dominant is lost from the germ plasm, no amount of breeding among recessives will bring it back. You will see in the latter part of this book how very useful that bit of information can be to us as breeders.

But as a mathematical proposition, if there are at least a pair of determiners for each external trait which we see, then how many ways can those pairs be combined with other similar pairs? The answer is six. Some years ago I bred a great many black and white guinea pigs to be used as exhibition material to show how Mendel's law operates. I wish these were dogs but you can see from the colors and the dots under each, what are the six different ways that the determiners can unite. Just imagine that the black guinea pigs are ticked English Setters, and that the whites are non-ticked. There you have the six ways that the determiners for these colors might combine, and they do combine that way in actual breeding practice.

Now, these things are not impractical theoretical happenings. They are useful. No matter what character about a dog you care to consider, if that character has been determined by research to

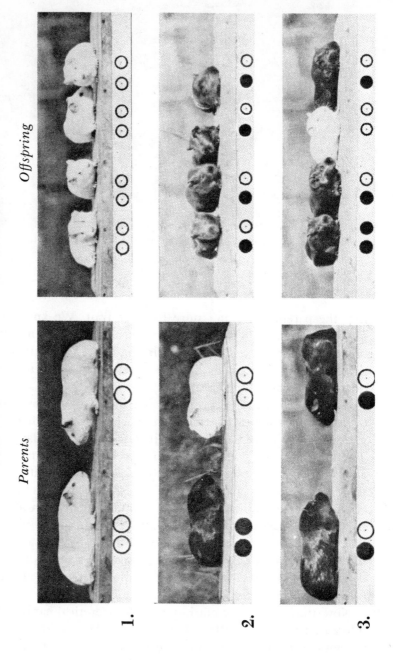

Parents

Offspring

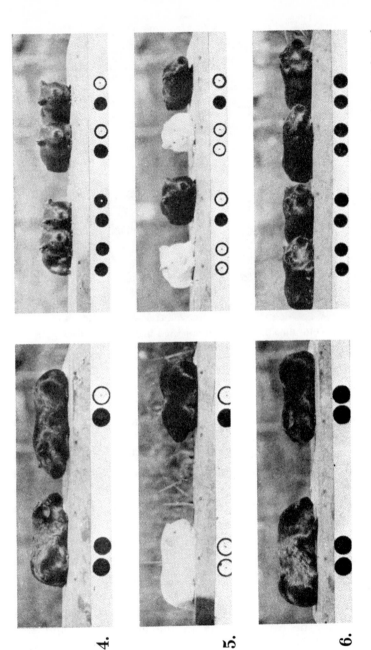

The six possible ways in which a pair of determiners can unite, and the expected results. Only in cases 1, 2, and 6 are the exact expectancies realized in every litter. The ratios apply where large numbers are considered.

A white Bloodhound which appeared in a litter of black and tans. White Setters sometimes appear in litters of purebred Irish Setters, and such recessives are not uncommon in all breeds.

be inherited as a simple Mendelian character, then you can apply this principle.

When you hear students of heredity speak of a 25-50-25 ratio you know they are likely speaking about the probabilities when two hybrids are crossed. When they speak of a 50-50 ratio, they are speaking about the expectancy when a hybrid is mated with a purebred, and that can be taken either way. The hybrid may be mated with a pure recessive or with a pure dominant.

It is only necessary to have one dominant present in the germ plasm and the character shows. When traits seem to skip a generation, it is because a pair of recessive genes combine. Recessives really do skip a generation and they may skip a dozen. A recessive may be carried along in the germ plasm and will never come out until it meets up with another like itself, or it may be lost at any generation. The Bloodhound pictured at the top of page 136 was the result of just that sort of thing. He could not be registered as his color disqualified him. This happens all the time and accounts for good and undesirable characters which often occur in what is thought to be pure breeds.

The following statement might be considered as "rules for dominant and recessive traits." It was drawn up by the old Eugenics Record Office staff, and is useful as summarizing our knowledge on the subject:

With Dominant Traits, note:

1. The trait does not skip a generation.
2. On the average a relatively large number of the progeny are affected.
3. Only affected individuals carry the trait.
4. With traits of this sort, there is less danger of continuing undesirable characteristics in a strain, than is the case with recessive traits.
5. The breeding formula for each individual is quite certain.

With Recessive Traits, note:

1. The trait may skip one or more generations.
2. On the average a relatively small percentage of the individuals in the strain carry the trait.
3. Only those which carry a pair of determiners of the trait, exhibit it.
4. Those carrying only one determiner can be ascertained only by mating, hence there is much more danger of insidiously contaminating the strain than is the case with dominant traits.
5. The trait must come from both sides of the family.

There are a great many characteristics of dogs which have now been worked out on a Mendelian basis, and are known to be unit characters. But then again, there are many others whose mode of inheritance is not known, and others again which are not governed by any one pair of genes but by so many as to make a Mendelian prediction out of the question. The entire third section of this book is devoted to these things. I mention them here because people often ask how body length is inherited, how head length, ear length, racing ability. "Are they dominants or recessives?" These are not simple matters.

Indeed, a great many of the things we find most valuable to us in dogs such as disposition, innate hunting ability and so forth, are not inherited as simple characters, but in some cases are the sum total of almost all the dog has. In such cases we have to study them in a different manner, which I shall outline later. Some are variations of unit characters too, and some are unit characters on which modifying genes effect changes.

Every dog breeder should know the underlying principle of Mendel's law. Then they would not be talking what percent of blood of his great grandfather this dog carried or that the blood of the dam is 69% of the inheritance of the puppies, and all such foolishness with which dog breeding is still water-logged. They would know that either a character is present or it is absent. They would realize that some characters are recessive and are carried that way in the germ plasm, only to crop out later, and some are dominant. They would realize that the sex in all but a few cases had nothing to do with the inheritance. They would not be saying that the great granddam controlled the color of the puppies. We know this is not so, and we know it is not a single ancestor, but that the controlling factor is the thing that controls it in every ancestor who possesses it and that it goes on and on creating, creating, and not being created by any dog in the line.

Think about the dog as the expression of the germ plasm. The dog and his near kin show what that particular germ plasm is capable of doing. If we keep this conception in mind we shall be better dog breeders.

Some breeders will naturally ask, "What happens when two dominants occur in the same dog, each of which affect color?" That is a reasonable question. For example, I am often asked to explain the result of mating a blue-ticked hound with a black-and-tan. The progeny is black-and-tan, but the ticking is not visible unless the dog has a white patch on the chest. So people ask, "Is the ticking factor recessive to the black-and-tan then?"

It would appear to be, but it is not. It cannot show unless

138

the dog is white. It is still a dominant trait even though it is carried in such a way that one does not see it. The saddle factor is a dominant when one kind of tan is concerned, but when the other is concerned it would appear to be recessive. The dominant tan dog can carry the recessive tan and the saddle factor also. The modifier (the saddle factor) , though masked in this case, is still a dominant.

So coat color modifiers can still be dominant and not show. In that case the modifier is generally written in genetic symbols as an initial written above and to the right of the character it modifies, i.e., W^t or S^T. Such traits we may call, "masked dominants."

Incidentally, when breeders talk about prepotency in a dog they usually mean that he or she carries a predominance of dominant determiners in his or her germ plasm. Thus the progeny tend to look more like that parent, no matter to what dog he or she is mated.

A point not often understood by dog breeders is that for every modifying gene there must be its opposite. Thus we say that there is a gene which dilutes black to blue and red to fawn and we represent them in small letters, as for example "b." We must also have "B" which is the opposite or full extension of color.

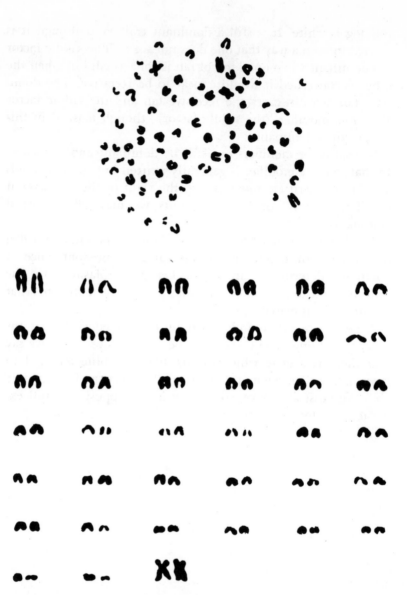

Normal dividing spread and chromosome "map" (karotype) of a 3-year old
Keeshond. Above: Chromosome spread of a dividing white cell cultured from
blood. Below: Karotype constructed from above spread by arbitrarily pairing the
chromosomes according to size. The two X-chromosomes (bottom row) are
conspicuous because they are the only metacentric (centrally located) chromosomes seen. There are 38 pairs of acrocentric autosomes (those chromosomes
other than the sex chromosomes). Illustration with permission from article,
Hereditary Diseases of the Dog, by D. F. Patterson and W. Medway, *Journal
of the AMVA*, vol. 149, 1966.

3

Sex—Ancient and Modern Beliefs

THERE are hundreds of theories about the cause of sex. Most of them have no sound data to support them. Only a few are worthy of consideration.

The modern sex theory holds that the sexes are different because of the differences in the chromosomes. Every mammal has an even number of chromosomes, each species having its distinct number. The human has 24 pair, the horse has 32 pair, the fruit fly has four pair, the crayfish has 100 pair, the fox 19 pair, and the dog 39 pair.

If we could look at the chromosomes under a microscope and sort them out we would see that the different pairs did not look alike. Some would be dots, some like hairpins, some like straight lines. We might label the pairs, A, B, C, D, etc. Now the two chromosomes which constituted the pair we call A would be alike in appearance. In fact, this would hold true of all of the chromosome pairs *in the case of the female*. But it would not hold true in the case of the male. There would be one pair of chromosomes that we should find composed of two that were not alike.

141

These are called the sex chromosomes, and a good deal of what we know about genetics has been determined upon the basis of this information. I have waited this long to explain sex so you would find it easier to understand because you had the key which corresponds to knowledge of the chromosomes.

If we designate each of the female sex chromosomes as X, then the female pair is XX. The male has one of these X chromosomes in his pair but the other is different and we call it Y. So the male pair is XY. Now let us do a little juggling.

Each offspring receives one-half of his chromosomes from each parent. The whole matter is one of chance. Every germ cell or ovum which the mother contributes has half the requisite number of chromosomes, that is, one from each pair. Each, therefore, has one X chromosome. In the cell division which produces the sperm, an X chromosome goes into one sperm and a Y into the other. So it is easy to see that half of the sperm cells have the X chromosome and the other half have the Y.

Don't you see, therefore, that it is simply a matter of chance as to which the offspring shall be? If a sperm cell with an X chromosome unites with the ovum, there will be an XX pair of sex chromosomes formed and the offspring will be a female, but if a Y joins with an X, the offspring will be a male.

Diverse Sex to Order Theories

Our forefathers didn't know this. Hence they elaborated theories to explain sex, some of which make us laugh. The moon, the sun, the season of the year, the wind, the climate, the period of the mating season, the ripeness of the sperm and of the ovum, the food eaten, the water drunk, the air breathed, the age of the parents, the number of times mated, the side on which the dog left the bitch, the size of the different sides of the body and even maternal impressions, not to mention a great many others were believed to have influenced the sex of the offspring.

A friend of mine paid a doctor $500 to prescribe the diet for his wife so she would have a girl, and she had a boy. This doctor used the sugar treatment.

142

Astrology was used by dog breeders, and is today, despite
the fact that it has no scientific basis whatever.

The originator of the sugar treatment apparently believed
that girls were sweeter than boys, judging by the fact that he had
his women patients eat sugar if they wanted a girl, while if
they wanted a boy, they were to eat as though they had diabetes.
All who succeeded were ardent boosters of the great doctor.
The half who failed were told they hadn't followed directions
carefully enough, and indeed were not allowed to know they
constituted as large a proportion as half. So they tried again,
and since the chances were even that the next child would be
what they wanted, half of the half thus were also convinced. It
was great business.

Another method which was much heralded was based on the
fact that the right side of the body was stronger than the left.
The right side was therefore where the males came from, because they were stronger than the females (all except mentally)
and the left side was where the females came from because the

143

female of the species was weaker than the male (all except mentally). The originator of the theory proved this nicely by taking the right ovary out of a bitch and the right testicle out of a dog, and upon mating them he got only female pups. He did the same with a sow and a boar with similar results.

Then an Englishman contradicted him, and got the agreement of the discoverer of this momentous idea that he would withdraw his claims, if the Englishman repeated the experiment with rabbits and got little rabbits of both sexes. The experiment was performed and both sexes produced whereupon the inventor backed down and claimed that all the experiment really proved was that his theory didn't work in the case of rabbits.

Of all the 1,900 odd sex theories that have been put forward in the past 2,500 years, not one has ever been demonstrated to stand up under test. I will say that there is just a little evidence in regard to one. There is more than enough to make many people stand up and shout that they know how to produce sex to order, but not enough to convince sceptical scientists. This little evidence is in regard to the time method. Whether it holds out hope in the case of dogs I do not know—my impression is that it does not hold out much hope in natural matings.

It is now coming to be held that there is a difference in size between the male producing sperm and the female producing, the latter being larger. Being larger they can therefore live longer in uncongenial environments. That is the starting point. It is a delicate proposition because all the sperm that would be required to start all the dogs in America, if they could be massed together in an Army, would make a speck about as large as the head of a pin. Nevertheless, by microscopic methods it is possible to measure them.

Now add to this fact another. If mating takes place before the ova are discharged from the ovaries, the sperm have to wait until they are. If there are conditions such as higher temperature, acidity, different concentration of medium, etc., in the female reproductive tract, where the sperm have to do their waiting, then the ones that are largest can best survive. This would mean therefore, that where mating takes place before ovulation, a somewhat greater percentage of females would be produced. It might also mean that the smaller male producing sperm would be somewhat more active, and that if mating takes place at the time of, or following ovulation, then they would be the first to reach the goal and fertilize the ova. That would mean that mating late in the period would produce more males and mating early in the period would produce more females. And as I say, there seems to be a little evidence anyway that such is the case.

If anyone wishes to investigate this subject further, the following table, showing the sexes of puppies of 7,462 litters which comprise 49,650 individuals, will be of interest.

The relative frequency of litters of different size in German Shepherd dogs and the total number of males and of females in each class of litters, follows:

Litters		No. in Litters	No. of males	No. of females
39	....	1	18	21
264	....	2	254	274
373	....	3	557	562
600	....	4	1218	1182
1000	....	5	2591	2409
1207	....	6	3716	3526
1281	....	7	4677	4290
1147	....	8	4743	4433
797	....	9	3714	3459
453	....	10	2290	2240
187	....	11	1052	1005
78	....	12	495	441
26	....	13	149	189
5	....	14	39	31
5	....	15	46	29

Total 7462 litters ____ 25,559 ____ 24,091

Total 49,650

Note that there were more females than males in the litters which were comprised of only one or two puppies. Note also that there were more males than females where the litters were comprised of 14 and 15 puppies. When dogs are mated at the optimum time, the greater activity of the male-producing sperm permits them to fertilize the ova in slightly greater numbers than female-producing. Or perhaps there is a selectivity on the part of the ova.

145

I have gone through my records for the last few years and chosen all of the litters which comprised 14 or more puppies. Add to these Mr. Ely's prize litter:

Number Litters	Number Pups in Litter	No. Males	No. Females
1	23	15	8
2	18	19	17
3	17	19	15
2	16	19	13
6	15	55	35
9	14	65	47
		192	135

This is a ratio of 142.2, males to 100 females, but no higher than another group as you will see later.

Several studies have been made and published dealing with the sex ratio in dogs. The principal studies have dealt with Greyhounds in England, and German Shepherds in Germany. Schmaltz cites Wilkins as showing that the proportion of males to females in dogs is 110:100. Combining the figures of Heape and Dighton for Greyhounds, the figures for 25,374 dogs born was 115.8 males to 100 females. My own studies with German Shepherds, which figures were derived from the official registry for the breed and covering 49,640 dogs, was 106:100.

Following the publication of my paper in 1927, W. Winzenburger in Germany made a calculation from records from the same studbook covering the period of 1928 to 1934. This embraced 22,281 litters with 159,304 puppies, making the average litter size 7.15 and a sex ratio of 105.5:100.

Repeatedly the point has been debated whether the proportion of males to females can be influenced by certain factors, such as food, climate, breeding at various times of the year. It is a serious matter that of the hundreds of theories which have been postulated, in each case the originators of the theories have proved to their own satisfaction that what we today consider theory was to them definite fact.

What influences are at work, if any, to modify the sex ratio, is always a matter of interest on which to speculate. In using records from kennel clubs or registry associations many factors must be taken into consideration. Naturally the dogs recorded in kennel association records have been fed on wide varieties of foods, have been kept under a wide variety of kennel and climatic conditions and, therefore, in studying the sex ratio one studies a composite of extremely varied conditions. It has seemed to me that it would be interesting if we could take the figures from at least one fairly large group of dogs which had been raised under as nearly uniform conditions as possible.

In my own kennels considerably over 12,000 puppies have been whelped, but of these a much smaller number has been whelped when the parents have been fed on the same food, many having been used in food testing experiments. Therefore, I went through the records carefully and selected all of the litters born to parents which had been fed the same food and also selected only those puppies whose parents had been raised from puppyhood in my kennels and had been mated to dogs which had lived at least a year in the kennels. All others were rejected. This was done in order to eliminate as many outside influences as possible and thus, within certain limits, to choose a group of puppies conceived under relatively similar conditions. All of my dogs are kept out-of-doors the year around with no artificial heat in their kennels. In all, 1,440 dogs were born to parents which had been kept under these fairly uniform conditions of feed and care. The sex ratio of this number of puppies was 124.31 males to 100 females. The table below shows the births by months.

Birth Months	Males	Females	Ratio Males to 100 Females	Oestrus Months	
December	40	33	121	October	
January	88	59	169	November	Average ratio for
February	50	41	122	December	colder months
March	34	24	141	January	143.1 Males:
April	34	26	130	February	100 Females
May	53	32	165	March	
June	78	64	122	April	
July	114	97	117	May	Average ratio for
August	84	74	113	June	warmer months
September	36	28	128	July	116.1 Males:
October	76	69	110	August	100 Females
November	111	102	108	September	
	798	642			

147

It is interesting to note that the puppies conceived during the warm months of the year show a sex ratio, males to females, of 116:100, whereas those conceived during the colder months of the year show a sex ratio of 143:100.

According to Dr. Marca Burns, who studied sex ratios in 18 breeds, the ratio of males to females was over 100 except among Airedales, Bulldogs, Bloodhounds, Retrievers and Toys, where it was more than 120:100.

There has been so much written on the question of the use of acid and alkaline douches to produce the desired sex that a word must be said on the subject. Students are finding that it not only does not work, but that it may be dangerous to the health of animals. This has been one of the most common methods proposed in the past, yet carefully controlled studies to test it produce negative results. In 1945, Quisenberry found it useless in the rabbits he studied.

4

Sex Linkage

AFTER the first work on Mendel's law was done by students of biology, it was found that it worked when applied to a great many characters in the species studied. A whole school grew up; a new science was started, that of genetics.

But there were many findings which did not seem to check. One of these was not discovered for many years. Then it was found that there was a strange phenomenon which students began to speak of as sex linkage, which upset predictions until the cause was understood. The cause was learned in fruit flies, which could be bred by millions and studied under microscopes.

Keep in mind the distinction between sex linked traits and sex limited ones. What we think of as masculine or feminine traits are the sex limited ones. These are caused by the influence of the gonads, the male and female reproductive glands. For instance, if the ovaries of a young pullet are removed she grows to look like something between a rooster and a hen, and if the testicles of a young male bird are removed he grows to have more nearly the same appearance. Such facts show us the influence of sex in limiting the body characteristics. But these modifications are not genetic in origin in the sense that truly sex linked traits are.

149

Poultry furnish the best example of the effect of the sex glands in modifying physical traits. The male and female look very different, but the pullet on left and the cockerel on right appear similar because of the removal of sex glands.

My experience with the spaying and castration of dogs shows me that the same facts apply to dogs. Clients who insisted that I spay six and seven week old puppies learned that at maturity they looked neither male nor female. Most veterinarians suggest that spaying be done when the pup is full grown, but before she first comes into heat.

If you will observe the pictures of the chromosomes herewith, which are diagrammatic drawings of the chromosomes in the fruit fly, you will note that they are in pairs and that all the pairs are alike except one. This pair is different in the male. In the female the corresponding pair has two chromosomes which are alike. There must be some traits which one of those chromosomes possesses, which the other does not in the case of the male. There could be some unmatched genes. In the female, with her pair of similar chromosomes, this would not be the case.

Female   *Male*

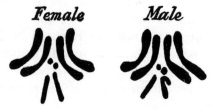

Chromosomes of the fruit fly.

150

This little chromosome which does not match the mate is the sex chromosome. If a newly formed cell which was created by the uniting of a sperm and an ovum possesses it, then the off-spring will be a male. If it has a pair of evenly matched chromosomes, it will be a female. Each male-forming sperm cell has one of each kind of chromosome including one of the smaller chromosomes. Each female-forming sperm cell has one of each of the chromosomes and the long one of the sex pair.

The reason that the sexes are evenly divided is because there are an equal number of sperm cells bearing the large chromosome and sperm bearing the small chromosome. Which of these will enter the ovum is a toss-up and that is equivalent to saying a 50-50 chance. The dice are not loaded so far as we know. The number of males and females born is another matter, however. This ratio is 106:100, but the reason for it is because 6% more females die in utero than males.

The sex linked traits which are quite common throughout nature and which must exist in dogs, as I have inferred, are those which lie on the large chromosome and are not dominated by the small. They are like any gene acting alone and without the influence of a partner. For that reason they do not seem to act according to the established principles of Mendelism. Some students have said that sex linked traits are recessive in females and dominant in males. In a sense that is true. The classic example is haemophilia, which is inherited through the mother, from maternal grandfather to grandson. The women do not have it, because the chromosome which accounts for it has a partner in the woman's germ plasm and the partner possesses a gene for normalcy which dominates the gene which causes haemophilia.

Dog breeders should be on the lookout for sex linked traits. Are there any characters which the maternal grandfather possesses which he passes on only to his grandsons and not to his granddaughters? Who will be the first dog breeder to find the first such character in dogs?

Another matter which we should understand also is that of linkage, as contrasted with sex linkage. There are many traits in all animals which are inherited in blocks, because the deter-

151

miners for them lie so closely together along the chromosomes. There is good evidence that the trait of yellow eye and liver nose in dogs are linked. I say this because among my own dogs I have found yellow-eyed dogs which did not have the liver nose. When we find traits which are thus linked it is quite difficult to break up the partnerships which keep them together. In some species, notably corn, mice and fruit flies, a great deal is known about these linkages and in fact it was the discoveries of them which enabled geneticists to actually draw maps of the chromosomes and tell where on each chromosome the definite genes were located.

What dog breeder will be the first to find other linkages? There must be a great many among all the inherited characteristics in our breeds of dogs.

5

Twins and Litters

THERE are two kinds of twins. One kind is identical twins, which are real twins. The other sort are fraternal twins. The former are exceedingly alike; the latter are no more alike than ordinary brothers or sisters. The former can be of only one sex; the latter can both be of the same sex or one of each sex. When an animal has what we term a litter of young, she is producing what, in animals which normally produce a single offspring at a time, one would call twins, triplets, quadruplets, quintuplets, etc. I never could see why there was any reason for calling ordinary twins, *twins*. We should reserve that word for the real thing, namely, the identical sort. What is the difference between a flock of sheep, all of the ewes of which have been bred up to produce say three or four lambs at a time, and certain dogs which have been bred down to producing only three or four young to a litter? We do not call the offspring of the latter triplets. We should call them both by the same name.

Possibly the reason we do not is because of the differences in the uterii of the various species. In the human the uterus is single, in the cow double, in the rabbit, the dog, the rat, etc., it

Identical twin calves on the left and ordinary twin calves on the right. The identical are not absolutely identical as to color, but other means of comparison showed their identity.

is simply a pair of tubes which join into one like the letter Y. That seems to be the only reason for this difference between litters and triplets, quadruplets, etc. But I contend that we should have more accurate designations. There are many human beings which have produced four children at a time which were all as unlike as are the four little puppies produced by a Pomeranian bitch. The cause of the four in each case is the same— four separate and distinct sperm fertilized four separate and distinct ova.

If a cell which was produced by one sperm, having fertilized one ovum instead of going on and producing a single individual, divides and the two separate, then the result is two individuals with the same inheritance. There are occasional twin calves, which are real twins, but there are many more calves which

When the fetal sacs of a male and female embryo join, the female will be sterile. She is called a free martin.

154

are born two at a time and which are simply ordinary brother and sister.

Sometimes a pair of twins are produced by a mother and they are of opposite sexes, and sometimes the female grows up and is sterile all her life. This happens more than occasionally in some species. It is caused by the joining of the two placenta. Such offspring are called freemartins. The illustration shows the cause. The blood of both becomes mixed and the developing glands of the male exert an influence over those of the female so that they never develop properly. It was commonly held that the effect was alone on the reproductive glands, but it is more likely that the influence is over the entire glandular system. It requires more than the functioning of the sex glands to produce the sex manifestations, so it is likely that the female gland balance is disturbed.

Ever since the publication of this book I've been receiving letters from persons who have seen two puppies born within one fetal sac, who have broken it themselves and saved the puppies. We know therefore that twins are not an uncommon occurrence in dogs.

The first case which came to my attention, which I believe was indisputedly a case of identical twins, occurred in a litter of Cocker Spaniels. Their pictures are enlightening. The illustrations (page 157) show the great degree of similarity between Twin Su and Twin So, American Kennel Club Nos. 790,747 and 790,748 respectively, a pair of Cocker Spaniel puppies bred by Mr. O. B. Gilman of Boston, Massachusetts, owner of the Idahurst Kennels.

Mr. Gilman had read a number of my articles in which I asked that any cases of possible identical twins in dogs be reported to me. Upon a visit to Boston, Mr. Gilman reminded me of my request and took me to his kennels to get my opinion as to whether two dogs were identical twins or not.

After careful study of all anatomical features, there seemed little doubt. One point in particular was striking, and it was indeed this point which called the similarity to the owner's attention. Under the eyes of each there was a small red spot. Sometimes a dog's eyes will run, and if the hair underneath is white will leave a brownish stain, but in this case it was not caused by the eyes running. No amount of soap and washing would remove the spots, because they were caused by different colored hair. The dogs were black and white, but these spots were deep red. Such a combination of color is apparently new.

But there was another feature, namely, the placement of the teats on the abdomen, which also pointed to their monozygotic beginning. From the anterior the teats ran along in pairs to the last pair, which in each case were irregular. The right teat of each pair, instead of being opposite its mate, was about an inch posterior to it. The placement appeared to the eye to be the same.

The color, however, was not identical, but no less so than the differences in color seen in identical Holstein calves. Note that the left ear is split lengthwise, being half black and half white in each pup. The face markings are very similar. The increased amount of black on the body of one, as compared to the other, seems to be the one point of dissimilarity.

There were, however, a number of points about the color which were indicative. For instance, there were many small black spots on the legs and body that were of the same size and identically placed. Some may be seen in the illustrations. For instance, note the spots on the lips, and the spots between the eyes.

The occurrence was reported by me to a number of psychologists who evidenced great interest in these pups. Accordingly they were kept separate from each other, one upstairs and one down in the large kennel. It was highly interesting to observe their similar methods of turning around before lying down; their similar positions of resting and general attitudes in sleeping. Unfortunately they both died. The cause is not known. They grew to maturity and one day one died after a very brief illness, which was not distemper. The very next day the other died from a similar illness. No other dog in the kennel was sick at the time.

Among the hundreds of puppies born while I looked on, I cannot say that I have ever known of two coming from the same sac, and for puppies to be identical twins, they must have been brought to that point within the same sac. The trouble is

Idahurst Twin Su and Idahurst Twin So, the first identical twin
dogs ever reported.

that many puppies are born and the mother chews off the umbilical cord and does not pull the afterbirth out and consume it.
Rather the severed cord retracts and after a while the afterbirth
is discharged, often just before or with the next puppy to be
born.

On that account it seems impossible to determine whether
solid colored puppies, black-and-tans, or others marked very
similarly came from one embryonic sac or from two. But I have
seen a number of pairs of puppies which had large amounts of
white which one would certainly not want to state emphatically
were not identical twins, and I am inclined to believe that they
were. It would be most interesting if every dog breeder would

157

The tendency to produce large litters is distinctly hereditary.

be on the lookout for these unusual occurrences and report them, for surely they occur in dogs as well as in the case of other mammals. Nothing would make quite as good material for study, outside of twin humans, as twin dogs. So if any reader finds them, please communicate with some psychologist or with the author and he will see that they are brought to the attention of some scientist who will greatly appreciate it.

Many breeders wonder if the tendency to produce multiple offspring is inherited. There isn't any doubt of it. Sheep have been bred so that they have become very much more prolific. Dogs, rabbits, guinea pigs and other laboratory animals also have. In human beings the tendency to have more than one child distinctly runs in families and is inherited through the father as well as through the mother. If you think it worthwhile, and many do, try selecting in the breeding of your dogs so they will have large litters instead of small. The fact they are smaller when born will not mean they will not attain their natural size. I know of no experimental evidence which shows that puppies from the same bitch which are small at birth have not just as good a chance to attain the full size for which they were destined by their hereditary mechanism, as puppies which are large at birth.

6

Inbreeding

INBREEDING is considered by geneticists to be mating first cousins or closer. Beyond first cousins we call it linebreeding. Is it desirable to inbreed dogs? What good comes out of the practice? What bad?

Inbreeding is the way to fix traits in a family. It is a way of bringing out the objectionable recessive traits so they may be eliminated. In agriculture it is the basis for producing hybrid vigor. Without hybrid vigor the world today would be a hungrier world. Hybrid vigor increases yields of foodstuffs by from 30% to 50%, increases the weight of swine, increases the number of eggs laid by hens.

Hybrid vigor does not depend alone upon the crossing of highly inbred strains or families; it can be caused by crossing different species. For example, a mare mated with a jackass produces a mule. Dogs of different breeds, or grains grown in two different parts of the world or chickens of the same breed but from distinct linebred flocks have also been crossed.

Technically, the increased vigor which usually results from hybridizing is called *heterosis,* a term first used by A. Franklin

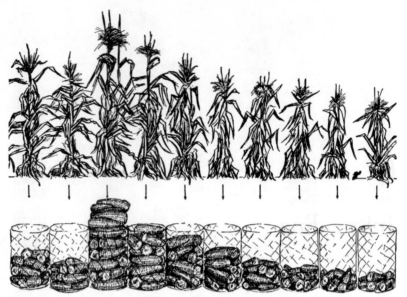

The two inbred strains of corn at left, when mated, produced corn like the third from left. But continued inbreeding makes it smaller again. Judicious inbreeding wtih selection should be good in case of dogs.

Schull of Princeton University. It is this principle on which geneticists depend for increased yields of crops.

The closest kind of inbreeding is brother to sister, next is parent to offspring, which is like crossing half brother to sister. A man is half brother to either parent.

Inbreeding not only brings objectionable features to light but also tends to cause infertility. In an inbreeding study of this author's using Pointers, the litter size decreased each generation. In the fifth generation there was complete infertility in one of the dogs I had kept to carry on with, and the experiment ended. With sufficient dogs it probably could be done. But would it serve any purpose other than an answer to a scientific question? It would make all of the dogs in the family so similar that they would appear to be identical twins. If they were out-crossed, the offspring would show hybrid vigor and the owner would practically have a patent on his efforts because the dogs would be such dependable breeders.

The result of crossing would produce the vigor, but what

160

would happen after that? Regression! Look at the illustration, which shows what happens to corn when two of the outbred-inbreds are crossed—back sliding! Only the first outcross is worthwhile.

Anyone attempting inbreeding would have to select the strongest individuals and most prolific of each generation. Experience with other species shows that if he got past the fifth generation of brother to sister mating, the next generations would show less degeneration. After the seventh, the stock is almost as strong and prolific as the original animals which started the inbred family. To repeat, both inbreeding and line-breeding are essential in establishing good or desirable traits and weeding out undesirable. Neither is harmful if the breeder wants to do best by his breed because if inbreeding brings to light a pair of hidden undesirable recessives, so much the better to have them weeded out of the strain. But it is expensive.

About one step away from being as black as black and
tan dogs ever come.

An intermediate degree of black and tan. His pups when
bred to bitches like himself were quite uniform as to color.

162

7

Complicating Mendelism

GREGOR MENDEL did not confine his studies to one pair of contrasting characters; he studied many in the same species. For instance, he predicted what would happen when tall peas which produced wrinkled seeds were crossed with dwarf peas which produced smooth coated seed; in other words, two characters at a time.

A dog is composed of a huge number of features which are inherited and most of them are not governed by pairs of genes. That's why we should see how to predict the outcome of more complicated inheritance. Some genes produce a character which, modified by other genes, make it appear very differently in different individuals. The color pattern of the Dalmatian, white with black spots, is an illustration. But why do some Dalmatians have no spots while others are nearly black?

The answer is that there are modifying genes at work producing more or less black. The same applies to the black-and-tan pattern of so many of our breeds of dogs. Basically the dog is tan with varying amounts of black covering it. The differences are enormous. Some tan dogs show but a few black hairs on the back, while at the opposite extreme we find a dog almost black.

163

Surely no one pair of genes could produce all that variation. Could two do it? They could, provided they all did not exert the same influence.

If we mate a very black dog with a very tan dog, we do not always get even an intermediate. Let us designate the determiners of these shades as follows, AaBb. These four are concerned in the ultimate color. Suppose that at one end of the scale we have AABB and at the other end of the scale aabb. There are at least 16 degrees of color variation with some variation from each degree. Some are seen more often than others.

Suppose we consider the very black dog with a minimum of tan as AABB and the very tan with a minimum of black as aabb. Then let us mate one from each end of the scale. The male cells would carry AB, taking one from each pair. The female would carry ab for the same reason. The offspring would be AaBb. The offspring would appear to be black-and-tan with the heads mostly tan but with a definite shading of black on them and on the ears.

I have tried to estimate the relative amounts of black to tan, which vary from about 4% to 96%. This has been done by stretching out skins and measuring as accurately as possible the black areas and the tan. At the one extreme one finds just two narrow patches of black along each side. Such a color is quite rare. At the other extreme, one finds only a small amount of tan. The black is extended all over the body except for a patch on each cheek, some on the underside of each ear, the inner sides of the legs and a little on the belly. Estimates of a large number of dogs have gone into this table, and as a result I have been able to predict quite accurately what sort of puppies the dogs would produce, once I knew the approximate composition of each of them, and that of course could be ascertained roughly from looking at them and estimating the black and the tan areas, but more accurately by considering previous progeny.

An interesting phase of this color question is that one can not tell from a puppy what color it will be when grown. This is very uncertain indeed. Some black-and-tan puppies are born with tan heads. Nearly all are born with black heads and those which will be toward the black extreme will have almost no tan showing at all until they are several days old, and then only on the cheeks. It is not possible to tell exactly what the ultimate color will be until after the first shedding.

Because of the distribution which I have found, I have given the genes the arbitrary values as follows: A—40, B—8, a—2, b—1. Suppose that we see, then, what the probable color would be if we mated a pair of the extremes, AABB with aabb. The product would have the following value, AaBb, or 40, 2, 8, 1. This makes 51.

Let us assume that we are going to mate a pair of the AaBb dogs. The sperm and ova could each have one A and one B and it would be a matter of chance which they happened to have. In fact, each might be any of the following compositions, AB, Ab, aB, ab. So we make a checkerboard and see what we could get.

SPERM

	AB	Ab	aB	ab
AB	AB AB 96	Ab AB 89	aB AB 58	ab AB 51
Ab	AB Ab 89	Ab Ab 82	aB Ab 51	ab Ab 44
aB	AB aB 58	Ab aB 51	aB aB 20	ab aB 13
ab	AB ab 51	Ab ab 44	aB ab 13	ab ab 6

EGGS

To summarize, we should expect 4 in 16 to be like the parents, AaBb, with a value of 51, and so forth. Here are the results:

4 AaBb 51	1 AAbb 82
2 AABb 89	1 aaBB 20
2 AaBB 58	1 AABB 96
2 Aabb 44	1 aabb 6
2 aaBb 13	

165

Or to arrange them according to what we should expect would be the whole range of colors we should find something approximating: 96, 89, 82, 58, 51, 44, 20, 13, 6. It is very much like that which I have found after studying many dogs. Some breeds, like the Doberman Pinscher, seem to have become stabilized as AABB and AABb. The same applies to all of the black-and-tan terriers I have seen. The same to certain strains of old-fashioned black-and-tan foxhounds. They seem to have the tan reduced to a very small amount, and the pumpkin seed spots over the eye are conspicuous because of it.

Most of the Foxhounds, especially those that are tricolored, are being bred in the great medium group of 58, 51 and 44. I say this because when they are ticked, the undercolor shows clearly and one can then observe the extent to which the saddle is spread over the body. But the Setters which are tricolored nearly all seem to be in the higher values with a very small amount of tan. So we see a dog with a black face and a small amount of tan on the cheeks.

Now observe how easy it is to predict the outcome of any mating when one has a good idea of the inherent value of the dog. I made several matings using a dog, AaBB and a bitch, AAbb. The puppies varied around 51 and 89. Why wouldn't they? All they could have produced was, AaBb, AABb. Then I mated one of the AaBb pups with an AABb dog. The pups were all very dark, but there were definitely two classes of them, one a little lighter than the other. They were obviously AaBB and AABb. I mated the bitch AAbb with a dog AABb. The puppies were all quite uniform and varied around AABb. There was not one AABB in the lot.

Occasionally one sees a dog with no tan on the chest and only a shading of tan on the feet. This is the AABB color and very rare.

When we consider only two pairs of determiners or genes at a time it adds slight complication to the Mendelian theory. The possible number of combinations taking two pairs of genes is therefore 16, which can be reduced to 9 types on the basis of appearance, when we give a value to each gene. When they have the same value, the 16 reduces to 4 types.

Most of the "old-fashioned" black-and-tan Foxhounds
show a wide extension of the black and a small amount of
of tan.

If we consider three genes all acting on the same end product,
the possible number of combinations is 64, and these can be
reduced to 8 types on the basis of dominance and recessiveness.
This is because wherever a capital letter appears representing a
dominant gene, even though it is with a recessive, the animal
will look like the dominant. Thus, if we were calling our characters, A, B and C, and letting a, b and c, respectively represent
the recessives, all of the following combinations would actually
look like ABC: AABBCC, AABBCc, AABbCC, AaBBCC,
AaBbCC, AaBBCc, AaBbCc, AABbCc, AaBBCc. But they
would not breed true, nor alike in all instances.

So the more characters one takes into account the more complicated the study becomes until at length one has to abandon
the Mendelian method of figuring and use other means. Where
the Mendelian law comes in handy is in predicting what will
happen when we consider a trait which has been found to behave as a unit character in inheritance, or where some trait has
been found to be governed by a pair of determiners. When one
understands the principle, he sees quite clearly that blood is not
the word to use in describing heredity, but that it is a case of
presence or absence, and it is wise to reiterate this many times.

167

Two great racing Greyhounds built for speed. How far would they go in a dog show?

8

Quantitative Methods in Dog Breeding

HAVING become acquainted with the multiple gene basis of many of the characters in our dogs, it becomes obvious that there are many traits which we value most in dogs which we cannot put on a Mendelian basis. Racing ability is one of these, because racing ability is really the sum total of all a dog has. There are many Greyhounds which have tremendous speed, but which are never raced because they will only run fast when they feel like it. There are some that have all the muscular coordination and rapidity of movement to make them speed champions but they lack an inch in leg length, and so are out of the running. Thus it is that one of the characters which compose the aggregate may often be the limiting factor, but usually it is several rather than one.

How are we going to put size on a Mendelian basis? How are we going to put the head length in dogs on such a basis, or stamina, or quickness of perception, or distance in vision, or quality of voice? There is so much variation in all of these things

169

that we must not try. But we cannot forget the principles of Mendelism, for after all, there are an innumerable number of factors working on the ultimate product, each of which is acting according to that law. Our only recourse then is to the adding machine method. Few dog breeders care to study the subject of heredity as deeply as one scientist has studied milk production in cows by the mathematical method, or as another has studied racing ability in horses, or as some have studied egg production in hens. Nor is it necessary to do so if we understand the principles and use them subconsciously. Therefore, I shall not outline the methods here, for it would take a whole book to do it. Let me simply reiterate what they have found. It has been learned that a hereditary index can be made of all horses, and their potential capacity as racers can be gauged fairly accurately, on paper, before the mating has been made which would produce them. It has been found that the milk production of some cows can be planned on paper and if the mating is made, the cow produced will give a volume of milk not very far from the calculated figure. The same applies to hens and their eggs. No one would be fool enough to declare that he could predict just the amount of milk or the number of eggs, but he can say within the limits of the pure line (See Chapter 9). He can predict that hens which would result from a certain mating will not lay fewer than 200 eggs apiece, if they are properly fed and cared for. He can say that the progeny of a certain mating will be able to run a mile in not less than 1.40, and be reasonably sure that his prediction will be true. He could not say that if he mated a plow mare with Man o' War that the colts will be great racers, nor can he predict the time of such colts at all accurately because no records have been kept on the forebears of the plow mare.

Records Needed

You cannot have reasonably accurate prediction unless you have ample records from which to predict. We have virtually no records in dogs except show records, with some exceptions in the case of some Greyhounds and Whippets. We have never sought to work out definite measurements for anything that dogs do. And yet we could work them out. Take the coonhunters, for instance. You will find that the field trials of these clubs of hunters are today among the most numerous of all the field trials conducted. But have they done anything in their new sport to standardize it and make it possible to know anything about records for breeding? Why have they not laid their trails over standard courses, say of one mile or four miles? Why have they not used stop watches and timed the line dog in each heat and each final? Or why have they not run their dogs in groups according to size? Or even by breed? These questions bring to mind the wonderful opportunities which we are overlooking, to make it possible to do something really of permanent value for our dogs.

We saw that when a characteristic was governed by only three pairs of determiners, that there were 64 possible combinations. So when one begins to study a character like racing ability in dogs, an ability which is the sum total of almost all that the dog has, one runs into thousands and thousands of determiners. The adding machine method is the only one to use under such circumstances. And to be perfectly fair and honest, the adding machine method comes pretty close to being an interpretation of common sense applied to animal breeding.

On the basis of the knowledge of records which have been made by various animals in the past by computing these records, averaging the near kin, one can form a pretty good idea of what the stock is able to produce. I think that the finest bit of common sense ever produced by any method for studying heredity is that which is so ably summed up by the Norwegian proverb: "Marry not the maid who is the only good maid in the clan."

What this proverb really means is that the individual is not of so much importance in calculating heredity as is the knowledge of the whole stock. A person *might* make a pretty good guess as to the kind of producer of high-grade offspring a dam would be, knowing her record. But it would make a vastly better guess if he were able to know the record of all her near

The will to work and the physical stamina of the sled dog are determined by everything the dog possesses.

kin and by getting a well-rounded picture of the whole stock he could then make a guess which would be pretty close to right. A number of dog breeders, whose kennels I have visited, have asked me how I thought they could improve their breeds. I always suggested the adding machine method and I am sure that these men have found out that I was right.

Most dog breeders already realize the importance of the stock. Very little more need be said about that as its importance is fully acknowledged.

Perhaps you think, then, that this admission on my part does not justify the writing of such a book as this, or the money spent by our research institutions, etc., on studies of plant and animal breeding. But such is not the case. I think that as we go along, we shall see little ways in which these studies can be of great help to all of us. Who is there who breeds dogs who doesn't want to know the foundation processes at the bottom of what he is doing? Most animal breeders are ingenious individuals. When they drive an automobile, they want to know how it works inside. When an advertisement tells them what constitutes a good dog food, they are not simply content with saying "Yes, I'll try it," but they ask "Why?" They are all from Missouri and so get much more fun out of life.

A real knowledge of genetics can multiply the pleasure derived from breeding many times and once in a while it can make a breeder some real money.

9

Variations and Pure Lines

ONE other point which needs clearing up is that which geneticists speak of as variation. We may consider any trait we wish and we shall find that every one shows some variation around a central standard. I think of a lot of yellow-eyed dogs in my kennels. If they are all standing up looking at me, I see that the eyes of each are definitely yellow, but when I look from one to the other very closely, I note that they are not all of exactly the same shade. Yet no matter which two I mate, their puppies all have yellow eyes. There isn't very much difference, but enough to be noticeable.

It matters not how pure a trait is, there is always some variation in it unless possibly we speak of albinos, and then there is no color, and so the white which we see is only one shade of white. But take the cream color which we see in Chow dogs. Every cream is not the same, but despite the fact that all the shades of it vary around a definite standard, they are all inherited.

There are some colors which are very likely shaded in different degrees because of several other genes which are working to

Variation in form and performance makes dog breeding more interesting.

affect it, as we saw in the case of the saddle factor affecting tan
to produce black and tan in varying amounts. These are called
modifying genes or determiners. Consider the slight differences
which are found among the animals, the progeny of the same
determiners. Notice the pair of twin dogs on page 157 or the
pair of twin calves on page 154. There you will see variation.
This is enough to show quite clearly that even the same pair of
genes does not always produce exactly the same result, but that
there is some slight variation—due to what, we do not know. So
do not expect too great uniformity even in twins, for there is
bound to be a little variation.

It is variation that gives dog breeding a large part of its kick.
It gives all animal breeding a part of its kick. If it were not for
this quality, we would soon be breeding our animals so they
were almost alike. It is a quality of the germ plasm to be more
or less elastic. But the limits of elasticity are limited. And that,
too, is fortunate. Because of the limitations of purebred lines
we see that we are able to keep the heredity of our dogs within
rather narrow limits.

What a geneticist calls a *pure line* differs from the usual layman's idea. The layman thinks of a pure line of dogs as a

175

Variation in ear length is common among Foxhounds.

"purebred" line all of the same breed. Not so the geneticist.

Suppose we photographed 1000 Dalmatians. We would have pictures of almost black or liver colored dogs and, at the other extreme, white dogs with but a few faint spots. If we mated the blacks we would have puppies ranging from black possibly down to ideally marked dogs. If we mated the ideally marked dogs which came from the blacks, we would produce puppies all from ideal to black. If we mated ideals from the white parents the puppies, when grown, would vary all toward the white end of this spectrum.

By long enough breeding we could segregate many groups within the spectrum, all of which would produce puppies varying around a certain standard. Then, no dogs bred within those groups (pure lines to the geneticist) would produce dogs more or less spotted than the limits of the pure line. Of course, if we mated a dog from each of the extremes we might have puppies ranging from one end of the spectrum to the other.

There are these pure lines within every complex character, even racing ability, hunting behavior, colors, size, height, or what have you. Certain well established families of dogs often represent genetic pure lines. Get one established and the outcome of matings can be predicted with greater accuracy than matings of dogs not from pure line families.

So to get back to our proverb, the maid who is the only good maid in a clan of a mentally inferior family is likely to have

176

children lower in the mental scale than she herself. The poorest maid, if from a mentally superior family, is likely to have children all superior to herself if her husband is also from a superior family.

A classic example of the pure line of Cocker Spaniels was one of the most famous studs America has produced—Red Brucie. He was a poor specimen of a remarkably fine line of Cockers, so poor that the only time he was shown he won a third. Yet, the first litter which he sired were all outstanding Cockers. After that the finest bitches were bred to him and he produced a large number of outstanding show dogs, including many "Best-in-Shows" when Cocker Spaniels constituted one-fourth of all the dogs in America and competition was keen. The Norwegian proverb applies to most everything in connection with breeding.

Here is what one of the most successful animal breeders in the world wrote me. "If you mated the two best outstanding Cocker Spaniels alive, none of the get would be as perfect as either of the parents. Yet every year someone produces a Cocker equal to the best from two "mutts," and it is hard to reconcile this." Well, yes, but with a knowledge of pure lines, their limitations and their potentialities in mind, it is not only not difficult to reconcile the occurrence, but it is the expectancy. It has been tried over and over again by mating animals of many kinds and very seldom do the offspring of these great individuals equal either of the parents.

Then along come two "mutts" that just seem to "nick" and produce a wonderful specimen. It is partly the chance of obtaining compensating traits and partly getting the pure lines, which we are constantly restricting, to give us the best of their extremes.

To be precise, a geneticist thinks of a pure line as all of the offspring of a single self-fertilized individual. But a breeder can also think of a pure line in a little different light. To him a pure line can be a strain that has arisen from close inbreeding. In a broader sense, a breed may be called a pure line. There are strains of Greyhounds which have been selected on the basis of speed, which are able to negotiate a quarter mile in between

177

25 and 26 seconds. Other strains have been selected for longer coursing races and while they have greater power of endurance, their sprint speed may vary at from 27 to 28 seconds for the quarter. If we cross one dog from each strain, we shall probably get something intermediate. Then if we cross some of their off-spring, the possibilities are for a distribution varying from fastest to slowest, with the great average varying around 26 to 27 seconds for the quarter.

Let us suppose that you are a breeder of Irish Wolfhounds. You have been breeding within your own strain now for twenty years. You have tried all methods of feeding and have never been able to produce a dog weighing over 146 pounds. You would breed to dogs belonging to another breeder whose dogs get to weigh 190 pounds, and size is what you really desire, but your dogs have been of such fine quality with the exception of size that you intensely dislike breaking your charm and going outside to breed. But how else can you get greater size in your strain?

That strain is to you what a pure line is to the geneticist to all intents and purposes. You have come up against a barrier. You cannot hurdle it. But then, too, not one of your puppies in the last five years has been a poor one. If you breed a pair of average dogs you find you are as likely to get very fine ones as you are to get less excellent specimens. All of them are good, but you want something better. For years now you haven't been able to get any but dogs varying around the same type. You have marked this strain with your own brand. People seeing their excellence come to know that they are your dogs but each person says, "Oh, if they were only larger, nothing could possibly stop them."

The pure line which you have developed is actually a greater help to you than you may have realized. The marked boundaries are so well established that even if you bred two of your poorest you would tend to get dogs all better than the parents. If you breed dogs at your best end of the scale you still get dogs ranging the whole length of the scale but slightly more near the top than near the bottom.

There is only one thing to do, if you do not want to go out-

178

After a pure line has been established, the only way to
increase size is to breed to stock which is larger despite
the loss in quality this might sometime entail.

side of your strain for new heredity. That is to breed a very
large number of pups and hope that among them there will be a
mutation which will allow the dog to grow larger. You hope too
that it will prove to be an hereditary mutation, and not just
one which occurred after the germ cells were established. You
might have to wait many dozen times longer than you will live.

But if you are wise you will breed to some giant dog outside

There are limits which pure lines impose, above or below which we cannot go. Note this very white St. Bernard has puppies, all of which have more color than she.

of your own strain, and be sure that this dog comes from a strain the members of which are all very large. By this method you will slowly build up your quality with his size and a little later incorporate more size until you gradually get what you want.

Probably the greatest breeders are those who have a great variety in type to begin with and constantly breed a very large number of puppies, and have a much wider selection from which to choose. But this is an expensive method. Their variety, however, is ever getting closer and closer to the breed standard. They are weeding out the dogs which are of undesirable type and the constant breeding to a few good males is making their strain increasingly more uniform. But even so they possess considerable variety.

The owner of popular stud dogs has an excellent chance to bring in outside heredity into his strain because he can watch the bitches which are sent to his dogs and choose puppies from them if he likes their type and wants them in his strain.

PART III

HEREDITY IN DOGS

A Basset Hound. This was the breed used by Francis Galton in the first color study ever made of dogs.

1

Coat Color Inheritance

In 1897, before Gregor Mendel was known to scientists outside of his community, Francis Galton, an Englishman, had studied color inheritance in Basset hounds. Chronologically, Galton's work was as early as Mendel's, and had he not only counted but also had in mind the dual nature of the hereditary factors, he would have been the man whom the world honored instead of Mendel, and dogs would have been the oft-quoted species through the medium of which "Galtonism" was discovered, rather than Mendelism, through the use of garden peas.

But Galton did not think of his tricolored dogs as having a pair of determiners which worked yoked together. What he was endeavoring to discover was the prepotency of the males and females. He had a theory that the black-and-tan males were prepotent over the tricolored females. It was another way of saying dominant. But he did not use the words dominant and recessive, nor did he guess apparently that the black-and-tan dog which, when bred to a tricolored bitch, produced approximately half tricolored and half black-and-tans, was really carrying the tricolor factors even though he did appear black-and-tan himself.

The next paper that we find in scientific literature dealing with color inheritance in dogs was one by A. Lang, published in Germany in 1910. He tells in this work how he secured a pair of mongrels which had resulted from crossing a brown-and-white hound-type female with a black Newfoundland. There were 14 puppies, all black. Lang mated a pair of these black puppies and obtained five black puppies and three brown. Had he obtained six black and two brown he would have had a perfect Mendelian ratio. But the 5–3 was not far out considering such a small number was presented.

In 1912 we find the next reference to color inheritance in dogs. Arend L. Hagedoorn, in a brief article, tells how he has never neglected to observe dogs of the color pattern which Galton described. He has a paragraph in which he attempts to show that the spots on a white dog always occur in the color they would if the dog were not spotted. In other words, a tricolored dog would naturally have a saddle if he had no white, and therefore when he has a spot on the back it is black, while one on the chest or belly is red.

He said, but gives no evidence to support his statement, that spotting with white is dominant in some dogs. He refers to white as partial albinism, and to the lemon of the Basset Hound as sable. We shall see more about that too, later on.

In 1913 three collaborators, K. Pearson, E. Nettleship and C. H. Usher, published a study of albinism entitled "A Monograph of Albinism in Man." They have a good deal to say about albinism in Pekingese dogs, and show how albinism was inherited as a recessive. They had dogs which showed very slight colors as young puppies that later faded to a white or almost white with pink eyes. Some showed spots which became indistinct. They had plenty of material to work with and doubtless established the principle of partial, as well as complete albinism in dogs.

In 1914, G. M. Allen turned his attention to white spotting and to red and black-and-tan. He used diagrams to show which color spots disappear last. Then he told how the red was sometimes dominant and sometimes recessive to the black-and-tan.

184

Next in chronological order came a study by C. C. Little, published in 1914. He called it "Inheritance of Coat Color in Pointer Dogs." He obtained his data from the stud book of the American Kennel Club.

In 1915, a year and three months after Little's report on his study appeared, a paper on color inheritance in Cocker Spaniels was published by Phillips and Barrows.

Herman L. Ibsen published a paper in 1916 in which he deals with coat color inheritance in Dachshunds. That old troublesome nuisance, the heredity of the black-and-tan, is dealt with, and here we find that sometimes it is dominant and sometimes recessive. He suggests that there is a restrictive factor R which inhibits the black and thus produces a red.

In 1918 Sewell Wright made a resume of all the work that had been previously done in coat color in dogs. He used letters to represent colors and, as nearly as I can determine, attempted to make these letters correspond as closely as possible to similar letters which are used to represent similar colors in other species. By 1918 a great deal of work had been done with mice, rabbits, rats and guinea pigs, so he had a good foundation upon which to base his studies. He made no original contribution, but he did make one prophecy which, as you will see, has come true. Previous students were bothered by the inheritance of the red and the black-and-tan. He was not bothered by it but suggested that if their data were correct then there must be two genetic reds.

In 1919 C. C. Little and E. E. Jones reported their study of coat color inheritance in Great Danes.

E. L. Pickhardt published the first study on Collie color in 1924 in a book, *The Collie in America,* and showed that black-and-tan is recessive to sable.

In 1927, D. C. Warren described his studies in Greyhound coat color inheritance. Greyhound coat color is the same as Great Dane color.

The next study, in 1928, was my own on the inheritance of the ticking factor. It also discussed flecking.

In 1930, C. Wreidt of Norway gave us information about the way in which gray mottling is inherited.

In 1931, N. A. Iljin's paper on Doberman Pinscher coat color appeared.

In 1934, my paper on the same subject was published. We agreed except on definitions. Iljin called liver-and-tan, brown. He called the dilute Isabella, but made no mention of its inheritance, whereas I called it fawn and showed the inheritance.

My paper on scent hound color inheritance appeared in *How to Breed Dogs* as did a report on the inheritance of the white collar pattern.

A. L. Mitchell reported a more detailed study of Collie color in 1935, and concluded that a pair of clear yellow sables cannot produce black-and-tan puppies. Otherwise, he agreed with Pickhardt's conclusions.

Chow coat color inheritance was first reported in *How to Breed Dogs* by me.

Dalmatian coat color inheritance was also reported in the same volume.

The different kinds of whites and their inheritance occupied ten pages of the text.

In the 1947 revision of *How to Breed Dogs* I reported that there are three kinds of white modifiers—ticking, Dalmatian spotting and flecking; the first two being dominant and the last recessive.

In 1952 Marca Burns in England published *The Genetics of the Dog.*

In 1957 a book by Dr. Clarence C. Little was published called *The Inheritance of Coat Color in Dogs.* This resulted from a questionnaire answered by dog breeders, to whom it was distributed by the American Kennel Club.

Since 1947 some new material has come to light. A history of the studies and a summation of what they all show follows—not in separate chapters, but all in this single chapter.

At this point it is pertinent to ask: How reliable is the information supplied by breeders? Comparison with what is known shows that most of it is reliable, but not all. Accidents occur.

Cabor and Kaliss analyzed data from registered Bull Terriers and found that some were inaccurate, based on what we know about coat color inheritance in the breed. They learned that brindle was dominant over the lack of it, red, black-and-white all being recessive to it.

Many veterinarians can attest to the chicanery which can be observed in the registering of dogs. One example is the Boxer. When I was studying the inheritance of coat color in the breed I realized, where the question of white was concerned, how unreliable registrations were. Having ear-cropped hundreds of puppies by a bloodless method I devised, I saw that many white puppies with a daub of tan or brindle were registered as tan-and-white or brindle-and-white dogs. How can one depend on such reports as the basis for a study?

Even where registrations are legal, as for black-and-tan in hounds, the breeder may register a tan hound with a tinge of black along the back as a tan dog, when it is genetically a black-and-tan of one extreme of the saddle factor. It is better to obtain facts by breeding dogs one's self.

When we look at a dog the first thing about him that strikes the eye may be his size, but more likely it will be his color. Nearly all the colors that we see in dogs are possessed by the gray dog. But there are some colors and color patterns which are most decidedly not. So let us consider a gray dog briefly and see what colors really go to make up the various shades of gray.

The Gray Dog

If we scrutinize each hair, we find that it is not a plain gray hair, but a banded one. We find both black and some shade of red or yellow on the hair. We note that the dog may be evenly colored all over or that he may be marked definitely with a darker shade of color on the back in the form of a saddle. We find, too, that he has one form of white spotting which puts a little white on the chest, or the tip of the tail, or possibly the feet or only a white toenail.

Thus, the gray dog is somewhat like a ray of white light which we know is actually composed of all the colors. Not quite, but the analogy is there. Let us pass it through a spectroscope and

The gray dog contains in his genetic origin many of the colors found in other breeds.

The black dog may be one which has lost the red or yellow pigments in the hair, which the gray dog possesses.

188

take it apart. Suppose that mutations occurred. What could they be and what are the results?

The dog could lose the yellow pigment, in which case he would be a black dog. He could lose the black pigment, in which case he would be a yellow or red dog. He could lose both, in which case he would be a dark-eyed white dog. He could lose even that pigment, in which case he would be devoid of all color and be an albino with a pink nose and pink eyes.

Other mutations could occur so that he would have dilute shades of color: either dilute black or dilute red, producing blue or cream. He could have mutations which affected the color pattern so that there was much more black showing than yellow, and yet not have lost the lighter color completely. He could have another mutation or a series of them which would limit the black pigment to only a very small part of the body, like a few stray black hairs on the back or the tail. And so on. He could have other mutations which also bred true which caused white spots which showed the white beneath to develop like windows in the color. These white spots might take strange shapes. Another mutation could cause the colors of black and yellow to mix in strange ways so that the effect was brindling.

These and many other modifications are actually what have happened to the dog. That is the way, in all probability, our many colors have come down to us. Each time a new one appeared, some enterprising human being took advantage of it, and by inbreeding or by breeding two such mutations which occurred at the same time, the new character was incorporated.

It is interesting to know a little of the chemistry of color in hairs. Each hair has a color base of chromogen as well as an enzyme which interacts with the chromogen to produce melanin in the form of granules.

Hairs have an inner portion called the *medulla* and an outer layer called the *cortex*. The distribution of the melanin granules in these layers produces the color we see. The many ways in which the granules are distributed accounts for the great variety in colors in dogs.

This information about color inheritance can be useful in a great many ways. If it is proposed to make any color mating, you

No more majestic dog has ever been created than a fine specimen of the New-foundland breed. The solid black is the type more often seen. The black of the Newfoundland is dominant over the black-and-white (Landseer pattern) also seen in the breed.

will be able to know what one can be relatively sure can occur on the basis of appearance where the colors of the grandparents are taken into account. In short, what may or may not happen when you breed dogs and know the ancestral colors.

It will also prove useful in certain cases in determining paternity. It may be helpful in preventing false pedigrees and other abuses. To illustrate, I knew a man who owned a champion cream Chow dog. Many bitches were sent to him to be bred to that dog. Among them were several cream bitches, and some of the owners of the cream bitches wondered why their puppies were black or red. Now according to our best information, if two creams are mated they are the ultimate in recessives, and could not produce a black or a red. When I visited this man, I saw a poor type black dog and knew the answer.

I have been instrumental in helping a number of people

to determine the paternity of litters by simply considering the recessive traits alone. Thus, while a pair of black Cocker Spaniels might produce puppies of any color, a pair of creams will not produce a black. Two black-and-tan hounds might produce a tricolored pup, but no pair of tricolored dogs has ever been known to produce a black-and-tan. You will see many such illustrations.

Observations of the results of inter-color series crosses in the previous edition of *How to Breed Dogs* showed what happens when dogs of such series are crossed.

There are a number of ways of presenting what is known about coat color inheritance in dogs. In the first editions of this book I devoted a chapter to each of the various types of dogs and explained what had been learned about the inheritance of the coat colors. A number of the chapters detailed my own studies, some of which had been published in scientific journals and others which were published for the first time in the book. All told, the studies cited covered 130 pages.

In this edition I have condensed the color inheritance, where it is known, for our breeds. The chief discrepancy between the new and my own work occurs in the inheritance of the saddle and brindling factors. My studies indicate it is a separate gene linked closely with tan or red and itself subject to variation. Dr. Little's interpretation is that black-and-tan or red-and-tan are a single gene color modified by a pair of genes which changes the black to red. To my mind the saddle gene is similar to that which produces brindling, another gene which also affects tan and also varies greatly in amount.

Color Loci on Chromosomes

Dogs cannot be bred in huge numbers like mice or corn to determine where on certain chromosomes the loci for definite genes lie. Surmise, based on a considerable amount of study by geneticists familiar with coat color inheritance in rodents—Sewell Wright, C. C. Little, for example—has suggested that the same principles apply to dogs as well, even though the different species have different numbers of chromosomes.

Little has proposed the following map of loci, and surely there is no more knowledgeable geneticist alive, nor one better equipped with information about rodent and canine coat color inheritance. He postulates the following loci for all of the colors: A, B, C, D, E, G, M, P, S, T—ten loci in all.

This book is written primarily to be of use to the practical dog breeder. I suggest that the reader deeply interested in the symbols of color genes, the loci of various colors, consult *The Inheritance of Coat Color,* by C. C. Little. It seems to me that knowing what the symbols are is sufficient, that what the practical dog breeder wants to know is what he or she can expect when certain colored dogs are mated. Therefore, I have condensed 130 pages by grouping the breeds which carry the various colors and presenting the results of proposed matings. There isn't much point in placing the breeds together on the basis of class grouping, i.e., Working Dogs, Hound Dogs.

These are the basic colors of dogs:
Black
Recessive tan or red
Dominant tan or red
Recessive white
Albino white
Dominant white

In America as of 1970, no dog with the dominant white has been seen, although it has been often reported in Russian dogs. It apparently is the equivalent of the white of the Yorkshire hog, which is dominant over the black of the Berkshire.

These are modifying genes which produce various effects:
Agouti, which causes banded hairs
Liver gene, which affects black
Full color gene, which produces the color undiluted
Dilution gene, which with black produces blue; with red produces yellow
Greying gene
Merle gene

192

> White modifiers
> Ticking gene
> Flecking gene
> Dalmatian
> Recessive tan modifiers
> Saddle
> Brindle

In an article in a hunting magazine, I outlined some of the coat color research of interest and asked anyone who had crossed breeds to tell me of the results. Some surprising letters came. The results are listed here. It will be argued that there may be mistakes. Perhaps, but observe how well these results tally with work done under controlled conditions:

White Samoyed with cream ears x all-red Chow: 9 all-red puppies.

St. Bernard x Newfoundland: 10 puppies—black or black-and-white.

Black Cocker x tricolor Beagle: Two litters. All black with white chest. All short hair. Open trailers. Excellent pheasant dogs. All pups were prone to lay on more fat than either of the parents.

Back cross of an F_1 to the Beagle: 2 black and 1 red-and-white (not tricolor).

Russian Wolfhound x long-eared Foxhound: Medium length ears. Stature of Borzoi. Short hair. Hunts by scent and open trails.

Two registered Pointers: 7 pups—3 longhaired, 1 rough coated, and 3 shorthaired. It was amazing how many reported two Pointers producing some longhaired puppies.

Airedale to Collie: Wirehaired tan or yellow dog.

Black Spitz x tricolor Fox Terrier: All black, short hair.

Irish Setter x Bloodhound: 4 black-and-tans, 3 all-black, 1 red-and-tan, 3 reds.

Newfoundland x sable-and-white American farm shepherd: All puppies black.

Black-and-white Setter x black-and-tan Bloodhound: 11 pups—4 black-and-tan, 3 all black, 1 red-and-tan, and 3 all red.

Brindle Great Dane x tricolor Foxhound: Two litters. 20 pups. All golden fawn or fawn and brindle with white collars.

Black Cocker Spaniel x tricolor Beagle: Two litters. All black with white on chest.

Irish Water Spaniels x Irish Setters: Many litters. Most pups solid black, with occasional dark seal color.

Airedale x Fox Terrier: Three litters. All black-and-tan.

Black Schipperke x white Poodle: 4 pups, black with white chests.

Great Dane x tricolor Foxhound: 20 pups, all golden fawn and fawn-brindle with white collar.

The Whites of Dogs

Among other species of animals, several different genetic whites have been shown to exist. For instance, if we mate a white leghorn chicken with a white Plymouth Rock, the result is all colored chickens, and no white ones in the lot. This is because the two whites are very different. In different species the whites behave differently in the mode of inheritance. Thus, there is a white in swine which is dominant. If a white Yorkshire is mated with a black Berkshire the pigs are all white.

But in dogs the whites behave as in rodents. There is no dominant solid white to my knowledge. But there are three definitely different whites and I think we have data which seems to show still another. Let us see.

1. The albino white. This is the absence of all color. It has been known to exist for many years in dogs, and there is a scattering of references in very old canine literature to its spontaneous occurrence. But no breed of white dogs has ever been developed from these mutations, although it would have been very easy to do so. Naturally the albino color in dogs behaves as in every other species, studied as a recessive. White rats, and rabbits, with their pink eyes are known to everyone. But not many have seen albino dogs.

In America there are doubtless at least fifty today. In my files I have correspondence from persons who, in total have ten dogs which are albinos. Three of these are Pekingese. Two are termed feists. A feist is the colloquial expression for any kind of small dog like a Fox Terrier, for example, in the Central South states. There are one each of five other breeds. All have pink eyes and even the toe pads are white or pinkish.

All have occurred spontaneously, but in the case of the woman who owns the Pekingese, she states that the color has occurred several times in her strain, to dogs belonging to other people as well as to herself. There is every evidence that it is inherited as a recessive. We have seen that Pearson and associates described their study of this character a number of years ago.

Dark-eyed white German Shepherd Dogs. This is a distinctly different white from the albino white.

While no studies have as yet been reported, there is every probability that the white of the Samoyed is either of the dark-eyed white or the third type, but extended so that no other color shows. Some Samoyeds have biscuit-colored ears and some do not.

Two Bloodhounds were mated with two Bull Terriers (*see top picture*).
A pup from each litter was mated together (*see middle picture above
and picture of male dog on opposite page for individuals used*).
Puppies of the four general color types (*shown in lower picture*) were
produced.

When the male bred of a Bloodhound x Bull Terrier cross (*pictured at top*) was mated to a pure Bull Terrier, the four puppies shown here were produced. Note the two whites and two nearly solid colored like the father.

The commonest type of white is that seen as spotting on most of
the breeds, such as Collies, Newfoundlands, and hounds.

Here the blue ticking is restricted to a few spots indicating the probability of
two distinct whites on the same dog.

In 1929, in England, Pearson and Usher upset most dog breeders' ideas of albinism by reporting the results of their experiments in crossing albino Pekingese with black Pomeranians. They had some puppies born with pale gray or buff coats due to what they call a diffuse pigmentation. These puppies they called Cornaz albinos. Some of them were "skewbald" (cornaz-and-white).

Two of their white albinos never gave rise to dogs with dark eyes, but did produce some Cornaz albinos. Nor did the Cornaz albinos ever produce puppies with dark eyes and color, but a Cornaz-and-white produced a puppy with pigmented coat and dark eyes. So Pearson and Usher refuse to accept the old idea that albinism in dogs is a simple Mendelian recessive.

We think of albinos as always pink-eyed, but as we have seen from the work of Pearson and Usher, there are more kinds than one. Dr. James McI. Phillips reported in the *Journal of Heredity* in 1937 the appearance of a blue-eyed white puppy in a litter of pigmented Cocker Spaniels.

2. Then there is the dark-eyed white. This is a very common color, especially in the German Shepherd Dog. Two of these dogs breed true. In 1926 I saw a litter of them in Arkansas, which were the product of mating two dark-eyed whites. Every puppy was white. None was an albino. This color has occurred in other breeds too. There are numerous Chows which have appeared with this color. It is not a very light cream but a clear white, very different from the cream which Chows also come in. Pekingese have also been found and bred so that it would have been a simple matter to originate strains on this basis.

There is some discrimination against the color because so many people believe that dark-eyed white dogs are deaf, which is not always the case. Breeders of German Shepherds have had dozens of them appear from their stock as recessives, one to three or four in a litter of blacks or grays, and they have continued to appear whenever certain dogs are mated. I have many figures on this but they are too common to relate. This too is obviously inherited as a recessive.

199

3. The third white, which should have been put first, is the common white which we see on nearly all dogs. It is the white we see on the chest of some, and covering all of others, such as white hounds, white Newfoundlands, the white of St. Bernards, of many of the breeds. It is the white tied up with the spotting factor which we have repeatedly considered. But are these three all of the whites?

In their paper on *Inheritance in Cocker Spaniels*, Barrows and Phillips suggested two whites in dogs. One they intimated is the white which covers the dogs in large spots and the other is the white which appears on the toes and throat and tip of the tail, although they did not mention that extremity. They said that the white spotting is dominant. Little and Jones in their paper on color inheritance in Great Danes agreed with Barrows and Phillips. Then came Warren and showed that in the case of Greyhounds their white spotting is inherited as a recessive.

At one time I thought there was some evidence to show that there might be a different genetic white which is inherited as a dominant in relation to some colors, but I have found differently. Even the Bull Terrier white is recessive to the black-and-tan of the hound.

Now, as to that second white which the former investigators mention as being different from the white which extends over the body, I think we have scanty if any evidence to show it. It seems from my extensive evidence that every dog has white in his genetic make-up, just as he has black. The black and the white are modified or restricted as to areas by a variety of determiners. And the little daubs of white which are seen appearing on the chest are only evidences of it. I think that I have seen only a very few dogs which were entirely without a white hair on the body. Only part of a toenail may show white to evidence that it is there. Only three white hairs on the chest may be the telltale sign.

But between that very small amount and an amount which shows as a completely white chest, legs white to the shoulders, a narrow blaze in the face, a white tip to the tail, there are many many degrees of white and according to my data all degrees are inherited as recessive to the solid color. In fact there are a few cases where there have been white spots above the shoulder which undoubtedly were inherited in that manner. It would seem that there are many modifying factors involved.

Also we must not forget that very often the condition where there is considerable white on the lower parts of the dog and the tip of the tail, is an indication of a hybrid or heterozygous condition for the color in the dog. For example when I crossed a Bloodhound with a solid white Bull Terrier, there was not a single completely black-and-tan dog in the lot.

Now, no matter how many black crosses this dog has made to solid-colored bitches, all the offspring are like the dominant form in appearance, but most of them will have the white on the chest. In F_2 crosses of the pair shown on page 196 there have been two black-and-tans which had a very little white on the chest like the one shown on page 197 as one of four puppies.

Then in the case of Bloodhounds, I have repeatedly crossed two dogs which showed no white on the body and had them produce puppies with varying amounts of white even including white feet. I have crossed dogs with white feet and have had them produce a puppy with no white. The point is that there will be a variation very gradual, to be sure, from nothing up to considerable. I think that the fact that we see three white hairs on the chest does not warrant us in assuming that the dog is very different, if any, genetically from one which has not those three. And by the same token, I think that the dog with three white hairs on his chest is very little different genetically from one with a spot as large as a man's hand, white feet, and a white tip to his tail.

Even the hybrid (heterozygous) condition need not show much white. I have several bitches which carry white recessively, as shown by their breeding records. They have been bred to white dogs and produced litters very close to 50-50 colored puppies. Yet they have not over a square inch of white on their bodies.

4. Several years ago I had a hound whose breeding I knew. He was one quarter white Bulldog. One grandfather was the Bulldog. One was a white hound. These dogs produced an almost white dog which was, of course, a mongrel, but an excellent

squirrel dog. He was mated to a blue-ticked hound. The puppies were all ticked. The curious thing about them was that some were ticked all over but some were ticked in spots only. Now this occurrence would have to have one of two phenomena to explain it, it seems to me. The first and unlikely explanation would be that there was a form of spotting which restricted the ticking to certain areas of the dog's body. The second and more likely, is that there are two kinds of whites in the same dog. The ticking could not effect the one kind of white and could effect the other.

Without the ticking one could not know that there was more than one kind of white. It would seem to indicate that there were very definitely two kinds. I am now trying to work further on this question by making matings to determine the facts. The one mating is apparently not enough. Dogs have already been procured and more will be made to try and get at the basis.

So we can say definitely that there are three kinds of whites and possibly four. But we still have another to consider.

Because of the fact that geneticists have always designated the white in laboratory animals as S to stand for spotting, I am not at all sure they have been correct. It would seem that there are are different genetic whites and that each deserves a name as much as the two kinds of tans. Who shall say that in a lemon-and-white dog the lemon isn't doing the spotting and so give the solid color the S? Indeed to the eye this is much more likely to be the case, and the spots are generally nice clear spots. Look at the beautiful spot on the hound on page 198. In such a case does it seem reasonable to call the white the spotting and the real spot by a totally different term? After all, we are considering the interaction of two distinct colors, and now that we know there are several kinds of white which behave differently, genetically, we had perhaps better use a different designation. I shouldn't wonder if we would in time use a term to apply to the intense colors to indicate that they were restricted and that because of them no color appeared, hence the area was white.

Would it not be proper to describe the ticking factor as W^T, rather than S^T? If we did that, could we not then consider a harlequin Great Dane as a white dog with still a different

202

The Beagle is of the "White Collar" color pattern. Dogs possessing this color pattern are usually solid-colored in the body except for the white which will show on the legs, chest, belly and extend upward around the neck. Sometimes dogs will have a blaze of white on the face which will vary considerably and the end of the tail will be white.

The white on the Boston terrier is a modification of the white collar pattern.

modifier present, i.e., W^H? For after all there is occasionally a completely white Dane, and might not these dogs be white Danes which have lost the H factor? Or white dogs with the H factor which in turn has been modified so much as to not show at all?

5. Probably not, because as Little and Jones have shown the harlequin white is dominant over solid colors i.e., tan, black, etc. This being the case we have in harlequin white a fifth genetic white, semi-lethal in nature.

The Dalmatian's white is not of this nature. In the first edition of this book I said it probably was. Since then I have crossed Dalmatians with dogs of solid color and they produced solid color puppies. One litter, produced by a friend, who mated a black-and-tan hound with a Dalmatian, was composed of all spotted puppies but had black and tan on the head and tan spots on the legs. This hound however was half-breed tricolor.

The Dalmatian, mated to several other white breeds, produces indistinctly spotted puppies.

6. There is one other white which is definitely different from the others so far described. It is found in Norwegian harriers and in Collies, both smooth and rough, and in Shetland Sheepdogs. This is a white of a semi-lethal nature. When one of these is crossed with a black-and-tan or tricolor, a curious color called "merle" is produced. This white, which almost invariably weakens the possessor, is a very undesirable character, but certainly a distinct white which we cannot overlook. It often is not a solid white because sometimes one finds faint patches of other colors accompanying it. And it may be, too, that it is the same white as number 5.

Still another white, one which Iljin says is dominant over colors, is found in the Russian shepherd and sometimes in the Siberian. He gives no data on its inheritance. I have seen several white Siberians and know of their having been crossed with colored dogs, in which case the white behaved as the Samoyed white—recessively. If it is established that Iljin's white is a dominant, we then may have seven genetic whites in dogs and modifiers of several as well.

Liver to liver Pointers cannot produce black, but may produce liver or lemon.

The lemon and white Pointer with liver nose, when mated to liver, sometimes produces black puppies.

Black color in Cockers is dominant over all other colors. Solid color is dominant over white splashed.

The orange and white of Spaniels is recessive to black and white, but the term orange and white is too inaccurate—the orange may be light red or dark yellow.

These two pictures also provide a remarkable study of the change in concept of the "ideal" Cocker. The photo of the black above represents the appearance of the show Cocker in 1971 as contrasted with the dog of 1925 in the lower picture.

Black and white is recessive to solid color, but dominant over all other colors combined with white.

The Papillon is subject to the same patterns of color inheritance as the Spaniels.

207

Here are examples of the five more common color designations of the Poodle. On this page are pictured the black and silver. On the facing page, top to bottom, are the white, apricot and brown.

The black represents one of the basic dominant colors in the breed. White in Poodles is recessive to all other colors, and the so-called brown is the same as the liver color in other breeds.

The standard for show Poodles requires that their coats be of an even and solid color at the skin. Dogs of two or more colors at the skin are termed "parti-colored", and are disqualified. Clear colors are definitely preferred, but the coats of blues, grays, silvers browns, cafe-au-laits, apricots and creams may show varying shades, just so long as it is of the same color.

The color patterns apply equally for all three sizes of the breed—Toy, Miniature and Standard.

COLORS OF GREAT DANES

First column:

1—solid black
2—black, white points
3—black and white
4—blue

Second column:

1—harlequin
2—harlequin with white
3—harlequin with too-solid spots
4—harlequin on blue background

Third column:

1—solid heavy brindle
2—solid heavy brindle with white points
3—light brindle
4—faint brindle with white points

Fourth column:

1—dark tan, black muzzle
2—same with white points
3—light fawn
4—light fawn with light muzzle

The tan of the Dane is recessive to the brindling. Both are the same color, with and without a modifier, in the author's opinion.

A harlequin Dane. The color is distinctive in this breed and is caused by a definite determiner.

In Boxers, the dominant brindle is favored by many. It is found in a variety of shades, from almost black to very faint pencil lines on the fawn background.

Fawn is recessive to brindle and black.

The brindling of the Bulldog is determined by the modification of tan.

A Bulldog without brindling.

This black Greyhound, mated with a brindle male, produced the puppies shown below.

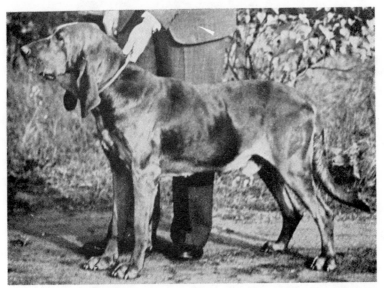

This dog produced puppies with all degrees of black. His puppies, in the picture below, show this variation.

The blackest puppy, at left, has faded to an intermediate. The lightest, at right, has only a small black saddle.

215

The ticking reveals the true genetic color of the dog which the white often covers up. The legs are red ticked and the saddle is blue ticked.

A Pointer showing flecking, but not ticking.

Here is a lightly ticked Setter, but not ticked heavily enough to warrant the title of "blue belton". (Blue ticking is a color, and the term should not be used to constitute a breed or strain, as many believe.)

The German Shorthaired Pointer carries the same ticking factor as hounds, Setters and some other breeds.

217

Dalmatian spotting is caused by a different determiner from ticking. When this book was first written there was doubt, but it no longer exists. (For discussion of an interesting physiological oddity that the Dalmatian exhibits, see page 327).

Cross of Dalmatian and Norwegian Elkhound. Note the loss of the Dalmatian spotting, the thin coat, and the dominance of the short hair.

218

The two dogs at top of the page produced puppies like the one pictured below, some of which were flecked, showing the recessive or inhibited condition of flecking as distinct from ticking.

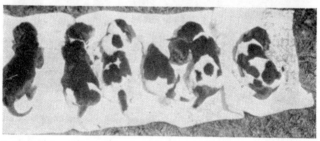

A typical story of hound color inheritance. *At top:* The black-and-tan Bloodhound was mated with the tricolored Basset Hound. The black-and-tan dog on the right in the middle picture was one of their puppies. He was mated with the Beagle bitch shown with him, and their six puppies (tricolored and black-and-tan) are shown below.

The tan Greyhound at left in the top picture was mated to the tricolored, ticked Foxhound at right. The pup shown below was one of the resultant litter. Some were ticked, some solid colored, some tan and white and one tricolored. (Interestingly, four of the ten pups had bob tails.)

The result of crossing two black-and-tan hounds, each of which had a white parent. Note that the white spotting is recessive.

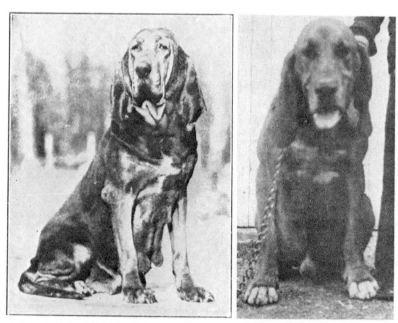

When mated to the tan dog at right, the Bloodhound bitch at left produced 18 tan puppies; when mated to a black-and-tan which carried tan recessively, she produced not one tan puppy. The dog at right never sired a black-and-tan pup, even when mated to many black-and-tan bitches.

222

An exceptional color in hounds. This deep rich red pup has no tan but a liver colored nose and foot pads, as though only the black were inhibited. Only one of this color has been produced in the author's kennels.

A solid red Bloodhound with black nose. Breeding definitely showed that this dog carried the recessive kind of tan.

What happens when a black-and-tan hound is
mated with a black-and-white Setter. Had the Setter
been a tricolor, the pup would have been a tricolored or black-and-tan dog.

A black-and-tan Bloodhound mated with a black-and-white Great Dane produced a litter of puppies of which the two above represent the extremes of color.
The father was marked like the nearer puppy.

Few people realize that scent hound color and Setter color are inherited in the same way.

The same facts which apply to the inheritance of scent hounds apply to Fox Terriers, both Wire and Smooth coats.

225

The Bloodhound at top left, mated with the double harlequin Great Dane at right, produced the gray-black harlequin below.

The gray-black harlequin on the opposite page, mated to a black-and-tan Bloodhound, produced the six puppies above. They are three quarters Bloodhound,
but note the combination of colors from both breeds.

The merling on the Collie is the result of the same color determiner as affects the hound.

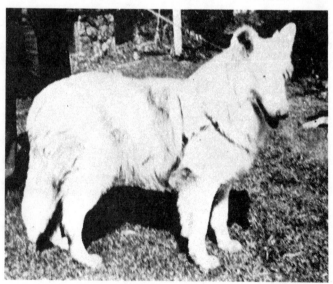

The imperfect white caused by a pair of merling factors combining. The result is undesirable.

Here is a dark sable and white Collie. Sable is dominant over black-and-tan. A sable, if it carries the black-and-tan color recessively, may produce black-and-tan puppies when mated to another like itself, or to a black-and-tan.

Here is a light sable Collie. From this color as well as from the dark sable, tricolors may be produced.

A contrast in black and red. These are the two primary colors in Chow Chows, other colors being modifications of these.

Blue Chow puppy. This color carries the dilution determiner and is in reality a dilute black.

230

The St. Bernard comes in various shades of sable and with more or less white.

A Newfoundland crossed with a St. Bernard produces black offspring. One of those puppies crossed with a St. Bernard produces puppies like this one, sable and whites, blacks, and black and whites.

231

Here we see a liver-and-tan Doberman. He carries the saddle factor but recessive determiners in the germ plasm repress the black.

Airedale Terriers are related to the scent hounds in that they
have the tan and the tan with the saddle.

The coat colors of the Pekingese are a mixture of Chow and
Collie colors.

233

The treeing aptitude clearly runs in families. Some dogs are such natural tree dogs that they never need training. This dog, for example, treed the family cat from the time he was three months old, and later developed into a great coon and squirrel dog.

234

2

The Inheritance
of Behavior Patterns

THE first study on the inheritance of what I then called "mental aptitudes" ever made with dogs was published in the December 1929 issue of *The Journal of Heredity*. It concerned the response of a dog following the scent left by an animal to that odor. Some dogs follow animal trails mutely; some bay or bark as they follow. I was told by a psychologist that I was not studying an aptitude, but a behavior pattern. The aptness for playing a violin by a human being would be an aptitude but a dog's following a trail and baying or being silent was a behavior pattern. So be it.

As a coon hunter I had used open trailers and still or mute trailers. When I crossed purebred open trailers with purebred mute trailers and trained the puppies to follow raccoon trails, all I had ever worked with barked on the trail, but with yap of the shepherd or house dog. They lost the beautiful bay of the hound.

I learned that not all dogs which looked as one would expect a still trailer to look were always still trailers. Many breeds

Three Beagles hunting. The trailing behavior of the "trailing" breeds is very different from that of the "tracking" breeds, for whom following a trail is unnatural. These Beagles are natural born trailers.

of dogs are very inferior at following trails compared with hounds. Some Springer Spaniels bark and some run trails mutely. Some farm shepherds bark on the trail.

I made many F_2 crosses and found no clear-cut segregation. One shepherd x hound cross produced open trailing offspring. Two of the F_1 offspring produced two puppies. One had long hair and barked on the track, while a shorthaired pup followed silently.

Most interesting of all the F_1 and F_2 were crosses of Bloodhounds with Bull Terriers. Two different pairs were crossed and their offspring mated together. One male F_1 was mated to his mother. The picture on page 194 of the four puppies and their parents is typical of the appearance of the F_2 dogs I raised from the F_1 crosses. There were none with ears nearly approaching the Bloodhound grandparents, nor as short as the Bull Terriers'. I had no time to carefully check the behavior and voices following trails of all these dogs. Most were given away. Some were used as guard dogs and others as hunters. Eight of one litter of 17 were carefully studied, however. Two had melodious voices on the trail. Two had the same squeaky voices as the sire, and the other four were silent during all our trials. On the whole they were an intelligent group.

The F_1 bitch, Mary, was mated once to a dog which was a cross of a Bloodhound and Basset bitch. It was a dog with intermediate length legs. There were 14 pups, pictured on page 108. These were all given to hunters. All that were trained and lived to hunt were open trailers. One in particular liked to fight with other dogs so much he was destroyed.

The white puppy shown on page 108 was, from early puppyhood, incompatible with his littermates, and as he grew older was such a ferocious fighter he too was destroyed. Psychologists would call it dominance. He did indeed dominate the littermates, but carried this behavior to the extreme.

The F_1 dog called Bill was a dominant dog all through his life but he never started a fight. Put in a pen with any dog, he

Pups of the mating of Bill and Mary, representing F2 crosses of Bloodhound x Bull Terrier.

was always respected, usually without growling. He became our doctor dog. If a dog had a cut or sore it could not reach, Bill would lick it for the injured dog. Sometimes there would be objections but Bill would, in some way we could not observe, communicate to the injured dog, who would then stand and accept the treatment.

I have never known a dog who would take so much abuse from puppies and sometimes older dogs. We once had a large hound with a nasty disposition with other dogs and decided to try to cure him. We left Bill with him for several days. He tormented the Bullhound, taking Bill's food if one of us wasn't there to prevent it, and pushed the dog about. Bill seemed to know his strength and took the abuse as long as he could. Finally exasperation or frustration built up to an explosion and we found the big hound so badly chewed and cowed that he was lying curled up in a corner looking about half his size. Bill was unmarked. He was a wonderful animal in many ways.

The one exception to the findings on the dominance of open trailing inheritance is work done by Marchlewski, who crossed silent English Pointers with German Shorthaired Pointers which "yelped" on a trail. The offspring were silent. This is quite astonishing in view of the fact that when the German Shorthair was first introduced, it was heralded as being a great trail dog. It is a truly excellent bird dog, but those which I knew which were tried for coon hunting were all still trailers. They did run with their noses close to the ground, however, indicating hound ancestry. Probably some were open trailers in the early days of development.

The Slow Steady Hound

There is a highly prized behavior pattern involving both gait and voice that the fox hunter, who hunts to kill, prizes above all other qualities in a Foxhound. When one hears of a Foxhound which ran a fox continuously for 24 or 36 hours, it is usually one of this type. The dog settles down to a steady,

238

not too fast lope—usually about 10 to 12 miles per hour. He opens at regular, not too frequent, intervals. Foxes soon lose all fear of such hounds, and I have known of many hunts in which the fox was seldom over 75 yards ahead of these hounds after the first hour. The hunter hears the hound, can station himself to shoot and usually ends the season with a prize bag.

In contrast to this type of behavior pattern we have the field trial dog before which foxes are not shot. They run fast and true.

A study should be made of the inheritance of these patterns. We know the field trial type breeds uniformly true because of so many generations of selection, but the lone hunter which charms the fox into losing its fear is such a rarity that the behavior needs study.

Some hunters have reported to me that they own open trailing Airedales. Quite possibly they are purebred dogs. Quite possibly, too, they are part hound, because the cross of Airedale with hound produces a dog with Airedale characteristics.

Scott, Shepard and Werboff found considerable difference in Shetland Sheepdogs and Basenjis with regard to their early treatment and subsequent mature behavior. They were studying what they called "kennel dog syndrome." The Basenjis were poor at four to six weeks of age in learning the particular inhibitory task, but increased their performance by 43 percent at later ages. The Shetlands stayed at a low level and then improved by 212 percent.

Scott, Bronson and Trattner, in studying differential handling and antagonistic behavior, found differences in Basenjis and Shetland Sheepdogs: their genetic background dictated how dogs of these different breeds reacted to the same situation. "Sensitive and easily inhibited Shelties accepted the position of ignored sibling, while the emotionally tractable Basenjis struggled against it but got into fewer fights."

The problem of studying inheritance of mental aptitudes is a psycho-genetic one. First we must select characters in the dog which are as nearly as possible independent of training, that is, those behavior patterns which exhibit themselves if the dog is allowed to be natural. Here are some contrasting pairs which fulfill this requirement and are to a great extent measurable:

1. Trail barking vs. mute trailing.
2. Hound drawl vs. choppy bark.
3. Hunting with head high vs. head to the ground.
4. Water going vs. lack of it.
5. Bird hunting vs. lack of it.
6. Independent hunting vs. packing.
7. Staying quality in trailing vs. early quitting.
8. Using eyes in hunting vs. using nose.
9. Mouthing prey vs. quick killing.
10. Retrieving vs. non-retrieving.
11. Pointing vs. non-pointing.
12. Inhibited vs. not inhibited.
13. In fighting, slashing vs. tenacity of grip.
14. Fighting mutely vs. fighting noisily.
15. Digging for game vs. non-digging.
16. Pugnaciousness vs. docility.
17. Energetic vs. lethargic.
18. Horse-wise vs. lack of it.
19. Sensitiveness of nature vs. coarseness.
20. Stubbornness vs. $\begin{cases} \text{cooperativeness.} \\ \text{willingness.} \end{cases}$
21. Herding vs. lack of it.
22. Flock responsibility vs. lack of it.
23. Smiling vs. non-smiling.
24. Quartering vs. non-quartering.

The above are those characteristics with which I have worked or observed. Here are others studied by researchers:

1. Mute trailing of English Pointer vs. yelping on trail of German Pointer.
2. Backing vs. non-backing.
3. Liveliness vs. subdued.
4. Auditory oversensitiveness vs. undersensitiveness.
5. Oversensitiveness to touch vs. its opposite.
6. Closeness to heel of horses position of Dalmatians vs. distance from heels.
7. Sluggishness vs. active behavior.
8. Carrying objects vs. non-carrying.
9. Passive defense reaction vs. active defense reaction.
10. Shyness vs. non-shyness.
11. Active temperament vs. lethargic.
12. Timidity vs. aggressiveness.

The first five in the first list are those to which I have given most attention. One very fortunate feature about studying behavior patterns in dogs is that one can observe several contrasting pairs in the same cross. For example, a setter dog is interested in birds, points, hunts with head high, retrieves his prey. In contrast, a hound is interested in animal tracks, does not point, hunts with head to the ground, is a poor retriever and crushes his prey. All of these aptitudes may be studied in one cross.

Here is a list of crosses which I have made which are pertinent to the study of these aptitudes we are here considering:

Litters		Pups
1	Bloodhound x Newfoundland	8
2	Bloodhounds x Irish Setter—11-5	16
4	Foxhounds x English Setter—6-7-9-6	28
2	Beagles x Cocker Spaniels—6-5	11
1	Backcross (Bl.-Ir. Setter) to Foxhound—11	11
1	Backcross (foxh.-Pointer) to Pointer—4	4
1	Backcross (foxh.-Eng. Setter) to Foxhound—8	8
1	Backcross (Bl.-Ir. Setter) to Pointer—3	3
4	F_2 Bloodhound x Irish Setter—3-5-8-13	29
17		118

Now consider the evidence on which the conclusions on these behavior patterns are based.

1. *Open trailing vs. still trailing.*

Some of the breeds I've used in these studies were:

Open Trailers	Mute Trailers	Open Trailers	Mute Trailers
Bloodhound	Airedale	Foxhound	English Setter
Foxhound	Collie	Bloodhound	Great Dane
Springer Spaniel	English Setter	Bloodhound	Newfoundland
Bloodhound	Norwegian Elkhound	Bloodhound	Irish Setter
Foxhound	Norwegian Elkhound	Foxhound	Pointer
Beagle	Cocker Spaniel	Greyhound	Foxhound
Foxhound	Airedale	English Setters	Farm Shepherds
Bloodhound	Bull Terrier		

Their grandparents were a black-and-tan hound and a sable Collie. (The hound barks on the trail, but the Collie trails mutely.) Their parents were sable-colored, shorthaired trail barkers. These traits have recombined in the dogs shown above, so that the longhaired dog is a trail barker, and the black-and-tan shorthaired dog trails mutely.

These and many more crosses I have made or observed, which I was sure were authentic, attest to the dominance of the trail barking vs. still trailing.

When I first bred Bloodhounds in 1922, many of the American dogs bayed on man trails. This was a nuisance. I found dogs which ran man trails mutely, and after 20 years of selective breeding every Bloodhound I bred, worked or sold was a mute trailer on human trails but open on animal trails. This was observable at times in training and occasionally embarrassing in serious man trailing with dogs not yet entirely dependable. I have been running man trails in difficult trailing conditions, crossed some area where deer had been lying and had a hound leave the man trail and run bellowing on the deer track. The same has occurred when rabbits jumped and ran ahead of an inexperienced dog. When I was studying in 1937 at Auburn,

242

Alabama, I presented many purebred trained Bloodhounds to several penitentiaries where nondescript "bloodhounds" were used on man trails and ran in packs. Each superintendent insisted that my dogs would open as they ran with a pack, but none ever did. I observed many such trials.

2. *Hound drawl vs. choppy bark.*

This is a companion trait of the trail barking aptitude, but in this case the hound type of voice is recessive. The long drawl and beautiful melodious voice of the pure hound is gone in all crosses so far observed and the more rasping voice of the other parent is dominant. The quality of voice is likely a matter of throat and vocal cord construction but the drawl is likely a behavior pattern.

Here, too, one finds segregation in the F_2 crosses but apparently it is not a simple matter. Certainly it is inherited and independent of training. One can usually tell about it from the first trail which the young dog follows.

3. *The aptitude of hunting with head high vs. head to the ground.*

Representatives of those breeds, like the bird dogs, are generally destroyed by hunters if they drop their noses and go to trailing. Generations of rigid selection have caused them to keep their heads up and hunt by air scents. The hounds, especially of the long-eared types, generally use their eyes little and keep their noses to the ground.

Crosses of these two types produce a dog which in a natural state keeps the head up in hunting but which will drop the head occasionally to pick up a hot scent. It could scarcely be called a complete dominant. However, I have never seen a dog of such a cross which anyone would consider a trailer.

In one cross of a Bloodhound-Irish Setter to a Pointer female, one of the pups looked like an excellent bird dog but his natural aptitude caused him to occasionally trail where his two litter mates never did. He made a splendid pheasant dog. He trailed and barked until the bird left the ground.

243

The Scottish Deerhound, like the other sight hounds, runs by sight and is not much good at finding game with his nose. Fanciers selected for the former and against the latter.

In some sections dogs of the hound-setter cross and hound-Springer cross are highly valued for pheasants simply because they will, if necessary, drop their heads and trail, although their natural mode is hunting with heads high.

In a Russian volume entitled *Genetic Studies on the Domestic Dog*, Marchlewski had published in 1930 many interesting observations and findings. He crossed German Shorthaired Pointers with English Pointers and found that when German Pointers which hunted with their head to the ground, like hounds, were mated with the high-headed English dogs, the puppies carried their heads high like the English Pointers.

Marchlewski found that the higher grade of pointing exhibited by English Pointers was incompletely dominant over lower grades in the German Shorthair.

The Newfoundland is one of the most natural water dogs ever developed. One will often dive to retrieve. The breed has been used in the development of many water breeds.

4. Water-going vs. lack of it.

If one takes a pack of untrained dogs of different breeds and crosses into the woods and notes their native behavior around ponds and brooks, one is immediately impressed by the way in which some dogs jump into the first water they find and wallow and swim, while others only drink, perhaps wade through the brook smelling for tracks on the bank and get out. These differences are very marked.

The bird dogs are retrievers and natural water dogs. Newfoundlands and the derivatives of that breed usually love the water. Newfoundlands frequently will dive deeply and bring up sunken objects. Hounds, while not afraid of water, do not love it as do the bird dogs. So far, I can say that the trait appears to be dominant and the F_1 dogs are just as good water dogs as

245

The Chesapeake Bay Retriever is a natural water dog and retriever.

are their parents. This applies to the offspring of Cocker Spaniel and Beagle, to Bloodhound x Newfoundland crosses as well.

5. *Inheritance of Bird Interest.*

The aptitude of what I shall call bird-interest is nicely observed by mixing dogs of breeds to be crossed and then observing their behavior when subjected to the same stimulus. This was done in the author's kennels with a variety of dogs. The observations could not be recorded by measurements but the differences in the breeds used was startling. These differences can be seen by people who know nothing about dogs.

In the summertime a pen of four Cocker Spaniels was observed. They were puppies six months old with no training whatever. Whenever a bird or butterfly flitted across the run, every puppy tried to catch it, danced, sometimes on hind legs, and rushed around the pen until it came to the wire fence. Then it would stand and watch the object of its attention until it went out of sight. This was done on a litter of Pointers and a litter of English Setters. All of these behave similarly except that Pointers and Setters freeze to a point more often than do Cockers.

Next, careful attention was given to pens of Bloodhound and Bull Terrier puppies, and crosses between them. These were not in the least interested in the birds and insects. It was proposed that, by putting the breeds together, the bird hunters would infect with their enthusiasm those without bird-interest. But it was of no use. The excitement of the bird dogs was enough to stir up the non-bird dogs but they all seemed to show no interest.

Crosses of these two types show the bird-interest to be strongly dominant. I have crossed farm shepherds with English Setters; Irish Setters with Bloodhounds; Pointers with Fox-hounds and several others, and observed dozens of the offspring. Without exception, these F₁ dogs are interested in birds and

The Setter is interested in birds, points, retrieves and usually enjoys going into the water, because these mental aptitudes have been bred into him by selection.

butterflies, and usually as much so as purebred bird dogs. And, as already reported they tend to hunt with heads high, except the Spaniel crosses.

6. *Smiling vs. Non-Smiling.*

Every dog owner has observed dogs that smile. Some people regard the expression as an indication of viciousness, but those who know dogs realize that the puckering of the face muscles is seldom done except when the animal is pleased. There are all degrees of it, and there are dogs which become trained to show their smile more and more as they get older and exercise the muscles more.

The trait is found in many breeds. In my experience I have seen more representatives among Pointers, Doberman Pinschers and my Bloodhounds than any others. But I have seen Beagles, Setters (both English and Irish), Foxhounds, smooth-coated Fox Terriers, Collies, farm shepherds, Samoyeds, Great Danes, Cockers, mongrels and others smile.

It has been most interesting to see it appear in one generation after the other of my experimental dogs. It first appeared in an imported Bloodhound, Marshall's Brutus. He smiled only slightly, but he had a ponderously deep lip which probably accounted for it. His son, Faithful of White Isle, was a clown. He would smile at the least request. A kind word was all he needed, and in shows I had to pinch him when a judged observed him so he wouldn't shorten his lip by smiling. Faithful was bred to dozens of bitches, of several breeds. He sired many litters of half-breeds (Bloodhound-Foxhounds). He sired Mary, the bullhound mentioned several times. He sired pups by a Bassett Hound, and of all the hundreds of puppies that came from him just about one-half could be taught to smile.

The teaching only consists of getting a dog in repose and soliciting his attention and then talking to him. If he is a smiler, a little puckering of the lip muscles will appear. The more he smiles, and the more the observer talks kindly and laughs and shows his appreciation, the broader the smile becomes. Day after day it increases. A smiling dog will show a far greater

The broad smile, coupled with panting, gives this smiler the appearance of laughing.

development as time goes by, provided he is given a chance to exercise his smile.

So far as my observation goes the smile is reserved for his human companions, not for his dog friends. I have watched dogs at play through a window when they did not know I was watching, and have never seen one smile at another.

The dog illustrated smiling showed definite degrees of the trait. If anyone approached her and evinced any interest in her whatever, she would smile very faintly, enough to make one laugh. But if that person spoke to her and chatted awhile, the broadest kind of smile would greet him. The full smile picture was taken on a hot day when she was trying to smile and pant at the same time. She did not stick out her tongue ordinarily, as this illustration might falsely indicate.

The trait of smiling that was inherited in my kennels from Marshall's Brutus has come down through many generations, never skipping one, and behaving as a Mendelian dominant. It has appeared in certainly over 100 puppies, and has been absent in another 100. Indeed the trait has caused embarrassment because several persons to whom I shipped puppies wrote to say they were vicious, but when they were told it was a smile and not a snarl the dogs were showing, they enjoyed it instead of fearing it.

In a litter of Doberman Pinschers with which I am well acquainted, three out of six puppies that have been raised show the smiling propensity, and only the mother smiles. The owner of the sire says he knows of no such trait in the sire's parents or grandparents.

No exact data are available for the greater part of Faithful's offspring, but of those raised at the kennel, obviously very close to one-half of the puppies have inherited the propensity. Thus, to mention a few:

Mated to a Setter, three puppies smiled out of seven in litter.

Mated to a Pointer, three puppies smiled out of six in litter.

Mated to two Foxhounds, seven puppies smiled out of 16 in both litters.

Mated to a Basset, 4 puppies smiled out of 8 in litter.

Mated to a Bull Terrier, two puppies smiled out of six in litter.

Mated to three Bloodhounds, ten puppies smiled out of 18 in both litters.

Another imported Bloodhound which could smile was mated to two Setters. This dog was a first cousin of Marshall's Brutus. Puppies which smiled appeared in both F_1 Setter x Bloodhound litters. A male from one litter was mated to two females from the other. Of the 11 puppies raised from both litters only two did not smile. One of these, a bitch, was mated to Faithful and to two other Bloodhounds. Some of her puppies by Faithful smiled but I am not sure of the numbers. Not one of her puppies from the other two litters ever smiled.

A brother of the bitch mentioned above (Gandhi) was a great smiler. He was mated to a Setter which smiled and which had previously produced two smiling puppies in a litter of four. Of their puppies, there were both smilers and non-smilers among them but I am not sure of the numbers.

One of the F_2 Bloodhound x Setter males, the same one

250

mentioned above, was mated twice to a purebred Pointer bitch. There were both kinds among their offspring. When mated to a purebred Setter there were both sorts among the puppies, six of which were raised.

I feel sure that while conditioning definitely accentuates the propensity, its fundamentals are a matter wholly independent of training and will be followed with care in the collection of further data.

7. *Quartering vs. Non-quartering.*

A further study of dogs of these crosses concerns their method of hunting. The natural bird dog, instead of finding birds by going in a straight line as a hound does, quarters. He runs from right to left and back again. In this zigzag fashion he covers the ground and finds birds. This way of hunting generally is lost in the first cross, although one does see some slight evidence of it. My Pointer crosses show it in the first generation more strongly than the Irish Setter and Bloodhound, and one cross of Pointer with Foxhound showed it in a very slight degree, as compared with the other two. One dog which I worked diligently to train for raccoon hunting was a back cross of a hound and Pointer to a Pointer. He knew exactly what was wanted of him and tried so desperately it was painful to watch him. He would find the track before any other dog, but he seemed entirely unable to put his nose to the ground and follow the trail with the hounds. Instead, he quartered and raced wildly about in seeming desperation until he usually gave up and stood and listened for the hounds. Then he dashed to them and tried again. But he knew from their voices when they were close to the tree and he was always there before any other dog. We tried to train this dog by dragging strong scents but, try as he would his hereditary propensity for quartering overpowered him.

In all studies of mental differences and behavior we are usually handicapped by a lack of measurements or measurable qualities. Certain aptitudes are going to be discovered which may be measured, but until that time, the judgment of scientists will have to be our only measurement. My own observations on the presence or absence of trail barking are measurable to some degree, but watching a cross of a Pointer and a hound trying to follow a scent of a raccoon can scarcely be measured with exactness. Several of us interested in this study have made the same observations.

8. *Backing vs. non-backing.*

Even the "backing" instinct so desirable in Pointers, is dependent on specific genes, Marchlewski says, but he does not detail the mode of inheritance of these genes.

9. *Liveliness vs. subdued.*

Iljin, a Russian, has published a book, as yet not translated into English, entitled *Genetics and Breeding of the Dog.* It appeared in 1932. Dog breeders will be indebted to him for this and other work. His studies with German Shepherd-wolf crosses have produced much of interest both as to behavior and coat color.

Among mental characteristics studied was liveliness. He holds that normal dogs are lively but that there is a factor which represses liveliness. Crosses of German Shepherd and Siberian Huskies are seldom lively.

Adametz, reported by Iljin, found that the active, almost nervous, temperament was incompletely dominant over the more lethargic temperament of the German Shorthair.

Gates observed the offspring of a very gentle, timid Old English Sheepdog with a playful aggressive Collie and in the F_2 generation found a tendency toward segregation of the traits.

10. *Auditory oversensitiveness vs. undersensitiveness.*

Humphrey and Warner in their excellent book, *Working Dogs* (1934), show that dogs which are easily startled by loud noises—called by them, auditory oversensitiveness—tend to produce few of their kind when mated to dogs with undersensitive hearing. They suggest more than one factor or gene governing this trait.

The same applies, they show, to the sense of touch, and both tactual and auditory over- and under-sensitiveness are associated with sex because they found more males undersensitive and more females oversensitive than chance would explain.

They also list several other mental qualities which are probably inherited but give us no conclusive evidence.

11. *Inheritance of Dalmatian behavior.*

Keeler and Trumble in 1940 published a study on a behavior pattern in Dalmatians. They found that some dogs run under a coach close to the horses while others take positions farther back. And despite the fact that only a few dogs were observed, they conclude that the preference in positions is inherited to some degree.

12. *Sluggishness vs. active behavior.*

James, in an excellent study, by measuring the reaction of dogs as to their adjustment to food taking, and to adjustment to a painful situation found that he could grade dogs into two extreme or "polar groups" as he called them. One extreme was the sluggish or inactive type, the other, the active group. He found types distributed between these two extremes. When dogs of the extremes were crossed, the harmonious relationship between behavior and physical form broke up. Then when these F_1 crosses were in turn mated, the ancestral characters recombined in new ways. He showed, for instance, that a dog could exhibit the form of the Basset and yet be excitable like a German Shepherd grandparent.

13. *Carrying vs. non-carrying.*

Krushinsky of Russia studied the inheritance of the natural behavior of carrying or "apporting" as he calls it. This is independent of previous training and such natural carriers were easily made expert by reinforcing the responses. When such dogs were crossed with non-carriers there was evidence that the behavior tended to be hereditary.

Beside these he also shows us how individual traits become incorporated in a strain, and how it pays to use a dog of a type best for the performance of a given task, to train to do the work for which he is best suited.

253

14. *Passive defense reaction vs. active defense reaction.*

Krushinsky also studied two inherited behavior patterns which he called "active defense reaction" and "passive defense reaction." The active form exhibits anger, the passive, cowardice. German Shepherds raised in isolation and many in "free upbringing" show the cowardly defense reaction "though in a weaker form." Doberman Pinschers and Erdel Terriers show the angry defense reaction. He concludes "the manifestation of certain behavior in response to the external stimulus occurs the easier, the more it is in accord with the genotype of the animal."

15. *Shyness vs. non-shyness.*

In another paper Krushinsky crossed German Shepherd Dogs with "Giliatzki Laika" and compared the progeny with that resulting from crossing dogs and wolves. By combining the shyness of the wild animals with the greater excitability of the dogs, the progeny, which possesses both, show a pronounced manifestation of shyness. The Giliatzki Laika, being much less excitable, does not show the shyness so much as the German Shepherd, but the combination is usually shy. It was found that small doses of certain drugs caused accentuation of the characters; thus a new means of studying them was applied with success.

16. *Timidity vs. aggressiveness.*

A behavior pattern, difficult to measure but easily observable and one which some observers would call cowardice and others would interpret as self-protection, is that which dogs of some breeds exhibit toward dogs of other breeds. This is seen exemplified by German Shepherd Dogs and many Doberman Pinschers. Almost all night hunters have observed it many times. In hunting raccoons some men train their hounds to hunt in the lights of a car. The men ride and the hounds lope or trot along within sight. One can observe many facts about hounds in this way.

As the hounds trot along, farm dogs or house dogs in suburbs rush out to protect the property. Farm shepherd dogs will stand

The Bull Terrier is pugnacious,
but one finds differences within
the breed as to degree.

ominously guarding. Never have I seen one turn and run from
the hound or hounds. German Shepherd Dogs, which are
popular and are frequently kept as watchdogs, invariably turn
and run away from the hounds. They seem to avoid a fight whenever possible.

17. *The bird hunting aptitude vs. lack of it.*

In the case of bird-interest it would seem that this is a genuine
aptitude—an innate aptness for hunting birds which other
breeds possess only in the same degree that all human beings can
learn to play the piano where others are so apt they do it well
as early as ten years of age, and with very little practicing.

This aptitude shows itself in all of the crosses mentioned
above, that of being interested in things that fly. And the
aptitude is clearly dominant.

Pups from several such crosses have been in the same pens
with my hounds and other types. These hybrids have been just
as attentive to butterflies, birds and airplanes as are their
purebred bird dog parents. And it has been very remarkable
to watch these pointing or trying to catch the butterflies, while
the other breeds would pay no attention whatever.

255

Bred of a sire that was half Bloodhound, half Irish Setter, and of a dam
that was a purebred Pointer, this bitch was a natural bird dog.

But in the field is where one finds the better test. Air drifts
of unseen birds excite these hybrids. They often point well but
not with the style of the bird dog parent.

18. *Reaction to vaccination.*

The reaction to a certain stimulus is one way of studying
a behavior pattern. One such stimulus is a hypodermic needle.
On the examining table of the Whitney Veterinary Clinic every
year are placed in excess of 1,000 dogs each of which receives a
distemper vaccination. The syringe and needle are the same size,
are soaked in the same sterilizing solution and the puncture is
made in the same place on every dog—under the skin over the
shoulder. The vaccine is always identical.

Now, if some puppies stand like statues never wincing at the
needle prick, or the injection of vaccine into both sites of
injection, that is noteworthy. If some puppies scream and snap,
urinate and defecate while being restrained, that too is worth
noting. And if some race about when placed on the floor, and
act as if they were having fits, that also is significant. But what

256

is more so is the fact that the behavior can usually be predicted by observing the breed to which the puppy belongs. There are distinct breed differences, and strain differences within breeds.

These breeds which appear stolid react much as might be expected. Boxers may be counted on to utter no cry, show little reaction to the injection, and only exhibit their discomfort by scratching. Cocker Spaniels show the greatest strain differences but as a breed can be counted on to squeal their protest most vehemently and usually react most violently. Airedales and Irish Terriers, as well as Scottish Terriers, are but little moved. All of the Bull Terriers and Staffordshires stand near the top in showing pain least, or perhaps feeling it least.

In strains the differences are so noteworthy that one may depend on the reactions by simply knowing the strain. One day, a litter of English Setters came to be vaccinated. They were nine weeks old. Each of the seven reacted in the same way, making a great crying but no biting. Soon after they had gone, another litter was brought. These six puppies never flinched. Every condition was practically identical. Another time a client brought 36 Springer Spaniels. Their mothers were sisters, all of which had been bred to the same dog. Every puppy emitted a little "yip" when the needle pierced the skin, but no cry beyond that. In contrast other litters of Springers could be mentioned which screamed and urinated as a result of the same injection.

Toward a Better Understanding of Behavior Patterns

City people far outnumber country dwellers today. Urbanites know about dog breeds by what they read or see of dog shows. And as of 1971 dog shows are principally those held under the rules of the American Kennel Club. Only those breeds of dogs which the A.K.C. "recognizes" can be shown. For a breed to be "recognized" entails the forming of a breed association by fanciers and after a large number of dogs have been bred and registered by those fanciers, the A.K.C. may then recognize the breed and permit registrations in its stud books.

257

If the fanciers of breeds have no interest in having the breed of their fancy "recognized" by the A.K.C. they may run their own association (Greyhound breeders), or register their dogs in a different kennel club (Upland Bird Dog breeders in the American Field Stud Book, or Redbone and other Coonhound breeders in the United Kennel Club).

It is a pity that urbanites seldom have a chance to observe these wonderful breeds not shown in A.K.C. shows. "Out of sight, out of mind." The hunting bird dogs outnumber the A.K.C. show type bird dogs by a vast proportion. Racing Greyhounds and Foxhounds outnumber the A.K.C. show type 100 to one. Redbone Coonhounds registered in the U.K.C. outnumber over three-quarters of the breeds recognized in the A.K.C. The Redbone Breeders Association has 900 members, making it one of the largest of all breed associations. But no Redbone appears in city dog shows.

All the dogs shown in a year in all the A.K.C. dog shows constitute something over 100,000, a pittance of the 25,000,000 or more dogs in the U.S.A. With 1,000 Coonhound field trials, and with about the same number of Beagle and bird dog trials, the total interest in field work is far greater than the interest in dog shows. But field trial enthusiasts have their shows too.

The important point is that, as the result of the cleavage among dog breeders, different types of dogs are developing among the different breeds, different both in form and behavior. What has already happened is that the A.K.C. show dogs are much less proficient for the work for which the breeds were intended than those fancied by the field trial folks. Look at the illustrations of the show type Beagle and the field type; of the show type English Setter and a big field type winner; of the proficient Bloodhound man trailers and the ponderous show type; of the show Greyhound and the track dog, the former chosen for a square appearance, the latter with the long back and long strides.

Much work remains to be done on the inheritance of behavior patterns, some of which are of real importance. As an example,

258

The Redbone Coonhound, a breed created in America. An extremely efficient dog for his work, his specialized behavior is inherited. The red color is dominant.

we have witnessed a great change in the behavior of Setters and Pointers, in their mode of hunting. Within two human generations the breeds have changed from dogs which stayed only a short distance in front of the hunter to those which dash off so fast and so far to find their birds that the field trials have to be judged on horseback. Today it is difficult to find American-bred Setters and Pointers useful for personal bird dogs. Why? Because owners of bitches breed them to the great field trial champions, and they are the fast wide-ranging dogs.

Beagles are registered in the A.K.C., but only as a matter of convenience to the field trial men. The show-type Beagle from which the modern field type has been developed is practically useless in field trials. Those who doubt that behavior patterns are inherited should observe the differences which these breeds exhibit.

While we know something about how certain behavior patterns are inherited, we know very little. It would be much more worthwhile if we had tests for innate mental capacity and something akin to the tests which have been used for human beings. We could not test reasoning ability in the broad sense because dogs do not reason in the same way as human beings, if at all. But there are means of devising tests to determine the speed of learning certain facts which we wish dogs to learn and in that sense we would be testing something highly useful to man.

What no one has been able to answer is this, "Why have not dogs been bred for mental qualities other than those which are useful to man in practical ways?" When you and I want to teach our dogs some useful tricks, or acts which we call tricks, we have to go through a carefully executed technique, and we do this either consciously or unconsciously. I have a friend who taught a dog over 200 words. He had a subject which was most responsive. Had he spent the same amount of time on some dog with a lower mentality, it might have taken him much longer to accomplish the same results. But on the other hand, if he had used a dog with a still higher mentality, it might also have taken him very much less time. Whatever that quality is which makes it possible for a dog to learn easily, it is a very fine quality for any dog to possess. That is, up to a certain point.

Now, why have some men not bred dogs for just that quality? We see the old-fashioned farm shepherds learn to take down the bars and bring certain cows home. Probably if we were to study them we would find among their number a higher percentage of learnability than that of any other breed. Now, I think I know the partial answer, and it ties up with the "certain point" which I mentioned above.

That reason is that today most of our dogs which are bred and sold for pets are kennel-bred dogs. What does a kennel owner want in his dogs that actually militates against the development of the very finest mental qualities? He wants compliance with his conditions. He does not try to comply with the dog's. And for that matter, so does the owner of one or two dogs if he has to keep them in confinement.

Elimination of Valuable Characters

I, like the majority of readers of this book, have been party to the eradication of some of the very finest canine mental ability. How? Well, I have killed the dogs which I found I couldn't keep confined, or else I have given them away, where they were finally killed, some by owners and some by automobiles, and so forth. I think of two which I had to destroy this very year which were probably brighter than any dog I now own. Only very heavy wire would hold them. They had been together once in a run made of heavy poultry wire. There was a broken strand and one got her nose through and worked on the wire until she had a hole in it big enough to crawl through. The other watched her and helped at times. They were thrashed for doing it, but were too cunning, and from that time on no wire fence was safe. So I moved them to a run that was enclosed with extra heavy wire, but they dug out. Then I put rocks under the wire so they could not dig out. They soon learned to jump up and over the six-foot fence.

I transferred them to another enclosure with another heavy fence seven feet high, but they were out in no time. So then I put them back in the six foot high enclosure and covered the top with poultry netting. One of them jumped up, caught her teeth in the wire, hung onto the side wire with her feet and worked on the top wire until she had a hole big enough to get out, and out she went. The other followed, of course.

I grew so tired of being waked up nights and worrying about disturbing the neighbors that I finally destroyed them, as they were not of any further use to me in my scientific work, nor had I the time nor inclination to struggle with them further.

Had I been able to work on a strain of dogs irrespective of breed which could be bred for mental ability of the sort I have described, then I should have kept these troublesome dogs and bred them, keeping them in a kennel out of which it was impossible to escape. But I, like most breeders, didn't have the time to make my conditions fit the dogs, but rather I made the dogs try to adapt themselves to conditions which had been

The most important mental ability should be even more highly developed by selection.

planned for the ordinary dog's intelligence. I actually have contributed to making dogs less intelligent, instead of more.

Some day a group of enterprising breeders is going to get the cooperation of a group of psychologists, and is then going to develop a breed of dogs which will be more responsive and more easily taught, more eager to learn, than any heretofore developed. It will take time. It will also mean that the conditions of housing and so forth will have to be developed to fit the dogs, rather than expecting the dogs to be conformists to present day kennel conditions.

The reason why the farm shepherds have become so much more easily taught, and why they learn so many more things than the ordinary run of kennel dogs, is because they are not expected to be conformists. They are not bred down to specified kennel standards but are allowed to develop the best there is in them. Of course it is true that not nearly enough care has gone into developing their best points, but still we see them taking the children to school, returning for them at the proper time without being told, putting the cows out and bringing them in again, doing almost unbelievable feats in the handling of sheep, amusing the family with little tricks they have learned and in every way showing sense that few kennel-bred dogs exhibit.

In short, why not breed for more intelligence, or whatever those qualities are which make dogs appear smarter? The innate ease of learning is inherited. This most important mental ability should be even more highly developed by selection. If it is, the dog will be a still more useful animal to man or to a greater number of men.

3

The Inheritance of Eye Color

MANY a case of human paternity has been settled on the basis of eye color and there is no reason why the paternity of dogs could not be equally well established by this method. The mode of inheritance is so well known in human beings that one can predict in certain cases just what color eyes a child from a given pair of parents will have.

In the case of dogs there are only two principal kinds of variations from the normal. The first kind which we shall consider is the light and the dark eye. We group them together because they are inherited as complements of each other. By dark eye, I mean the usual dark brown eye which is inconspicuous because it does not stand out in great contrast to the rest. We do not especially notice the eyes of the dog when they are brown. It is common and very likely the best eye color for the sake of the dog, because it most perfectly protects the eye from the rays of the bright sunlight. The lighter the eye color, the more the dog needs to squint when in a bright light.

The albino lacks all protective coloration in the eyes, all pigment. His eyes show red because we can see right through to the blood. In this case eye color is associated with hair color and

264

The light eye and the dark eye are inherited in a definite manner, the light being recessive. These dogs illustrate the yellow or light brown eye. This is distinct from the pearl eye, but both kinds are similarly inherited.

skin color. Or to be more exact we should say "the lack of color or pigment."

The contrasting character of the dark eye is the light brown eye, sometimes mistakenly called the yellow eye. This is not a yellow color but a brown.

There we have one complementary pair of factors, the dark and the light brown color. But there is another pair, the pearl eye and the dark eye. There are certainly cases where the pearl eye is inherited in association with hair color. We know this because very occasionally we see dogs with one pearl eye and the other brown, and in such cases we usually find that the hair color around the pearl eye is different, usually lighter than that surrounding the brown eye. I am not referring to that kind but rather to the case where both eyes are a clear pearl.

Then, there is another pearl eye which is inherited in a totally different way. In the case of the former, quite often one eye is pearl and the other not. Harlequin Danes often have it. Some dog and horse breeders speak of this eye as a "watch eye." Occasionally it will be found in sable Collies which are descended from merles.

First, inheritance: I have now observed many crosses involving all types of inheritance of this trait. I have never yet found

265

a pair of light-eyed parents giving birth to dark-eyed pups. I have often seen two dark-eyed parents produce litters in which all the pups are dark-eyed. In fact, this is the usual result. And I have had two litters of hounds in which the number of pups showed quite conclusively that both parents were duplex for the trait, that is, that each had one determiner for light and one for dark, but while they themselves appeared dark-eyed, nevertheless they produced close to 25 percent light brown-eyed puppies.

Among my Bloodhounds I had the yellow-eye factor fairly well entrenched. There were sufficient individuals to make an interesting study.

If we designate the dark brown eye as Y and the yellow as y, we find four litters where a Yy dog was mated with a Yy bitch. Of the 39 pups 33 were brown-eyed and six yellow.

One YY stud dog was mated with many bitches, some with yellow eyes and some Yy. Every puppy was brown-eyed.

2 Yy with yy gave 16 puppies, nine brown and seven yellow.

4 Yy with yy gave 36 puppies, 17 brown and 19 yellow.

A puppy's eyes are bluish when they first open and one must wait until the eyes change to their adult color before counting the product of matings being studied. Some of the litters in the above resumé were larger at birth and the puppies died from one cause or another, but this probably does not affect the conclusion.

The yellow eye always accompanies the liver-and-tan color pattern. This is left out of account in this study. All of the dogs included were solid-colored black-and-tans. Note the illustration of two dogs, one dark-eyed and one light, which were repeatedly mated and produced only dark eyes.

There is a type of pearl or watch eye whose inheritance is in no way related to the pearl eye of the harlequin or merle colored dogs. It was common a generation ago in Pointers, and because it gave the possessor a wild and startled appearance was discriminated against much more rigidly than yellow eyes in dark colored dogs. I have seen it in blacks and liver Pointers. Liver and white Pointers always have yellow eyes but the eyes of those with pearl eyes had the same appearance as they did in black dogs. My data are meager because they were

266

derived in 1920 from the records of one breeder with whom I was closely acquainted. Naturally he was trying to eliminate the defect from his dogs. He had one litter of black mated with liver in which there were two pearl-eyed black puppies; two other litters of liver mated to liver in which two pearl-eyed liver puppies appeared. We used to joke that they always came in pairs. He gave me one of the bitch puppies which I raised and mated to a liver male owned by a neighbor. There were only two puppies in the litter and both were pearl-eyed. None of these dogs was deaf. This pearl eye is therefore a recessive.

Another eye characteristic which has come in for study is the ruby eye. Iljin found it in several breeds—Beagles, Great Danes and mongrels—and learned that it was best observed when certain light conditions were met. Most dog breeders have probably seen it. When a dog is kept in a fairly dark place and then looks at a light coming from close to the observer, one sees a ruby reflection. There is a similar light reflected from the eyes of some, but not all, raccoons. This ruby eye Iljin found to be recessive to the usually pigmented eye, but dominant over the albino eye.

4

Inheritance of Coat Characteristics

IN THE case of many species of animals it has been amply demonstrated that, where the length of the coat is either long or short, the long hair behaves recessively to the short. The example of long-haired guinea pigs is generally cited in text books on genetics as classical. The evidence which I shall present shows that without exception long hair when mated with short behaves recessively in the case of dogs as in the case of other species.

The study is the result of observations from among many dogs which I have owned and bred in the past, and on dogs belonging to others where the results have proved interesting, and where matings have been positively controlled.

Two observations many years ago called to mind the probability of the recessive character of long hair: The first was the finding of two long-haired dogs in a litter of Pointer puppies. These were dogs owned by a close friend and I knew that the bitch had been mated to only one dog and he a registered Pointer. The usual doubt naturally could not be dispelled, nevertheless, until, upon inquiry and wider knowledge of the practices of men interested in breeding bird dogs for field trials, it was a common practice to mate Pointers (short hair) with Setters (long hair). The puppies commonly called *droppers* are all short-haired and often erroneously referred to as Pointers. This has been done, and it appeared as a possible explanation that a pair of these hybrids which looked like excellent pointers had been mated and the result was two long-haired puppies in the litter.

The second indication appeared as the result of the mating of a pair of wirehaired Airedales, on which the coat was not much longer than a hound's, but wiry and curly in character. In every litter which this pair produced there was one or more long-haired and silky-haired puppy. Then I learned that this was not at all unusual, and that it occurred because the Airedale was a new breed, still in the process possibly of losing its masked recessives.

Among the progeny of Weimaraners, which are said to be an old breed, doubt is cast by the rather common occurrence of long-haired puppies being whelped in some litters. Likewise were the frequent production of long-haired pups in litters of German Shorthaired Pointers. If both were old, pure breeds, even if one had been bred to an English Setter the puppies would be short-haired, provided the short-haired parent carried no genes for long hair. When two short-haired parents produce a long-haired pup, that is prima facie evidence that both had a long-haired ancestor. This hints at the fact that English Setters may have gone into the creation of the breed.

Having available at the time a Great Dane (short-haired) and a Collie, I mated the pair, and the puppies were all short-haired. That was in 1916. Since then, many crosses have been made to determine inheritance of certain genetic traits, and from these the following observations show that long hair behaves recessively in the case of the dog as well as those other experimental animals.

The table shows some of the various breeds crossed. All of the progeny were short-haired.

Collie with Great Dane.
St. Bernard with French Bulldog.
Shepherd (farm) with Foxhound—2 matings.
Cocker Spaniel with Beagle—3 matings.
Irish Setter with Bloodhound—2 matings.
English Setter with Foxhound—2 matings.
Collie with Foxhound—5 matings.
Collie with Bull Terrier.
Cocker Spaniel with Boston Terrier.
Cocker Spaniel with Boston Terrier.
Collie with Pointer.
Russian Wolfhound with Bloodhound.
Collie with Airedale.
Setter with Pointer.
Pomeranian with German Shepherd.
Bloodhound with Newfoundland.

Besides these F_1 crosses several interesting F_2 crosses have been made, as well as back crosses, and these are listed in the following tables together with the results:

Parents	Appearance of Parent	Appearance of Puppies *
6 crosses F_1 Irish Setter-Bloodhound	Short-haired, slight fullness under tail	20 puppies; 17 short-haired; 3 long-haired
1 cross F_1 Collie-Foxhound	Short-haired, slight fullness under tail	6 puppies; 2 long-haired 4 short-haired
1 cross F_1 Beagle-Cocker Spaniel	Short hair	4 puppies, all short-haired
1 cross F_1 Irish Setter-Bloodhound	Short hair, slight full- under tail in both cases	6 puppies; 5 short-haired 1 long-haired
1 cross English Setter-Bloodhound with Irish Setter F_1 Collie-Foxhound	Short hair, both cases. Fullness under tail of former, none in case of latter	8 puppies, 2 long-haired, 6 short-haired.

* Sometimes the long hair does not become fully apparent until puppies are seven months old.

270

The following back crosses show the same thing as the previous table, namely that short hair is dominant and that there is Mendelian segregation:

Parents	Appearance of Parents	Appearance of Puppies
4 crosses Irish Setter-Bloodhound to Setter	Short-haired Long-haired	33 puppies; 14 long-haired; 19 short-haired
3 crosses Irish Setter-Bloodhound to Bloodhound	Short-haired Short-haired	18 puppies; all short-haired
2 crosses English Setter-Foxhound to English Setter	Short-haired Long-haired	10 puppies; 6 long-haired; 4 short-haired
1 cross Cocker Spaniel-Beagle Beagle	Short-haired Short-haired	5 puppies; all short-haired
1 cross Greyhound Bloodhound-Irish Setter	Short-haired Short-haired	11 puppies; all short-haired

There are great variations in the length of the hair of dogs. When we speak of long or short hair, we ordinarily refer to a general class. Within the long-haired group there is tremendous variation. For instance, the hair on the tail of one Russian Wolfhound was ten inches long, and on another it was only five inches. I have measured many specimens of hair from different parts of the body of many dogs, but it serves little purpose to list these measurements because of the great variation within the separate breeds.

The same applies to variation in hair length within short-haired breeds. Bloodhounds used in these crosses had hair of different lengths and yet all would be classified as short-haired dogs. Within this breed there are two different hair lengths which are sufficiently different to make them distinct and these two classes are caused by different genes.

The denseness of the coat often affects its appearance. The denser it is the less likely it is to lie flat on the body. The coat

The result of crossing a St. Bernard with a French Bulldog distinctly shows the dominance of the short hair.

which stands erect appears much longer than the coat of the same length hair which lies flat. This sometimes deceives the casual observer but it need not if this point is kept in mind.

In all my experience and observation no case of two long-haired dogs having short-haired puppies has ever come to my attention. As shown above, short-haired dogs sometimes produce long-haired offspring. In known matings the numbers of long-haired and short-haired puppies in litters from short-haired parents closely approximates the 1:3 Mendelian ratio. Back crosses produce close to a 1:1 ratio. Thus, apparently we are justified in assuming that the inheritance of hair length in dogs is similar to the mode in other species.

Lang, Anker, Iljin and Little also agree that short hair is almost completely dominant over long and governed by a single gene, and that wire coat is a single gene dominance over smooth coat.

There are different kinds of long coats. That of the Old English Sheepdog and that of the Collie are so different that when Gates crossed the two and got longhaired pups, he was surprised that a pair of the F_1 produced among the F_2 some short-haired, smooth coats. This would indicate that the genes for the two kinds of coats lay on different sites of the chromosomes.

Hairlessness is due to a single gene. It is incompletely dominant as anyone acquainted with the characteristic knows. All of the hairless dogs show some hair often over the hips. If a dog inherits both dominant genes, according to Stockdale, Plate and Letard, he probably will not live.

In my cross of St. Bernard x French Bulldog, the legs were shorter in proportion than those of the larger dog. Lang crossed a St. Bernard and a Dachshund and says the body and trunk form of the Saint was dominant over that of the Dachshund.

That there are degrees of hair length is best illustrated by the transition which came over the whole Cocker Spaniel breed when it became permitted to exhibit dogs which had been barbered instead of bred for coat. The Cocker had become America's most popular breed, so that one in every four of American dogs was a Cocker Spaniel. They were formerly exhibited unbarbered, although the use of a razor to smooth the ears and neck was not objected to. With the advent of electric clippers the Cocker quickly was transformed. Fanciers looked for the longest haired dogs they could find and finding too few, bred only to the longest haired studs. The longer coat being recessive, the transition was dramatic. Within two dog generations Cockers became show dogs only with such long dense coats that only show fanciers and wealthy persons who could pay for frequent clippings could cope with them. The breed dropped dramatically in popularity.

Coat Density

Next we consider the thickness and the thinness of the coat. One of the thickest coated dogs is the Scandinavian Grahund (Norwegian Elkhound). If we counted the number of hairs to the square inch we should find that it was many times the number which is possessed by a Foxhound, for instance. I have not counted the hairs on many dogs in this way but enough to make

273

The dam shown is the result of crossing a Bloodhound with a Norwegian Elkhound. She was mated to her brother, and the six puppies shown below were the result. Note the color segregation as well as the coat. (This was probably the first planned F2 genetic experiment ever undertaken with dogs.)

274

The coat of the Norwegian Elkhound is probably thicker than that of any other breed.

me able only to generalize. In the first place, climate has a tremendous influence not only in regard to the diameter of each hair but also with regard to the density of the coat. Just how it causes this effect we don't know.

Dogs in the southern United States, with such thin coats one can blow the hairs apart and see the skin, will develop much denser coats by fall when moved to New England in the spring.

When a dog with a dense coat (like that on a Norwegian Elkhound) is crossed with a dog with a thin coat (like that on many Bloodhounds), in a general way it is correct to say that the thin coat is dominant over the thick.

We get segregation, as can be seen in the puppy pictures on page 274. The F_1 bitch was bred to a brother and her pups are all shown. The thick coat on the greyish looking one stayed when it was mature so that, with its lop ears and a tail that curled over its back and its thick coat, the dog looked odd.

But here there was not a clear-cut Mendelian segregation. Instead there was considerable variation and the puppies had coats which differed considerably, one from the other. There was not a distinct cleavage. But there is great variation even among pure bred dogs. I have counted enough hairs to be able to say that the variation is so great that only within rather wide limits can one predict the outcome from any mating. But even so, those limits are indicative of dominance and recessiveness, probably caused by multiple factors. Certain it is that sometimes two thin coated dogs produce puppies which grow to have very thick coats. This was not a matter of climate or feeding, as all of the breeding has been done in the same locality and on the same diet.

Inheritance of Undercoat

Some fanciers call undercoat "double coat." This is part of the furnishings of all of the northern dogs and the wire-haired breeds. Plucking the long coat on the wires reveals the softer undercoat. Breed crosses such as the Elkhound x Bloodhound gives us dogs with the undercoat lacking, and appearing in some dogs in the F_2 generation.

Inheritance of Straight and Curly Hair

In human beings it has been found that curly hair is dominant over straight. In dogs I found that this is not the case. Not many people realize what causes the hair to be straight or curly. If you watch a machine making wood dowels, you will see the straight round sticks produced by the cutters, and they are straight because they are round. The more oval they are the more curl the dowels would have. Shavings are tightly kinked. In the same way, the formation of the hair follicles will be found to be round or oval according to the kind of hair that is produced, and the more oval the tighter the curl. If one takes a hair from an Irish Water Spaniel and looks at it through a microscope it will be observed to be thick in one dimension and thin

276

The cross of Airedale and Bloodhound produced puppies, of which this is one, with a coarse coat but not as wavy and considerably shorter than that of the Airedale parent. No plucking was ever necessary.

in the other, actually very much of an oval in cross section. If one observes the hair of a Beagle, he will find it to be round.

Here is some evidence to show that the dominance is always toward the straight, as though the whole matter of curliness in dogs' hair were a question of multiple factors, or else of a pair of factors, one for straight, the other for curliness, and several pairs of factors in turn affecting the one for curliness.

A pair of straight coated dogs sometimes produces puppies with a wave in their coats. An Airedale with a wave, mated to a Bloodhound with a very slight wave, produced a litter of pups which when grown appeared as the one shown here. This dog has the wiry coat but not the very wavy hair of the Airdale.

There is a great difference between the doormat type of coat, that which stands up on end, and the wavy type of coat. I am not referring to the doormat coat nor the coarse coat which data show are inherited as dominants, but I refer here to the

277

The kinky coat of the Irish Water Spaniel is recessive to the straight hair of the other breeds.

curl. The Borzoi (Russian Wolfhound) to which I have previously referred, which was mated to the Bloodhound, produced puppies without the slightest wave in their coats. Another Borzoi which was mated to a Foxhound had pups with similar coats. But two Borzois, one of which has a straight coat and the other a wavy produced seven puppies, three of which had straight coats and four with wavy. Two of the straight often produce wavy-coated dogs.

The long hair of the Irish Setter is recessive to short hair in crosses.

That the kinky hair of the Irish Water Spaniel is recessive to the straight hair of the long-haired dog is evident from the following crosses: Irish Water Spaniel x Cocker Spaniel—(two crosses) 14 black, long-haired, straight-haired puppies with long hair on the tail, whereas the Irish Water Spaniel's tail is very short-haired, as is his face.

Irish Water Spaniel x Irish Setters—eight puppies, all black with a straight coat. The manager of a western kennel wrote me upon receipt of my inquiry, after I had learned that they made dozens of this mating for special hunting purposes: "We have made a great many matings of Irish Setter and Irish Water Spaniels and have yet to have the first pup born from them that was anything but black. Most of them have a little wave in their coat but I guess you would call them straight-haired dogs. They all look just like Setters having long hair on the tails, but are often much larger than the dogs that were mated to produce them."

Another kennel in Iowa also makes a specialty of this cross. A letter from the owner states essentially the same facts except that he has seen a few dark seal puppies from such matings. He too says the puppies are black with straight hair like the Setter.

This might be called hearsay evidence on my part, but I trust the word of these men who have made the crosses for business purposes, and the large number represented indicates that it is worthwhile material for study. The wave in the coat can be partly explained by the fact that some Irish Setters have slight waves in their coats naturally.

A cross of a pure black Belgian Shepherd with a wavy-coated tan Irish Water Spaniel resulted in all black wavy-coated puppies.

In Cocker Spaniels one finds great variation in the type of coat, and it is common knowledge that a pair of curly-coated dogs will produce puppies with straight coats, and that a pair of straight-haired dogs not infrequently produce puppies with wavy and slightly curly hair. Mating among the wavy and curly coated Cockers produces great variation. Mating among the straight does likewise but the great part of the puppies are straight-haired. I have endeavored to obtain data from Cocker

279

breeders on this point but those whom I have consulted have not kept data, and tell me that there is so much doctoring done for showing purposes that one cannot tell from the appearance of a Cocker whether his coat is naturally straight or curly. The curly kinks have been cut off and sometimes the neck has been almost shaved. Among my own Cockers it is very evident that the straight hair is dominant and the curly recessive. Some breeders believe that there is a linkage of coat characters with coat color in Cockers. Reds are thought seldom to have as good coats as blacks.

The Lakeland Terrier is a good example of the wirehaired breeds. Nearly all of them have longish hair which has to be plucked in order for the dogs to look as they are pictured.

Inheritance of Wire Coat

Next, to briefly consider the so-called wire-haired coat. This is, more often than not, wavy as well as wiry, and coarse in the

280

bargain. The hair stands up or nearly so, and the heavy guard hairs become loose twice a year and come out with great ease, almost like the quills of a porcupine, which are also over-developed hairs. But the hairs in a wire-haired dog stay in a long while if not pulled, and a goodly part of the plucking is done for style rather than to prevent the spread of dog hairs about the house.

In a great many crosses which I have made using wire-haired breeds and smooth-haired breeds, the wire-haired type has always been dominant. The waviness tends to be recessive. Hence one seldom sees a pair of wire-haired dogs producing pups which are both smooth-coated and straight-haired. Indeed I have never observed such a case. But I have seen a number of litters of puppies produced from wire-haired dogs which were straight-haired. In a litter of wire-haired terriers, two smooth-coated Fox Terriers appeared.

Not only have I made the first cross, but I have produced F_2 generations for this trait, and back crosses as well. In an F_2 mating of an Airedale x Beagle cross there were both wire-haired puppies and smooth-coated dogs. But the smooth-coated ones had wavy hair. In a back cross of one of these dogs to another Beagle they produced three with wire coat and two with smooth, but in this case all of the puppies had straight hair.

There is just one small "give-away" which one cannot always overcome, and which may be caused by a different pair of factors. I refer to the whiskers on the face. Quite often in some litters the puppies have been smooth and straight-coated but with a few whiskers which would not lie down, especially under the lips. They were apparently inherited independently of the other characters.

Inheritance of Coarseness of Coat

In all the matings of setters with hounds the coats were coarser than the setters, and I believe that we have evidence enough to make a tentative assertion that coarseness in coat is dominant. I have examined dozens of puppies which were produced by such matings and in no case was the very fine texture coat inherited in any other way. But as for saying that the F_2 puppies showed perfect segregation, I cannot, as there was always great variation in the hair from then on. Among several such litters there are all grades in the texture, and yet the grandparents had two distinct types of coats.

Airedale breeders have often found soft-coated puppies in litters with coarse hair.

It is well known that some dogs possess two distinct coats. The wire-haired breeds are noted for this, as are the northern dogs. It is the development of one of these against the other which gives the great variety in coat, to say nothing of the length of the coat. The outer coat is harsher and not very thick in some breeds while the under coat is shorter and generally exceedingly thick, and this protects the dog from the heat and cold as an excellent insulation.

A further study on the inheritance of the wire-hair when crossed with smooth was made by C. C. Little when he crossed Brussels Griffons. This breed comes with both types of hair. He found that the wire-hair is dominant, which finding is in keeping with studies of breed crosses. His study was done in 1934.

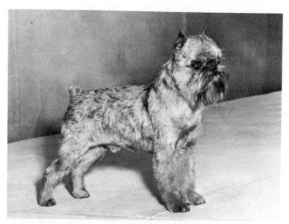

There are two varieties of the Brussels Griffon—the rough coat (as pictured) and the smooth. In crossings, the rough coat has proved dominant.

282

Color and Hair Length

All breeders of long-haired dogs know that certain colors are associated with longer hair or shorter hair. Breeders of Cocker Spaniels and English Setters often note that the hair growing on black spots which appear in white dogs is very much longer than the white hair surrounding them. I have measured the difference in a group of Cocker Spaniels. Ignoring the large patches of color and measuring only the hair growing from restricted spots and the white hair immediately adjacent, it was found that the black hair was four or five times as long as the white background.

There is, of course, very great difference in the hair-length in different dogs of the same breed, but taking black dogs in general the coats grow much longer than the coats of red brothers and sisters in the same litters. Thus we have a definite linkage between the red and the length of coat. For instance, to find a red dog that grows long hair on the top of the head is a rarity. There are those which develop a faded, longer fuzz, but not the long hair of the blacks. There are blacks which never develop long hair on the top of the head, but most of the better show dogs are those with it, allowing for trimming by experts which helps to convince judges that they have heads differently shaped from what they really are.

Black-and-white puppies usually have larger pigmented areas and less white than do the red-and-white puppies. These are typical of this phenomenon.

Not only is there this association, so often found in Cockers and Setters, but another similar fact comes to light when litters of puppies are compared. The illustration shows a litter of Cocker Spaniel puppies. Note that the black-and-white puppy shows more color than do his four brothers and sisters. At first glance one would say, what is odd about that? But when one observes many parti-colored Cocker puppies and notes that the black-and-whites are pigmented over much larger areas than are the red-and-white, the picture changes.

This fact has a definite application practically. How many times have Cocker breeders been advised not to mate reds with parti-colors because so often the puppies are foul-marked? And this is true. It is a very rare thing to see a black Cocker with a white blaze in the face and white feet, but very common in the case of reds. The red color seems to be less formidable in asserting itself and covering the white, as it were, while the black is much stronger. Perhaps this is not the correct expression to use in this regard, but it brings the point home. It would seem that if a red is to be mated with a parti-colored Cocker, then the parti should be one with a lot of color.

It would seem that the foul-marked red should not be considered a parti-colored dog at all, but be classed with the solids, while a black with that much white is genetically a true parti-color. On that account, it should be classed as a parti.

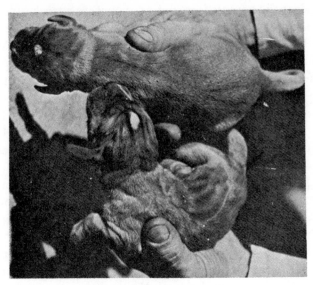

Non-ripple and ripple coats.

Inheritance of Ripple-Coat in New-Born Puppies

Most puppies are born with a coat that is smooth. The character here discussed involves the skin. It is shown clearly in a day-old puppy. A puppy possessing it shows long regular waves or ripples running from his neck to his hind legs and spreading slightly as they travel posteriorly. Puppies have these ripples at birth, or do not have them at all. I had seen hundreds of puppies with them among my Bloodhounds, and others without them, and it was many years before it struck me that it was an inherited genetic character. And even then it was some years before I was sure whether it was inherited as a dominant or as a recessive. Then it was apparent that in many litters all the puppies had them, while in others about one-half of the pups were so marked.

To look at the parents it is not possible to say whether at birth they were rippled or not. In fact, at the age of a week one cannot say, because the ripples are outgrown. One has to know what the parents were before they were a week old. Knowing what kind of puppies the parents have previously sired also helps. Fortunately, many such records were preserved. Most of my Bloodhound litters have been composed of rippled puppies but there was one dog, Jack, which sired three litters in which all the puppies were smooth. So was the litter of puppies which produced Bill, the male bullhound shown on page 106. Brutus, an imported Bloodhound never sired a smooth pup. His son, Faithful, sired many litters in which part of the puppies were rippled and part smooth. Mary, the female bullhound, was one of his puppies, whelped by a Bull Terrier. This litter was born at a time when I was curious about the inheritance of the trait. Mary is recorded as being one of the puppies with the rippling.

So here we had a purebred dog for the smooth coat mated with what was most likely a hybrid. I counted the smooths and ripples in the first five litters and the last, a total of 85 puppies. Of these, 40 were rippled and 45 were smooth, which comes close to a 50-50 ratio.

Frederick of Barchester, another Bloodhound, never sired a smooth puppy. One of his puppies has sired a litter of 11, of which six are rippled and five smooth.

Another Bloodhound, bred to a yellow bitch of the same strain, sired seven puppies, of which three are wavy and four smooth.

Malilda, a smooth, mated to Smarty, also a smooth, produced six puppies, of which only one was ripple-coated.

It would seem, in the face of less data than might be desirable, that the coat or skin characteristic which I have called rippled, is inherited as a recessive, and is definitely not sex-linked, appearing in either males or females.

The characteristic has no economic value, but is interesting in that apparently it is a clear-cut "presence or absence" factor. It might be useful sometimes in helping to determine paternity. It occurs in Cocker Spaniels and other breeds as well as Bloodhounds, but no attempt has been made to study it in these breeds.

5

The Inheritance of Body Form

A NY observer who has the opportunity to see the results of crossing breeds of dogs must be struck by the fact that the result usually is a blending inheritance, due to the great number of genes contributed by both parents. The mongrel offspring seldom exhibits a clear cut dominance or recessiveness of forms. Color is another thing; here we are interested in body form, leg length, tail characteristics and so on. This book shows pictures of many crosses made by the author beginning in 1920 and also pictures of crosses made by others. Breed crosses (mongrels) which afford living illustrations are everywhere. Some of us have published observations on the results of mongrelizing which can be of help to others who contemplate making crosses in the future.

Body form in dogs is of endless variety, so much so that it is difficult to more than generalize when we discuss its inheritance. There are dogs with legs shorter than those of other breeds, and those with shorter backs, shorter heads, and so on. There are some dogs of the roly-poly build and others which appear to be all angles.

A number of crosses between breeds of different form were made by Stockard and his assistants. These included Basset Hounds x German Shepherds, Boston Terriers x Dachshunds, French Bulldogs x Dachshunds, Dachshunds x Brussels Griffons, Great Danes x St. Bernards.

Stockard found mostly intermediate form features in all of these crosses. He says the St. Bernard x Great Dane puppies all became paralyzed in the hind quarters by the time they were five months old. Today there is evidence that this could have been due to diet or to the kinds of dogs with which he worked. I saw both parents and was impressed by the fact that both were weak in their hind legs. The Dane was one of the type fancied at that time which moved stiff-legged behind, more or less as if the hind legs were clubs. Today's Danes must show suppleness and move their hind legs in straight lines, not have to swing them.

Wreidt crossed a Rottweiler with a Doberman Pinscher and found the pups to be intermediate in body build. Lang crossed a Dachshund with a St. Bernard and found the St. Bernard body build to be dominant. In general body proportions the St. Bernard and the French Bulldog which I crossed were more or less similar. The illustration shows a dog much like either but intermediate in size. (page 272).

From several hundred crosses which I have made, and back crosses as well as F_2, I should not want to go on record as saying that the characters were determined completely by single pairs of genes, or inherited in typical Mendelian fashion. There are so many modifiers that with a few exceptions it is impossible to make such a statement. Stockard, in *The Physical Basis of Personality,* 1931, claims that the short leg length of the Basset was imperfectly dominant over the normal leg length in the German Sherpherd.

Dr. Marchlewski, studying Pointers for skull type and body build, found that the narrow chest of the English Pointer was dominant over the broad chest of the German Shorthair. He also found the cat foot (compact) was imperfectly dominant over the harelike type of foot in the breeds he observed.

288

Head Shape Inheritance

Wreidt crossed a Schnauzer x Dachshund (with a long nose) with a Pekingese with its short nose. The offspring were intermediate. He claims, on the basis of back crosses, that the broad skull and shortened face were determined by a single factor.

Marchlewski crossed narrow shepherd dogs with broad headed hounds and found the narrow type of head to be dominant over the broad head. He found in F_2 dogs that clear segregation occurred.

Iljin crossed wolves and dogs and determined that the so-called orbital angle, which is the angle formed by the intersection of a plane across the eye with a horizontal plane across the top of the skull, is not a simple genetic factor but is probably controlled by at least two factors. In F_1 animals the angle is intermediate, but closer to the dog type. The same applies to the zygomatic process and maxillary angle (cheekbone and angle at its anterior end). In this case the offspring were intermediate but closer to the wolf.

Leg Length Inheritance

Years before he had made any breed crossings I had mated a Dachshund with a Fox Terrier and a Dachshund with a Boston Terrier. All of the puppies from both crosses were more intermediate than they were short-legged like the Dachshund. I felt positive that since all the parents were registered dogs from good stock that I was dealing with pure breeds. The implication was that I was dealing with impurely bred Dachshunds. But subsequent research has shown unmistakably that my contention is correct. The result of mating a pure finely bred short-legged breed with a pure long-legged breed is much more nearly intermediate than short-legged. It seems to me that if we are going to make comparisons we should choose breeds which are as much alike in all respects except the one under consideration. Hence I tried it again and chose the two show dogs shown in the illustration on page 220, Bloodhound and Basset. The cross produced nine puppies which I raised, most of which I gave to hunters. There was some variation in these puppies but the dog

289

with the shortest legs was not nearly as short-legged as the mother.

The picture shows the cross, which is most interesting as a hunter and has legs almost intermediate between the parents. Now, back crosses of this dog to his mother, a short-legged bitch, resulted in puppies which varied from very short up to his leg length. There was no clear cut segregation, in the lower crosses, but there was a more definite segregation in the case of mating to the longer. There was a long skip between the intermediate and the long, there being no puppies in the interim. The dog was crossed with a Newfoundland, with a Foxhound and with an F_1 Bloodhound x Bull Terrier.

Besides the very short legs, such as those represented in the Basset and the Dachshund, there is another leg length in hounds which I have studied. This is a three-quarter appearance. It is illustrated by the hound in the picture. A great many of the old-fashioned Black-and-Tan hounds had this leg length. In its case

A short-legged Foxhound of a strain once popular with some hunters. This leg length is dominant over the normal leg length.

Result of crossing a Beagle with a Foxhound. The leg length corresponds to the Beagle's.

there does seem to be only the difference between the normal and that length which is determined by one pair of genes. More data, however, may dispel this possibility. But I have mated dogs with this leg length and all of the puppies have been short legged. Here, there seems to be simple dominance. A pair of the short-legged dogs have given rise to long-legged puppies, but I have no record of the reverse having occurred. In Vermont there is a strain of these dogs which has been crossed and re-crossed with long-legged hounds. There seems in this case to be a reasonably clear cut difference, but even so there will tend to be variations around either type.

If dogs of this short-legged strain are mated with long-legged dogs the puppies will be either all short legged or about half short and half long. This has occurred in the case of both males and females. The dog shown in the illustration, when mated to a long-legged bitch, produced a litter of five long-legged and four short-legged. There were 11 puppies in the litter but only nine lived. It is difficult to tell in the very early stages which puppies are going to have either short or long legs.

There are many breeds with naturally short legs, such as Clumber Spaniels, which do not have legs as short as those of

291

the Dachshund or Basset. Several of the terriers have leg lengths which are just above those of the very short-legged breeds. It will be interesting to determine whether these are all the same genetic character and different only because of modifying genes, or whether they are different.

Stockard finally came to the conclusion that short legs are dominant and that there are modifiers which he called ss and sl. When a dog has ss, he has a Basset Hound type of leg, but when he has sl, he has a little longer leg. He crossed Salukis and Basset Hounds and German Shepherds and Basset Hounds. He also crossed Bulldogs and Basset Hounds. His illustrations show the F_1 crosses to be more intermediate in leg length than very decidedly dominant. The Bulldog and Basset Hound cross appears very short legged, but the Bulldog has shorter legs than the German Shepherd anyway and a cross of a German Shepherd with a Bulldog produces offspring with legs slightly shorter than the German Shepherd's.

Among the individuals of some breeds there are allowable differences in leg length, even though the breed standard calls for only one length. Bloodhounds vary because handlers have preferences. Many of the greatest man trailers ever used in America have been dogs with legs much shorter than the standard prescribes. They have excelled to such an extent that they are remembered and therefore sought by men whose business is to trail men.

In the black-and-tan hound breed which the A.K.C. registers as Coonhounds but which are regarded by hunters as a type of foxhound, one finds the same kind of variation. It is probable that early Bloodhounds went into the development of the black-and-tan.

Because of the many Bloodhounds I raised, there was material for study, and my friendship with V. G. Mullikin of Lexington, Kentucky, gave me an opportunity to observe his dogs. The illustration shows very old Crusader Jr., a long-legged Bloodhound, and a short-legged dog, one with a splendid record as a man trailer, both the Captain's hounds.

A cross of Crusader with a short-legged sister of the other dog produced four short-legged and five long-legged dogs. One

These two Kentucky Bloodhounds, both very famous man trailers, illustrate the two leg lengths of the breed very well. The dog in the background was 13 years old.

of my short-legged bitches descended from this pair was mated with four different long-legged dogs, and of the 36 puppies raised, 19 were short-legged.

Jim, short legged, bred to Tessa, a short-legged imported bitch, sired eight puppies, three of them short-legged. Of all the litters sired by Jim about half were long- and half short-legged. No count was kept because most were sold as 6 to 8 week-old puppies.

In many matings made by the author, dogs with long legs crossed with dogs with short legs produced intermediate length legs, as we have seen. Stockard, who likened the short-legged breeds to human achondroplastic dwarfs, tells us the offspring are all short-legged. His illustrations, however, show dogs with

293

intermediate length legs. The cross of F_1 produced F_2 pups showing what he calls "full short" legs. When an F_1 Basset x German Shepherd was mated to a German Shepherd, about half the pups were intermediate in varying degrees and half long-legged. This was what I found with my Basset x Bloodhound cross mated to a long-legged parent.

Others—Lang, Stockard, Wreidt—agree that the leg length of the short-legged breeds is incompletely dominant to normal leg length, but they cite breeds having normal length legs such as the English Bulldog and French Bulldog, which have somewhat less than normal leg length, as well as Salukis, Schnauzer and Fox Terrier, which have normal length.

It would seem from what we now know that, with an exception soon to be discussed, shorter legs are dominant over long. The very short of Pekingese, Dachshund, Basset Hound are dominant over the next standard by length—probably represented by the Corgi. (A friend of the author's crossed a Corgi with a Dachshund and the puppies have very short legs.) The short-legged Foxhound is dominant over the full length Foxhound. We also know the Beagle type to be dominant over the long-legged type.

Many Beagles have been crossed with Foxhounds and the progeny of all I have known were Beagles in leg length. I crossed a Beagle bitch with a Redbone Coonhound. All of the red puppies had Beagle length legs. We called them "bebones." They made excellent rabbit dogs, especially for snowshoe rabbits and hares.

I can now report here a new type of short leg.

A mutation, occurring in a line of Cocker Spaniels, first came to light in my kennels. It is definitely a recessive. One of these is shown in the illustration. The sire was a normal-legged dog named Champ. The dam was another normal-legged dog named Compact. The first litter produced one such puppy out of five. The second litter produced two out of four. The third litter produced two out of eight. The fourth produced one out of five. This was six out of 22. The parents had a common ancestor in Playgirl. She was Champ's mother and Compact's maternal grandmother.

294

These puppies were littermates. The short legged puppy inherited his deformity as a Mendelian recessive. This is a different character from the Dachshund type of short legs, which is dominant.

Champ was mated with a red bitch that also had Playgirl for a maternal grandmother. She produced one out of four puppies with short legs.

Champ was the sire of over 100 puppies and had never produced a puppy with short legs until mated with these two bitches. When Compact was mated with a different dog she whelped six puppies, all of which were normal.

Both males and females have been born with the short legs so the trait is not sex linked.

Inheritance of Dewclaws

Dewclaws are those fifth toes situated on the inside of the legs close to the ground. Some dogs exhibit the toe as part of the foot, while others have them showing so far up the leg that they appear to be useless appendages. In swimming breeds and some others they may be desirable; for show they detract from the clean-cut appearance. Most Poodle breeders have them removed from front and back legs. Almost all dogs have dewclaws on the front legs, where they are often useful, but those useless ones on the hind legs are often removed.

Occasionally a dog will have only one, while some dogs have double dewclaws. Other dogs may have them attached to the leg only by skin. Because the nail in a dewclaw does not touch the ground and cannot wear down, it often grows in a circle and pierces the pad, causing irritation, so the nail must be cut. Then there are other dogs which have dewclaws entirely under the skin so they do not show. So in order to study the inheritance we must be sure where presence and absence leaves off.

In 1928 I published a study which showed that of the dogs I studied, dewclaws on the hind legs was always dominant.

Stockard in 1931 published a study showing that single dewclaws was dominant over double dewclaws.

In 1938, Keeler and Trumble showed that in the dogs they studied, known to be hybrid for the trait, should have all exhibited dewclaws—but only 47% did. When hybrids were crossed 25% should have been free of them, but 41.7% were free. If the dewclaws under the skin had been counted, possibly the figures would have been different.

The length and placement of dewclaws is also a matter of inheritance. I have insufficient data to show the mode of inheritance, but I often find dogs among my clients' packs with dewclaws in such a position that they are serviceable to run on, whereas most of them are pulled up so high they are only impediments. One family of Beagles shows the dewclaws so low and so serviceable that one wonders why some enterprising breeder could not establish it and make the dog better able to travel on snow.

The presence of dewclaws is dominant over the absence. This Setter is an exception in having only one extra toe instead of two.

Inheritance of Foot Characteristics

With so important an adjunct as sound feet, more research should have been done on the problem than we can find. Marchlewski crossed, as we have seen, English and German Pointers. He says the compact foot of the English is incompletely dominant over the open, harelike foot of the German. Humphrey and Warner tell us that among German Shepherd Dogs the tight or closed foot is dominant over the open foot, while the short foot is dominant over the long foot.

Occasionally one finds in a litter, one or more pups with such splay feet that the digits appear more like fingers instead of toes. This characteristic is one which incapacitates the dog. Those of us who have tried to use such dogs as hunters soon learn that

297

the feet become cut and sore, rendering the dogs useless except as pets.

The illustration shows the foot of a Spitz dog which has a development of the dewclaw to be the equivalent of a thumb. Unfortunately, the inheritance of this oddity was not studied.

Dewlap Inheritance

Dewlap inheritance is important in show dog breeding. Dogs of breeds in which the standard calls for clean necks and throats must never show dewlaps, so Marchlewski's finding that dewlap is clearly dominant over the lack of it is important. He crossed German Shorthaired with English Pointers. Breeders of pure breeds, some of which show "throatiness," would disagree (Cocker Spaniel and English Setter breeders, for example), because they find too many intermediate degrees of the defect to ever agree it is a simple matter.

Is Hip Dysplasia Inherited?

As of the year 1971, the serious defect in many dogs known as hip dysplasia is one of the most interesting problems in dog breeding. It is especially serious from the viewpoint of the breeder who sells puppies, because what appear to be sound pups often develop shallow hip sockets or even none at all, and the buyer returns with the pet and demands a replacement.

The armed forces demand sound hips in the dogs they buy and their criterion is severe. Many specialty clubs have set standards as to the depth of the sockets and discriminate against any dogs, however strong and sound they appear when moving, if X-rays submitted to a committee of experts show certain degrees of joint looseness or socket shallowness.

In case you are not acquainted with the terminology, you should know that the large thigh bone has an offset protrusion in the form of a ball which normally fits into a socket called the acetabulum. Failure of the joint to be normal according to some standards is called hip dysplasia. The joint is held together by ligaments and muscles. The ultimate dysplasia begins with laxness in the joint. The defect is seldom found in very active running breeds like Greyhounds or Whippets. In my experience it is most often found in large breeds which are pampered, permitted insufficient exercise and over-vitaminized and mineralized.

Some of the best work done so far on the subject, using a large number of German Shepherd dogs and dogs of some other breeds, has been conducted by members of the faculty of the Royal Veterinary College, Stockholm, Sweden. They reviewed the possible causes of the defect in human beings, many of which were attributed to hormone imbalance and compared the findings with canine abnormalities.

The Swedish investigators summarized their findings after all of their own studies and consideration of the work of others as follows:

> *The disease cannot be diagnosed at birth. The most severe cases can be picked out at an age of about 14 days.*
>
> *It seems doubtful that the disease is congenital in the dog. There is strong evidence that the primary cause of hip dysplasia is a joint laxity very early in life. This laxity is genetically controlled but environmental factors are responsible for about 50 per cent of the variation of the severity of hip dysplasia. The cause of laxity is unknown and future research has to be focused on this problem.*

Tail Characteristics

The general types of tails which are possessed by the pure breeds of our dogs are as follows:

1. The straight long tail.
2. The very long tail as of the Borzoi.
3. The straight stubby tail which is generally associated with such breeds as Beagles.
4. The straight whip tail which is commonly seen on the Pointer, the Bull Terrier and others.
5. The straight short tail which some strains of hounds possess.
6. The very short straight tail, occasionally seen in Cocker Spaniels.
7. The virtual absence of any tail as in the Old English Sheepdog, the Schipperke, the Doberman Pinscher.
8. The short screwtail as in the Boston Terrier and some English Bulldogs.
9. The stub screwtail most common in the English Bulldog.
10. The curled tail of the Pug, the Grahund.
11. The partly curled tail of the Eskimo, Chow.

All geneticists who have crossed dogs without tails or with screwtails have come to the conclusion that short tail or absence of tail is due to several factors. These include Klodnitsky, Spett, Iljin, Little, Stockard, Vilmarin, Koch and myself. Koch feels that screwtail is based on defective functioning of the pituitary growth hormone.

Many long-tailed puppies are born each year with kinks in their tails. These may occur at different places in the tails. While these kinks might appear to be hereditary, there is evidence that the kink is due to the embryonic tail becoming bent. After birth it attempts to grow straight. It often does, which causes an offset jog. In some dogs the tail shows a distinct angle. Such puppies should not be included in our considerations. After all the many breed crosses I have made it would seem that there is a potentiality to produce short or screwtails and that other genes are necessary to cause the various lengths and shapes of tails. (See 1947 edition of *How to Breed Dogs* for the breeds crossed to reach this conclusion.)

Naturally, most of the crosses which I have made have been with dogs with tails of natural lengths. By that I mean the length commonly seen in the shepherd, hound, etc. But there are many exceptions, as you will see, and it is interesting to note

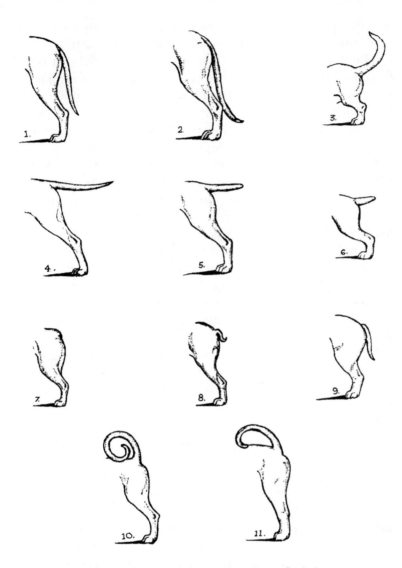

Illustration of the eleven types of tails listed on the facing page.

how true these established characters continue to breed, many of them almost if not entirely as unit Mendelian characters.

The Basset Hound, with its short tail, when bred to a Bloodhound with its normal length tail, produced nine puppies all with long tails, and these in combination with the intermediate length legs appeared rather incongruous. This cross also shows that the factor which produces the shorter legs is not the same factor which affects the tail length as some have claimed.

Crossing one of the above-mentioned puppies (Basset x Bloodhound) with a pure Beagle resulted in six puppies which had tails of varying lengths, not all in keeping with the dog's size of body. One puppy had a tail which was too long for harmony of appearance. It was noticeable, however, that none of them had large bodies and short tails like the Beagle and Basset. Where disharmony occurred it was in too much length of tail, not too little. (See photo, page 220.)

Crossing a Foxhound with a Beagle produced dogs with intermediate length tails. The illustration on page 291 shows what happened and the dog shown appeared representative of the litter which was uncommonly uniform. Why the tails here would have been shortened while the Bloodhound x Beagle cross produced tails which were long like the Bloodhound, I do not know.

Crossing a Borzoi with a Bloodhound resulted in a litter with long tails, slightly longer than the Bloodhound's, but not as long as the Borzoi's.

Crossing a French Bulldog with a St. Bernard produced pups with the normal length tail of the big dog.

Crossing an English Bulldog with a German Shepherd resulted in puppies with normal length tails.

Crossing a German Shepherd with a Grahund resulted in a litter of pups which carried their tails curled over their backs like the Grahund.

Crossing a Collie with a Chow gave the same result.

Crossing a Chow with a Boston Terrier produced a litter with tails that were normal length but straight and were inclined to bend forward but not curl tightly.

302

This puppy, result of a cross between a Foxhound and a Greyhound, had a short tail with the last vertebra bending at right angles, downward. A sister was likewise affected.

A blue-ticked hound pup was the only one with a short tail in one litter. This was not short like a Cocker Spaniel's tail after it has been docked, but half normal length. I bought and bred her to a splendid Greyhound and of the litter of ten puppies, four had short tails like the mother's and one had a tail just about three-fourths normal length. Two of the four short-tailed pups had, as further abnormalities, the last vertebra on the tail bent at right angles so that it pointed downward or inward.

This matter of short tail runs in families, but sometimes is a most unpredictable matter. Take two bitches, for instance, from the same litter. One has a "natural bob" tail, the other has a full length tail. They are mated to two dogs which are no relation to each other and neither of the dogs has ever been known to produce a short tailed puppy. Yet both of these bitches whelped puppies with short tails. The one with the "natural bob" produced four puppies in seven with short tails; the sister with the long tail produced three puppies with short tails in a litter of eight.

Thus we might say that the thing that is inherited is the ability to produce short tails, and that as yet we do not know what are the other factors which determine the ultimate result. This

303

ability seems to be inherited as a dominant. The ability is a rather rare possession. May it not be that this incomplete explanation applies to all of the breeds where it is so difficult to learn the mode of inheritance of the bob tail?

The Bloodhound mated with the Grahund produced pups with tails that were straight and of normal length, as may be seen in the illustration shown on page 274.

A Cocker Spaniel mated with a Chow produced puppies which had tails that were almost straight but with a slight curl, enough so that they drooped forward and almost touched the back.

A Boston Terrier and a Collie produced puppies with tails of normal length.

A Pointer crossed with a hound produced tails intermediate in length.

A Pointer crossed with a fighting bull with a screwtail produced pups with tails longer than the Pointer's, which appeared slightly shorter than normal.

A Chow crossed with an Airedale produced puppies with tails that were slightly curled but not bent in a circle.

A pit bull mated with a Bull Terrier produced five pups. Four had straight short tails like the Bull Terrier; a fifth had a jog in the middle of its tail.

Now as to tail abnormalities which have occurred among my dogs, I have to report that not a single one was inherited, at least so far as my investigations went. Here they all are:

In a litter of Bloodhounds there were four tail abnormalities. One was a perfect screwtail which any Boston Terrier fancier would have been proud to have on one of his dogs. One was a tail with an offset joint, so to speak. One joint turned right and the next left so that the tail had a jog, but otherwise was straight. The third had a bend at right angles of the third joint from the end and this part was pointed back toward the dog. In attempting to straighten it, by breaking, I broke the entire end of the tail off, and this disfigurement ruined the appearance of the pup. This same crook in the tail has also appeared in three

Bloodhound puppies in three other litters and the one previously mentioned, the jog, has appeared in one other. The fourth mutation in this litter was a short tail about one-third the normal length.

In a litter of F_2 Irish Setter–Bloodhound puppies there was one pup which we called Gandhi. He is shown, rear and side views. He had a perfect screwtail and after I was through with him he was X-rayed and killed and then dissected by a Yale University scientist so that his skeleton was preserved. This looked so genuine that it appeared it must be hereditary. I bred him to an English Setter. The puppies were all born with normal tails. I raised two of these puppies and bred them to their father. Again all the puppies had normal length tails. I concluded, therefore, that it was probably not hereditary and if so, not in a Mendelian fashion.

In a litter of Foxhounds, one puppy had a tail with a jog in it. This was bred to several different dogs but never produced a pup with anything but a normal tail. No pups were bred back to the mother, however, and no jog tails have ever appeared among any of the offspring.

To a pair of Borzois a litter of seven puppies was born which had one member with a perfect corkscrew twist in the very middle of the tail with the result that the tail appeared shorter than normal but had it been straightened out would have been natural in length.

A Cocker Spaniel in a litter of pups with normal tails had a short tail, which when grown was of just the right length. From correspondence with others I have several records of Cockers which have been born with tails of this short length.

A tricolored Foxhound appeared in a litter of purebred puppies of excellent stock, with a tail that curled over his back fully as much as does the tail of an Eskimo dog. None of his brothers and sisters had other than straight tails. Several Foxhounds with tails that curl have done good work in field trials and their owners openly brag about how tightly their tails curl. I have known the stock from which my dog came for many years, and have never known of such a tail either in the ancestral lines of this pup nor in the collateral. Possibly this was a recessive cropping out but more likely it was a mutation.

If we inquire into the mode of inheritance of tail characteristics within any single breed, we seem to arrive nowhere so far as any definite Mendelian mode of inheritance is concerned. I have collected data from the breeders of Schipperkes, for instance, from breeders of English Sheepdogs, from breeders of Boston Terriers. In the case of each, even though large numbers of data were collected, one could not say whether any condition was a recessive or a dominant.

I found that when two Schipperke dogs with natural bobtails were mated they frequently produced pups with long tails. I found also that when two dogs with long tails were mated they frequently produced bobtailed pups. The same thing held true with the Old English Sheepdogs. And then again another consideration must be noted in these breeds. I refer to the inadequacy of knowledge on the part of the breeders as to whether the dogs were born with bobtails or with long tails. Some breeders have owned no more than three generations of the dogs. Many have been imported and the owners did not know, so their letters told me, whether their dogs were natural bobtails or whether they had been trimmed by previous owners, and neither had they taken the trouble to learn.

The Old English Sheepdog breeders have done better and their data show that there is no rule of inheritance for the bobtails whatever. Sometimes they have tails and sometimes only

The Norwegian Elkhound tail is tightly curled. Crossing a
Norwegian Elkhound with a German Shepherd Dog resulted in
a litter of pups which carried their tails curled over their backs.

stubs. But they all have stubs by the time the breeders are
through with them.

Some Old English Sheepdogs are pure for bobtail and so potent in their dominancy that all of their puppies are bobtails.
One of my neighbor's pure English Setter was mated accidentally with a splendid Old English, and every one of the 11 puppies had perfect bobtails.

In his study of inheritance in Brussels Griffons, Little found
that the short tail is dominant over the long tail.

The number of kinks in the Boston Terrier's tail likewise
appears to be something that cannot be predicted. We know
that almost all Bostons are now born with short screwtails,
but even in inbred strains all the tails do not appear just alike.
In the case of English Bulldogs the same situation exists. No
fancier can predict what form the tails of his pups will take.
About all they can say is that the tails will be short and generally with a kink or two. Whether the kinks will be in a vertical
or in a horizontal plane cannot be predicted so far as existing
data reveal, although time may come to our rescue and more
data reveal a Mendelian basis. Likewise, more data may show

us a basis for predicting the outcome of crosses of the bobtail breeds. The Doberman Pinscher, the Boxer, the Corgis, etc., are all born with long tails, and so far no case among them has come to my attention from among these breeds where a pup was born with a bobtail, or no tail at all.

In a cross of a hound with a fighting Bulldog, all of the puppies had straight tails although the Bulldog had a definite kink in his about two-thirds from the tip. One of these pups was mated back to the Bulldog again and three puppies had kinks in their tails and one of these had a tail half normal length.

The mating of an American Pit Bulldog to an English Bulldog produced three litters—20 pups. Only one had a screwtail and "that was not perfect."

Rcheulishvili in Russia studied the short tail of the Georgian dogs and its inheritance in 1937. He mated a short-tailed male which was from a long-tailed parent and a short-tailed parent, with a dog which had had two long-tailed parents. From these matings he produced 13 with short tails and 11 with long. Therefore, the author concluded, short-tailedness is dominant.

I do not know the Georgian dog, but as already reported, in dogs I have studied, the short tail, even though it seems to be a dominant, is not always such. It would appear that the propensity of being able to produce short tails is hereditary.

From crosses and back crosses of Bulldogs, Boston Terriers and French Bulldogs with breeds having long tails, Stockard believed that there were two pairs of determiners concerned. One pair for long and short tail (long, dominant) and a pair for straight or bent tail (straight dominant). If a dog received the two recessive genes pure, he would have a tail like that on a desirable Bulldog.

My own results do not show it to be so simple a matter. Any Bulldog breeder of long experience can mention many instances where a pair of Bulldogs with perfect tails have produced puppies with tails so straight and long as to practically disqualify the puppies for show. In my work I was constantly being asked to cut tails short for Bulldog breeders. Some of these tails are perfectly straight, yet came from parents with short kinky tails which had never been touched.

308

The difference in the required tail carriage for show Setters as opposed to field Setters is graphically shown in these photos of two outstanding English Setters. Ch. Aspetuck's Shadow, at top, illustrates the straight tail ("not above the level of the back") called for in the AKC show standard. Field trial Setters, on the other hand, carry their tails straight up when hunting, as in the lower picture of Field Ch. Johnny Crockett.

Or take the red hound type shown on page 305. He has a perfect screwtail, yet his parents for generations have never had any such deformity. Nor is it probable that a dog would have two mutations occur at one time.

All the puppies from the French Bulldog x St. Bernard cross (see page 272) had long tails. A Dachshund x Boston Terrier produced all straight long tails as did, too, litters of Bulldog x Foxhound crosses.

Stockard claimed that the normal tail of the Basset is a simple dominant over the screwtail of the English Bulldog, a questionable statement because as we have seen many Bulldogs have such wide variations in their tails.

Koch came to the conclusion that the normal tail was a simple dominant over the screwtail in the French Bulldog before Stockard.

In the case of Schipperkes, taillessness is said by some breeders to be non-existent at birth. They are those who have started with dogs whose tails have been docked. One Belgian veterinarian wrote that some breeders have tried to breed the dogs taillessly, but they only succeeded in producing puppies with abnormal pelvises. The breed in America must be made of sterner stuff. Here are authentic matings, some of which I inspected at birth and one of which I owned:

A tailless bitch, mated to four different studs born with tails: 18 pups—13 tailless.

Tailless bitch x dog with tail, four litters: 17 pups—13 tailless.

A prominent doctor, long a fancier of the breed, says he could eliminate the capacity to produce puppies with tails in a few dog generations, by selective breeding.

In another case of Schipperke, the male, tailless; female docked, there were five pups, four tailless, one with tail.

In several matings of Schipperkes where the female was tailless and the male had a tail there were 22 puppies. All females born tailless, males with tails.

Iljin showed that the short tail of Schipperkes was dominant or incompletely dominant over the long tail. What Americans know as Schipperkes may be quite different from the Schipperkes in other countries. In Belgium the "little skippers" are often short-haired with stub tails.

Doubtless there are other genes for tail form yet to be discovered. Certainly the dominant short tail I previously described and Rchenleshvili further studied is one, and it will be interesting in the future to observe crosses between dogs with these different tail types.

Head Shape

Marchlewski crossed a narrow-headed sheepdog with a Pointer with a broad, dished type of head and found the narrow head dominant. Stonhege and Wreidt found the long type of head of a Greyhound was dominant over the Bulldog and Pug type of skull formation. Iljin found the opposite among German Shepherds and also in crosses between dog and wolf. Stockard found that Boston Terrier x Dachshund and French Bulldog x Dachshund produced intermediate head shapes and decided multiple factors were involved. When we crossed an English Bulldog with a Basset Hound, the wide head was incompletely dominant. Iljin observed that what he called the "Brick-shaped" head of an Airedale Terrier was incompletely dominant over the Doberman Pinscher, and that the Bulldog type of head is incompletely dominant over the Doberman Pinscher head type. The length of the heads show an intermediate type of dominance, but a short head crown is dominant over long crown. He found cheekbone breadth to be controlled by at least two factors and produced a blending type of inheritance.

Wreidt crossed a Schnauzer-Dachshund with a Pekingese. He deduced that the broad skull and retrorse nose of the Peke were produced by a single pair of genes.

The Inheritance of Jaw Anomalies

One of the most disappointing things that can happen to a dog breeder is to have what appears to be an almost perfect

311

specimen born and raised, only to have it become "undershot" in the last few months of growth. There are puppies born which develop this misfit jaw characteristic in their first few weeks of growth, others which develop it at three or four months and others not until after five months. And it is not necessarily those which are most seriously affected which show it early. One of the worst examples of this protruding lower jaw I have ever seen was in a Cocker Spaniel which up until teething time had a perfect fitting set of teeth; the lower incisors fit right behind the upper, when the mouth was closed. When she was seven months old her lower incisors protruded three-quarters of an inch.

Is this character inherited? Most certainly yes, but in what strange manner, no one has yet been able to say with certainty. And there is the opposite character in which the lower jaw is too short for the upper, known as "overshot." There is as yet no definite measurement for us to say whether the trouble lies in the mandible being too short or the upper jaw too far forward.

Such peculiarities might be expected to appear in crosses between different breeds, like a Collie mated to a Boston Terrier, but they appear within a pure breed.

Undershot Cocker Spaniels, in a closely bred strain, throw some light on the problem. Among my Cocker Spaniels there was not an undershot puppy or adult in the kennels. But every year a goodly number of undershot puppies appeared. Therefore, one might reason that the character is recessive. But let us see. In the first place when they do appear, they do not necessarily appear in a 25 percent ratio. A very wonderful bitch named Charm, whose mouth was perfect, was mated to a dog named Red Brucie, whose mouth was also perfect. They produced four puppies, every one of which was badly undershot, and one with a perfect mouth. Her name was Kathlyn.

Kathlyn was bred to Champ, a son of Roderic. In all the puppies of Roderic, I have not had an undershot puppy, and he was bred to many bitches. But when Champ was mated to Kathlyn on many occasions, there were always one or two undershot puppies. But their puppies were so fine that it paid to mate these dogs and destroy the undershot puppies. They had seven litters, of which ten puppies were undershot. So here it would seem that the trait is recessive. But let us look further. Some undershot puppies have appeared from other parents. I mated a pair of these, which were not badly deformed and, of five puppies in a litter, not one was undershot. If undershot is a recessive, then all of these puppies should have been undershot.

Again, we have a case of a character which runs in families, which seems to be inherited as a recessive, and yet does not behave that way consistently. There are all degrees of the defect. In fact, if we believe that dogs' teeth, to be a correct bite, should allow the lower incisors to slip behind the uppers, than an even bite of the front teeth is a little undershot, and possibly there has been so much selection for an even bite that dog breeders have unconsciously been breeding undershot dogs. If they are undershot a little, then a little addition to that little makes them appear badly undershot. And it is hard to draw the line.

An interesting study in a strain of long-haired Dachshunds was made by Gruenberg and Lea. Their dogs were so badly overshot that the canine teeth of the under jaw (mandible) occluded behind the upper teeth, instead of in front of them. The tooth size was reduced by the factor and the lower jaw appears to be shortened, and the upper jaw lengthened. This is seen in many breeds. A strain of Borzoi was so badly affected that some of the puppies could not eat out of a pan naturally. Gruenberg and Lea found, upon conducting some matings, that this trait was inherited as a simple recessive.

The lower jaw or mandible sometimes is much too short. Phillips found this condition to be a recessive, with modifying factors, so that when the maximum expression of these factors occurs the jaw is so short as to cause the death of the dog.

Inheritance of Missing Teeth

In the case of German Shepherds, Humphrey and Warner found that the condition of having the normal complement of teeth was dominant over incomplete complement, but must have more than a single factor controlling it. This is a moot problem with show dog breeders, because judges are often hunting for some little imperfection to "put dogs down." When they find a missing tooth they sometimes exaggerate its importance. The standard may give only one point for all the teeth, so a missing tooth might be 1/36th of a point. There are some teeth barely protruding through the gums. Should dogs with a missing tooth be kept from breeding?

Inheritance of Double Nose

Iljin describes a character which he calls "double nose," which he found in Siberian Huskies, Boxers and a Boxer-Bulldog cross. It is an incomplete dominant.

Ear Length Inheritance

I have made a great many crosses of dogs with long ears with dogs having short ears. Many illustrations of such crosses can be seen in this book: Bloodhound x Grahund, Bloodhound x Airedale, Bloodhound x Bull Terrier. Also, many F_2 pups from such crosses have been produced. The F_1s are never even halfway between the two extremes, and no F_2 pup has ever approximated the length of ear of the long-eared parent. Undoubtedly more than two factors are responsible.

Marchlewski crossed a German Shepherd with a Pointer and observed that the smaller ear of the German Shepherd is dominant over the longer ear of the Pointer. He also observed a cross of English Pointer's triangular type of ear and found it dominant over the "larger lobed" type of ear of the German Shorthair. He crossed a Pointer x German Shepherd with a Ceylon Hairless x Dachshund and found the pendant ear carriage incompletely dominant to erect ears.

Iljin postulates three allelomorphs for ear carriage:

Ha semi-erect, H lopeared, h erect.

Ha completely dominant over H and h; H incompletely dominant over h; HaHa—HaH—Hah semi-erect Collie type; HH lop; Hh semi-erect; hh erect.

It would seem that there are too many factors involved for such a simple explanation. Ear carriage runs through so many degrees that it is a complicated matter. Even within the same

314

breed one finds degrees—one ear erect, one lop, both ears tipping forward near the tip.

The lopear is definitely dominant, as Marchlewski and I found.

In the old-fashioned American Cocker breed one would find wide ears at the head attachment over which the dog had considerable control, raising the ear up to aid in hearing. Others had ears which attached to the head with a roundish form, and these dogs had little or no ability to even start to cock their ears.

Humphrey and Warner show that erect ear carriage in German Shepherds seems to be partially dominant over faulty ear carriage.

Inheritance of Heart Size

Some wonder at the endurance and speed of the racing Greyhound. G. R. Hermann studied the size of the hearts of ten dogs, all of which were racers, and compared them with hearts of ten mongrels. The Greyhounds had much larger hearts when the sizes of the hearts were compared with the body weights. He also found there was a definite correlation between the size of the heart and the speed of the dog, suggesting that there may be heart enlargement from the racing and that this very capacity is what makes some dogs better racers than others.

For many years it was believed that, in proportion to size, the deer had the largest heart of any mammal. Hermann's study also showed that the Greyhound's heart is larger than that of the deer. The long selection for speed has developed a breed in which even the puppies have large hearts.

Inheritance of Blood Groups

Most dog breeders and scientists ask whether dogs have blood groups as human beings have. I have given many transfusions without regard to blood grouping, but there are blood groups nevertheless—three, so far determined.

Iseki and Terashima injected dogs' blood into rabbits and

produced pure sera with which they could test for blood groups in dogs. They called the three types D_1, D_2, D_3. Then they studied the inheritance of the groups.

By a series of matings they found that D_1 and D_2 were unit characters. These were the matings used:

5 D_1-D_1 with D_2-D_2 produced only D_1-D_2 type. (hybrids)
4 D_2-D_2 with D_1-D_2 produced 10 D_2-D_2 and 11 D_1-D_2

Since there were no D_1-D_1 individuals, they had demonstrated that these blood groups were hereditary as unit characters.

In the blood and tissues of all animals there is an oxidizing enzyme called catalase. Allison and co-workers, in studying dog blood, found that although some dogs carry less than the normal amount, they nevertheless are not anemic. The researchers designated the gene for normal amount of catalase as C. Dogs with CC or Cc had normal blood, but those with cc had much less catalase than normal.

In the case of human beings, donor's blood must be carefully matched to that of the recipient or disastrous consequences may follow a transfusion. All dogs seem to be what in the case of human beings would be called universal donors.

Canine Hemophilia

In human beings two kinds of hemophilia have been designated, A and B. This is a sex linked ailment which usually kills the person within five years of birth because the victim's blood lacks the ability to clot. Some hemophiliacs have lived quite long. The affliction shows itself at from three weeks on. The joints often bleed, causing lameness, blood lumps appear under the skin, legs may be paralyzed. Any abrasion or scratch bleeds because the blood fails to clot. Even at teething a pup may bleed to death. Dogs with the A form carry the gene responsible on the x chromosome, so a hemophiliac bitch is a rare occurrence. When a male from defective parents is normal, he is as safe to use as a breeder, as if he were not related to the brothers which may have it. Bitches may appear normal but be carriers. The only way to determine whether a bitch is a carrier is to let her have puppies.

The B form, also called Christmas disease after a family of human beings in whom the disease was first reported, is not so severe as the A form. It, too, is a sex linked ailment. It was first reported in dogs in Cairn Terriers, and its mode of inheritance found to conform with that of human beings.

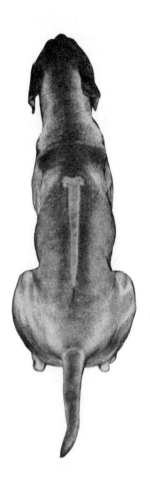

Ridgeback Skin Inheritance

The Rhodesian Ridgebacks possess a peculiarity of having a ridge along the back, caused by what Hare calls "tubular invagination of the skin in the middle of the back." This abnormality is hereditary, he says, judging from family and breeding records of this "Ridgeback" dog. But he does not say how.

Skeletal Abnormalities

The results of crossing a French Bulldog bitch with a Whippet male produced some very interesting results for Klatt, who published his study in 1939. From the original cross he produced four puppies, two of which were bred together. One of the first cross pups was bred back to his mother. The author tells us that nearly all of the puppies showed skeletal peculiarities like those of the mother—split arches, split centra, crooked tails and one feature which even the mother did not possess. The last rib was grown solidly to the vertebra with which it articulated.

Anyone interested in studying a careful, long time research project would do well to obtain, *The Genetic and Endocrine Basis for Differences in Form and Behavior.* Leg length and skeletal difference in the several breeds used are shown and their inheritance indicated. Much careful work was done on endocrine glands, and their differences in breeds, and what occurs to them when breeds are crossed. It represents painstaking work at great expense, in a study financed by the Rockefeller Foundation. Several authors contributed to the volume.

Giantism

Sometimes, instead of producing an improvement, a cross may produce deterioration. Stockard crossed Great Danes and St. Bernards. One might expect that the offspring would be giants with great vigor, but they were only as large as the St. Bernard with short hair, and the cross resulted in paralysis of most of the thigh muscles due to an abnormality in the motor neurons in the lumbar section of the spinal cord. They moved very much like large dogs with acute cases of hip dysplasia.

Crossing large breeds can result in soundness and hybrid vigor—as witness the giant which was shown at county fairs in

318

the Midwest. The dog was a cross of a Borzoi with an Irish Wolfhound. He was allowed to become fat and sometimes carried a saddle like a pony, and permitted children to ride him. I saw this dog many times. He was taller than any Wolfhound I ever saw. The owner said he stood 40 inches at the shoulders and I believe him. The coarse wire-haired coat stood out making him seem even larger than he was.

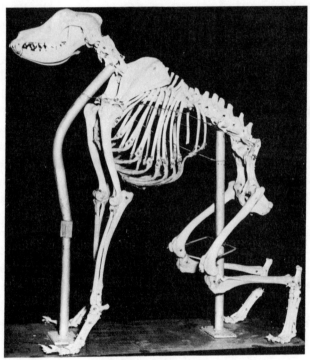

Skeleton of the Baboon Dog.

Baboon Dogs

In the Transvaal, South Africa, Dr. H.P.A. DeBoom found a mutation in dogs which shortens the spine and causes the dogs to sit most of the time instead of standing. The front legs are

319

held forward while they are sitting. Locally they are called "Baboon dogs." The defect appears to behave as a simple recessive.

Hereditary Ataxia in Smooth-haired Fox Terriers

A dog, or perhaps more, was imported into Sweden from England many years ago which occasionally produced a puppy with a brain defect which caused a staggering gait and bouncing dancing movements known as ataxia. In some cases the defect doesn't show until the fourth month of age, when the dog becomes restless. It is unable to climb stairs. Some affected dogs rub their heads against solid objects. Some seem able to compensate for the defect. In America it has been most common in Boston Terriers, of which I can remember several which lived to a good age.

Scientists at the Royal Veterinary College at Stockholm found a total of 27 cases which had appeared, all descended from the original imports.

The author and Dr. John Fulton at Yale University studied the effects of breeding two ataxic Fox Terriers. Of four puppies born, three were ataxic and one died soon after birth, apparently too weak to exist.

This defect had been previously described in Boston Terriers, Airedales, a French Bulldog and others, but only rarely. Some thought the defect was a mutation, but the Swedish investigators had enough material to demonstrate the inheritability, which they conclude is caused by a simple recessive gene.

This is a trait like glaucoma which can only be eliminated from a family of dogs by test breeding.

6

Disease Resistance

STUDENTS of human types have concluded that there is great difference between people in their susceptibility to diseases. Some tend to be "prone to" tuberculosis, others to kidney disease, still others to diabetes and so on. Those of us who have owned large numbers of dogs of many kinds have been struck with similar facts: the ease with which some breeds succumb to distemper or other diseases, and the remarkable ability of some breeds to live through them. Then too we have all heard of the wonderful vitality of the mongrel as compared with the purebred. Let us consider these ideas. Perhaps that is all they really are, ideas, or perhaps they are based upon solid facts.

We cannot dispute the students of human types, their data are derived, as in the case of Draper's, from thousands of measurements of human features.

As a dog breeder and later as a veterinarian, I have carefully observed thousands of dogs. I believe that the same conclusions will some day be applied to dogs.

In my dog breeding days I lived with over 500 cases of Carre distemper. This is nearly gone as a disease from my section and Hardpad disease has taken its place. But when it was so very prevalent among my dogs, so much so that I had 90 cases at one time, certain facts appeared that it would be difficult not to observe. First, it was obvious that among my Bloodhounds, pups and old dogs, the mortality was so great that after each epizootic, there were not many Bloodhounds left, and it was fortunate that so many bitches were pregnant (pregnant bitches seem to have much lighter cases than non-pregnant ones), or I might have become discouraged to the point of giving up the breed. Secondly, it was just as obvious that my bullhounds, which as has been seen resulted from crosses of Bull Terriers and Bloodhounds, had the most wonderful resistance. Where the Bloodhounds died so quickly, and in such large numbers, the bullhounds mixed right with them and, infected with the same virus, used to have a mortality of no more than 25 percent, and further, that among the bullhounds, those which, in the second filial generation, appeared most like Bloodhounds, had the least chance to survive. It was this very reason that made my bullhounds look more like Bull Terriers or like the members of the first cross, and so little like Bloodhounds. I bred and gave away several hundred of these tough dogs, and all the owners found them to be as tough in other ways as they were in resisting distemper.

So there is no other conclusion than that among these two types, we find one resistant and the other with a minimum of resistance, possibly the lowest of any breed of dog known. But suppose that we consider two types of Bloodhounds, the recently imported English type and dogs which had stood the tests of American natural selection, what then do we find? I had a good many of each type in my kennels. The English type was the beautiful show type with the great amount of loose skin and the phlegmatic disposition, whereas the American type that had survived was the less wrinkled dog with a more buoyant disposition, but not in the same class with the English type for showing. Going back over the records, I find that in five litters of the imported dogs distemper took every single puppy. In not one case of the American type did every puppy die; the mortality was nearer 50 percent, and that takes into account puppies of similar ages and during similar epizootics. For instance, a bitch

322

named Timid had 11 puppies which were ten weeks old. In the next pen an imported bitch had ten puppies nine weeks old. These were a lovely sight. Distemper struck us and when it was over in three months we had five of Timid's litter left and none of the imported bitch's. Sappho had ten puppies and she had been bred to an imported dog. Gloria, an imported bitch, had seven puppies and she was bred to the same dog. When it was all over, Sappho had four puppies and Gloria none. These two litters were five months old. There are definitely types within breeds which show greater or lesser resistance to Carré distemper.

And how about the idea that the mongrel is so much tougher than the purebred dog? It is a statement that requires qualification. My Bloodhound–Great Dane crosses were no hardier than the pure Bloodhound, but my Bloodhound–Bull Terrier crosses were far more resistant to distemper than the Bloodhound and probably as resistant as the Bull Terrier parent. From what I know from the owners of Bull Terrier kennels, there was very little dread of Carré distemper. The breed is probably hardier than most mongrels. Now that we are doing so much vaccination and Carré distemper is gradually becoming more rare, there will be less opportunity to observe breed differences.

About 1940 a new disease swept through the dogs in several northern sections of the United States. It lasted as an epizootic for about ten or 12 years and has not been seen since. It may come again. It seemed to be a disease principally of city and housedogs, but when farm dogs did contract it the mortality was high.

Symptoms took two phases. At first, with a temperature of close to 102.5° C, the dog appeared to have a cold and often gagged as if it had a bone in its throat, frequently leaving gobs of white froth on the floor. After two or three weeks from the initial symptoms some dogs, seemingly recovered, began to show symptoms of encephalitis (inflammation of the brain). The dog might twitch in a group of muscles (chorea), show disorientation and often convulsions.

We found in the practice of veterinary medicine, there was even some breed difference in whether the dog had the throat

323

phase of the disease. This was determined by a comparison of the number of dogs of various breeds presented for treatment at our hospital, which gives a fair picture of the number in our locality, and then comparing the numbers of dogs of these breeds which are brought to the hospital suffering with the throat phase of the disease. This shows that Scottish Terriers very seldom contract even the throat phase, Cocker Spaniels are in the expected proportions, German Shepherds and Dachshunds are in far too great proportions. This is interesting and illuminating, but when it comes to the breeds which develop encephalitis after the throat phase has subsided, we find a tremendous difference. Most of the dogs die with it if they show severe symptoms. The broad-headed, short-faced breeds very seldom develop encephalitis. The pointed-nosed breeds develop it far oftener than the other types. Note the figures.

BREED INCIDENCE OF ENCEPHALITIS

Breed	Number of Dogs	Number Developing Encephalitis	Percentage
Cocker Spaniel	70	14	20
Mongrel	40	10	25
Irish Setter	17	3	17
Boston Terrier	16	2	12
Farm Shepherd	15	4	26
German Shepherd	14	6	42
Collie	12	3	25
English Setter	12	2	16
Smooth Fox Terrier	11	2	18
Dachshund	10	3	33

But even within any breed the same kind of difference exists. While we have no true method of measuring, it is very clear that the dogs which are best described as "high strung," are those which most often develop encephalitis. One gets what has been called a "clinical hunch." In our hospital, my assistants and I made prophecies of the dogs which would be returned with encephalitis, on the basis of how nervous and hyperkinetic the dogs appeared to us during the initial infection. It was astonishing how well we guessed. But we feel it was not a guess at all. Nor did we forget the ones on which we were mistaken. Very often we were surprised to see a dog with a phlegmatic disposition returned with encephalitic symptoms, but surprise is the proper word, because many fewer dogs are returned among those we guessed would not be, than among those we guessed would be. It has even been suggested that the disease is performing a service to dogdom by tending to eliminate the nervous ones from the dog population.

Skin Disease

Every veterinarian knows that certain breeds are brought to him more often with skin diseases than are the other breeds. He also knows that some breeds are more likely to have skin diseases, which appear to him to be similar, than not. Thus Chow dogs presented to The Whitney Veterinary Clinic have a very characteristic kind of summer skin disease. The infected areas usually look the same and the same remedy cures most of them.

Scottish Terriers and other wirehaired breeds are noted for their susceptibility to what the breeders of them usually call "Scotch itch." It is probably of fungous origin, the breed is especially likely to have it and most of their infections look alike.

Predisposition to Fever Fits

In going through some old notes on a distemper epizootic I came across many observations on fits exhibited by dogs of various breeds. There were about 200 dogs, including puppies, in the kennels. Ninety of them had distemper, the real Carré distemper. Certain conclusions were obvious, that some breeds showed a much greater susceptibility to the fits that so often occur in the first rise of temperature from this dreaded disease, than do other breeds.

It was so apparent that when another epizootic developed in the kennels in which 75 dogs were affected, I again noted those which had fits. Lumping the two, there were 165 cases, and nearly all of the dogs were youngsters. Now, it is obviously unfair to compare adult young dogs of one breed with puppies of

325

another, so it is fortunate that there were enough puppies of several breeds or breed crosses of similar ages to make a comparison.

Several dogs exhibited fits in the last stages of the disease. Most of these died but they are not counted in the data; what I have reference to are only those fits which occurred in the first rise of temperature. Generally after that period the fits subsided. Fanciers of some types of dogs will wonder what I am talking about, because they never saw such a phenomenon, while others will wonder that all breeds do not behave as their dogs have. This, of course, applies to the older breeders, because real Carré distemper is becoming increasingly more infrequent due to vaccination.

Any such observations must be inaccurate because one would have to stay with dogs every minute of the day and night if an exact study were to be made. It is altogether possible that other dogs had fits during the night when no one was on hand to witness them, and there were many times during the day when dogs could have been affected, and no observations made. However what applies to one breed applies to all, and it is possible therefore to say that the tendency observed was not vitiated by this objection.

Some might suggest that some breeds are subject to higher temperatures, which may cause the fits, but this apparently is not true because inspection of the temperature curves shows no very great differences. It was fortunate that I was studying the disease, and taking daily temperatures on all of the sick dogs during both epizootics.

Breed	Number	Number exhibiting fits
Beagles	18	14
Bullhounds	18	2
Bloodhounds	30	20
Scottish Terriers	10	0
Coonhounds	12	8
Cocker Spaniels	22	0
Bloodhound x Great Dane	7	0
Bull Terrier x Bullhound	4	0
Greyhound x Foxhound	5	1

Beside these there were other mongrels and purebred dogs of different ages; all of the above were growing puppies. It is significant that the Beagles and coonhounds, both of which breeds are keen hunters, should show a higher proportion than the Bloodhound puppies, also keen hunters, but the last is a much more phlegmatic breed. There is no case of a Scottish Terrier or Cocker Spaniel showing the fits, even though the Cockers are a vivacious breed.

The bullhounds referred to above were F_2 and F_1 F_2 puppies, the latter representing a litter of a first generation cross mated to his daughter.

No attempt was made to study the inheritance of this propensity, and it may be that another strain of the virus of Carré distemper would affect other dogs very differently. The data are presented as indicating that there is a definite breed difference, and if so many of the members of a breed react so differently to the same virus, when kept under the same conditions, then we can conclude that there is an hereditary difference among dogs in this respect.

Dalmatian Urine

While it is not a disease, there is a distinct physiological oddity which the Dalmatian dog exhibits which makes it more or less unique. So far as study has revealed, most dogs have the power to break down uric acid in the body and form allantoin from it. The Dalmatian, however, in the cases reported by H. Onslow, shows a lesser ability. Onslow made crosses and found that the hybrids were like the normal dogs and not like the Dalmatian, and thus that the normal condition is dominant over the abnormal.

Dalmatians have come in for considerable study in regard to their urinary tract, and its difference from that of other dogs. We have H. L. Weatherford and his associates to thank for their studies on the peculiar crystals found in the nucleii of the cells of the liver in ordinary breeds and in the Dalmatian, and hybrids of the Dalmatian with the Collie. He found from chemical analysis that these crystals are in some way associated with the excretion of uric acid and not of allantoin. The presence of these crystals were found to be hereditary, and anyone interested in this unusual phase of heredity will find it by reading the published papers.

Dalmatians appear to be more susceptible to kidney stones than dogs of other breeds, according to Keeler and Trimble. They report on a limited number of autopsies and find the highest prevalence in Dalmatians. But this should not frighten persons interested in the breed; kidney stones were rare, even though they were more frequently found in the breed.

There has been so much discussion of urine in Dalmatians, that some people think they are abnormal to the extent of illness. As we have seen, they are unusual in the production of allantoin, but some dogs in all breeds produce urine of greater uric acid content than others. Trimble and Keeler studied this and published their report in 1938. These investigators found that in ordinary dog urine the uric acid content varies from 4 to 10 milligrams per kilogram of body weight; in Dalmatians it is usually over 28 milligrams. They show that the production of urine with high uric acid content is due to an almost completely recessive gene that is not sex-linked. They also show that the genes for this character and the genes for Dalmatian spotting segregate independently and are thus unrelated. In short, it isn't necessarily true that because a dog has the Dalmatian spots his urine must be higher in uric acid than that of other dogs.

Cryptorchidism

In 1935, in a German journal, W. Koch published a study showing that cryptorchidism (undescended testicles) is a simple Mendelian recessive to the normal condition. This conclusion is open to question. In the first place, a dog with both testicles undescended is sterile. Dogs with undescended testicles, in my experience, tend to develop cancers in them or on them in a high percentage of cases, and are thus rendered infertile. Taking these things into account makes it impossible to make a clear-cut study of the defect. That it is inherited can scarcely be doubted when one observes the way the character tends to run in families. But when in a litter we find one puppy with neither testicle outside of the abdomen, another with one in the scrotum and the other still in the abdomen, a third with one in the scrotum and the other under the skin between the scrotum and the external muscular ring through which the testes descend, and four bitches in the same litter, how can anyone conclude what the mode of inheritance is, especially when the stud which sired these puppies has both of his testicles in the scrotum?

In my work I come across many litters of puppies, some of which have undescended testicles, and often find that associated with this condition is some sort of weakness in the hind end of the dog. The very fact that the litter was born shows that both parents were fertile. I have endeavored to trace the inheritance and always it seems to be found coming from a bitch, usually not more distant than the second generation back. For example, a Collie bitch, which was the progenitor of many very wonderful dogs, has at least four grandsons which are crypt-orchids. Although she has been bred to dogs which have repeatedly produced sound puppies, and these puppies in turn mated to bitches and dogs of sound stock, here and there will be found a cryptorchid.

Among Boxers of my acquaintance cryptorchidism is par-ticularly prevalent. But I have cropped the ears of a great many litters and have had a splendid opportunity to study them carefully. In one litter, three dogs each had one testicle retained in the abdomen. When these testicles were removed two of the dogs became fathers and in one of those litters there was one puppy which was a complete cryptorchid, and two that were half. And of course as already mentioned, but so often overlooked, is the important point: the bitches are also able to pass on the propensity. From my observations I cannot say the defect is inherited as a recessive nor as a dominant, but that it clearly runs in families, and it is therefore obvious that all such dogs should be castrated and sold for pets. Cryptorchids usually develop sour dispositions and from every point of view should be castrated. They cannot be shown: if the judge sees the defect in the show ring, he may disqualify the animal. And it is one of the things that can so easily be bred out.

329

The Inheritance of Cleft Palate

The first study made to determine the inheritance of this characteristic was attempted in 1916 at the Carnegie Institution of Washington at Cold Spring Harbor, N.Y. Dr. Charles B. Davenport and Dr. H. H. Laughlin conducted it using Boston Terriers. So far as I have been able to learn, they never published a word about their work and I am reporting here what they told me about it many years ago. They used a number of bitches and produced a good many puppies, but came to the conclusion that you just couldn't say how the defect was inherited. It was difficult to raise a puppy which couldn't suck because of cleft palate, and often with harelip which is so often associated with it, so it was very difficult to use dogs with cleft palates to breed from. They found that sometimes dogs with partially cleft palates produced normal puppies and normal dogs produced cleft palates in their puppies. So they discontinued the experiment.

In 1935, Koch came to the conclusion that the normal condition is a simple dominant over the abnormal. He thought it was due to disturbance in the pituitary growth hormone.

Among my own Cocker Spaniels I have had many puppies born with cleft palates and some with harelips and several with the defect extending so far that it involved the nostrils. So far none of these puppies has been able to survive, and among the latter ones to be born, all were destroyed at once.

In order for this condition to be a simple recessive, we should expect to find 25 percent born to parents, if they produced so much as one. Such may be the expectancy and the realization in some breeds but my experience does not bear it out. Take, for instance, the pair of Cockers mentioned on page 338 as having produced the recessive short-legged puppies. This pair produced 22 puppies in the four matings and one only of them had a cleft palate. A pair of red Cockers have been mated four times and have produced one puppy out of 27 puppies. So far I have yet to have more than one puppy with a cleft palate born in any litter in my kennel.

Clients of the Whitney Veterinary Clinic have Boston terriers which I have known to produce three cleft palate puppies

330

in a single litter. That there is a greater tendency to perpetuate the trait in the short-nosed breeds can hardly be doubted when we see so many more puppies having to be destroyed in these breeds than in the long-nosed breeds. We might say that sloppy breeding, without elimination of strains which tend strongly to produce cleft palate, is to be blamed for the condition. But such may not be the case at all. In my experience puppies with cleft palates can and do crop up in the most unexpected litters, almost as if the defect were an oft recurring mutation.

So it seems safe to say that cleft palate and harelip are not dominants nor recessives inherited in the simple Mendelian manner, but rather that they tend to be more prevalent in short-faced breeds, and that they run in families. At any rate it is usually a lethal defect.

Now comes evidence that cleft palate may be entirely a nutritional problem. It has been found that a deficiency of riboflavin in diets predisposed puppies to harelips and cleft palate when the deficiency occurred early in the embryonic stage. In pigs, vitamin A deficiency produces the same defects. Possibly dogs react similarly.

Inheritance of Eye Defects

When many individuals in a breed appear to suffer from a defect, it is generally concluded that that trait must run in families, or run through the breed. Glaucoma is such a defect. There have been investigations in human families which indicate that glaucoma, or hardening of the eyeball from internal pressure, is inherited as a Mendelian dominant. There has been slight criticism of these studies.

The statement is often made that the same must apply to dogs. But where are the data to support such a statement? Probably the most noted breeds in this respect are the Wire Fox Terrier and Welsh Terrier. Without any doubt there are strains which produce many individuals which develop glaucoma in their middle life. One of the curious facts seems to be that the glaucoma may not always develop in both eyes, as is the case with man. Wire Fox Terriers exist with glaucoma, neither of whose parents have shown any trace of it. We can hardly conclude then that such cases are necessarily inherited.

But there are instances within my acquaintance where the defect has been passed from one generation to the next through three transfers and in such cases it has been known only in one side of the family. Thus we might say it was a dominant.

Obviously, glaucoma does not need to be inherited but can start in other ways such as from injuries, and injuries can come about from pugnacity, and Wirehaired Terriers are pugnacious. There is always the possibility that an inherited pugnacity is responsible for glaucoma at certain ages. Until someone has the time to study the problem, the best we can say is that glaucoma, from whatever cause, tends to run in families, and is probably present more frequently in the Wire Fox Terrier than in any other breed.

Cataract is an opacity of the lens of the eye; glaucoma, which we have been considering, is an internal pressure and eventual swelling of the eyeball, sometimes producing a complete displacement of the lens. The cornea, or the outside transparent part of the eye, sometimes becomes opaque in glaucoma. Dogs afflicted with it often scratch at their eyes and injure the cornea, making their owners, who may not understand the anatomy of the eye, believe that the dog has a cataract. Such is not the case unless the lens is affected. The lens is situated behind the iris. This opening in the iris is the pupil. Thus, if the pupil appears opaque right at the point where the iris moves, you may be sure the dog has a cataract. But if you can look through the pupil and see a bluish color in the eye of an old dog, that is not a cataract; that blue is a normal accompaniment of old age.

There are cataracts due to injuries, but there is also an inherited type. Hippel, in 1930, mated a German Shepherd Dog male to his sister. Both had what he thought were congenital cataracts. They produced 11 puppies in two matings and of these puppies two were normal and nine had cataracts.

Then he mated a blind male to a normal female three times, and produced 15 puppies, two with cataracts and 13 normal.

A blind female was mated with a normal male, and of the six puppies, five had cataracts and one was normal.

He concludes that the character is dominant and follows Mendelian rules.

Much has been written about defective vision in male Collies. In some the eyes are much too small and vision is obviously far from normal. In some with normal appearing eyes, there is partial blindness. What can we say about its inheritance? Only an association, because we do not find one without the other. Mitchell, and also Pearson, Nettleship and Usher, have published their observations on these facts.

Inheritance of Retinal Atrophy

Although we frequently hear it stated that the drying up and disappearing of the rods and cones in the retina of dogs' eyes is an hereditary ailment, there is one important reason to doubt it. My opinion, previously expressed on several occasions, is that the defect is caused by the virus of hepatitis. I first observed the fact that hepatitis can cause retinal atrophy in 1942. I returned in October from a coon hunting trip with my four hounds. There was a litter of puppies with the disease in the same end of the kennel where I put my big hounds. All four contracted the disease, which caused them but little inconvenience except that three of them developed white eyes. One had only one eye affected, two had both. After several weeks, the white disappeared from the corneas and we hunted more. By January I noted that my best tree dog was suffering from night blindness, which proceeded to become worse. And the hound with one eye affected scratched that eye several times, indicating he was not seeing on that side. A Yale ophthalmologist diagnosed the trouble as retinal atrophy. The next year two of the hounds were so blind they could not hunt properly, although they tried.

By asking clients who brought dogs to our hospital with defective vision, it was not surprising to me to find most of them remembered a time when their dogs had had blue eyes.

Where hepatitis runs through kennels it would be easy to conclude that retinal atrophy was inherited. The virus of Carré whitens the outside layer of the cornea, whereas the hepatitis virus whitens the inside layers. So is there any reason why it may not deteriorate the delicate rods and cones in the back of the eye as well as blueing the front, which is caused by accumulation of white cells acting as a protection?

Hereditary Hernia

It has been shown that there is a strong tendency for the ordinary inguinal hernia, so common in human beings, to run strongly in families. Phillips and Felton, in 1939, published a report on their study indicating that umbilical (navel) hernia runs in dog families. These hernias are generally represented by a large bubble of skin due to internal pressure forcing out the peritoneum (lining of the abdomen) and some of the omentum in the form of a lump. This is possible because when the abdomen grew together at the point where the umbilical cord enters it, the junction was not complete and a small ring was left. The opening is generally so small that only a bubble one-half to three-quarters of an inch is pushed out, and this bubble often becomes solidified as the dog becomes older. Nevertheless it often worries owners of dogs. Generally it is entirely benign.

These students found that it was either a single recessive factor or multiple factors which accounted for the hernia; that it was independent of deafness, or color, or sex, or other forms of hernia in its mode of inheritance.

Inheritance of Deafness

Deafnesss may be determined at this early age by making a squeaking noise with the lips. Deaf puppies will not prick their ears up in the least, while the normal ones will indicate that they can hear it in that manner.

Deaf dogs assume a peculiar attitude of alertness. One who is familiar with this after observing many such animals in contrast to the normals can spot them with ease. They will generally stand away from the other dogs, will usually not be as responsive and will indicate in many ways their abnormality. Unfortunately, these indications are frequently taken by owners to indicate shyness, or unfavorable temperaments, and they are often not recognized as being deaf. When they learn to bark, their voices, curiously enough, are not unlike that of other dogs in the litter, although several may have done considerable growling as well as barking. Since they do not hear a human voice raised in disapproval, they are often thought to be stupid.

In rearing puppies, deaf mothers tend to lie on more puppies than those which can hear their squeals. Thus, in general, the sense of feeling does not compensate for the deafness. Nor are such bitches prone to be more careful in pushing puppies out of the way before lying down. This observation has been made on many deaf bitches which the author has owned.

In the case of harlequins and merles, deafness usually is associated with color. But what about the form of deafness found very often in Bull Terriers? It is commonly believed that this character is associated with the all-white dog. My own data may serve to throw some doubt on this assertion and belief. These data show quite clearly that the color is not associated with white because of necessity, but may be because of lack of proper selection.

Mary had enough puppies to make a nice study in genetics, as we have seen. Now, among her puppies there were some that we thought at first were stupid, or stubborn, but it soon developed they were totally deaf. Some of these compensated for their deafness by their alertness to such a degree that we did not realize that the first litter had deaf puppies until the next litter was two months old. Her first litter consisted of 17 puppies, all of which we raised. There were two deaf ones among them. In all we found that we had nine deaf puppies and some partially deaf among the 129 which she whelped, many of which we raised.

This is not 25 percent, which would be the Mendelian expectancy. We had no way of knowing about the hearing of all of the puppies, but we always noted great difference among some of them. The important point is that of all the deaf ones there happened to be not a single one among the tricolored dogs, that is, the ones that were mostly white.

Another interesting observation is that in every litter save one,

one or more deaf puppies appeared. And that litter was Mary's only litter not sired by Bill. It was sired by a Bloodhound-Basset cross male. He could thus not have carried deafness recessively as Bill and Mary must have.

It would seem that this kind of deafness was not a color-linked character, but merely one that was associated with Bull Terriers in general and probably could be bred out completely. Surely it could not be said to be a character that behaved in Mendelian fashion, but there is strong evidence that it runs in families, and positive evidence that it ran strongly in this family.

Deafness is found as a common defect in Dalmatians. With them it may or may not be associated with color but the result of sloppy breeding. Among my clients was the owner of a pair of excellent Dalmatians whose dogs in two litters (total of 16 puppies) produced three deaf pups. Another client bred a deaf bitch to a sound dog and none of the ten puppies was deaf.

PART IV

SOME PRACTICAL CONSIDERATIONS

The Puli, a Hungarian sheepdog. Sometimes the rarer, useful breeds afford more pleasure as a hobby than the more popular dogs.

1

How to Start the Dog Hobby

I KNOW a man who wanted to start with a breed of dogs. He used the kind of knowledge that I have tried to set down in this book. So he knew that "If you would have fine children, marry not the maid who is the only good maid in the clan." In other words, he knew that family stock was what counted. He took a very small chance, therefore, when he counted his hard earned money and said to himself, "I haven't much money. Now I can either spend it to buy a dog which is a good specimen, which will very likely win prizes in small shows, or I can buy a dog which is himself not outstanding but which comes of a family that has produced many champions and grand dogs of the breed." He decided on the latter. He bought a dog which was of the finest stock but which was so far from the ideal that a judge before whom he was shown had the courage to put him third even though he was the only dog in his class. This happened many years ago.

This man kept the dog for awhile and finally saved some more money but found he didn't have to spend it because a friend had a bitch which was much like the dog, in that she came from grand stock but was not too good an individual.

He traded a service from his male for the bitch. The bitch produced 15 puppies. Of these he raised ten. He sold those he didn't want for $375 and kept the three best for himself, and one of these went best of breed at Madison Square Garden.

There is a lesson in that. I was the man. I have done as well several times since then by putting the same principle to work. As every Cocker Spaniel breeder will tell you, Red Brucie was the greatest stud dog in American dog history. Although he was not a show dog—he placed third the only time he was shown—he produced more champions than any other stud dog on record. The same rule applies to other great sires.

The way to develop your dog hobby then, if you have not unlimited means, is to buy the poorer specimens from a great family rather than the best specimens of a poor family. If you do the former, the general excellence level will be closer to the ideal, and if you do not, the trend will be downward.

How many of the great champions which have been brought to public attention are the sires of great dogs? The extremes always tend to breed toward the average, and that applies whether the extremes are good or bad. It is not only the dogs at the extremes which carry within their germ plasm a happy assortment of genes which, when they nick with other happy genes, produce stock close to the ideal. Many dogs at the upper extreme are those which most consistently produce just the kind of dogs which are far removed from the ideal.

We see then that the dog to buy, whenever possible, is the tested dog, and as such is very expensive. What is the solution? Buy no male dog at all, but attempt to breed one instead. Buy the right kind of female, breed her to a tested male, which has a reputation for producing the finest puppies and your chances are good of doing well with your breed.

This is the method used by many experienced persons. It is somewhat risky because when you ship your bitch away you do not stand as good a chance of her becoming pregnant as though you bred her to a stud of your own at home. But when you do use this method you are using what geneticists call the pure sire method. As contrasted with the method employed by monogamous animals which mate for life, the dogs are mated by

340

Start with a good bitch from a strain which produces uniformly high class stock.

their owners and only a very few of the males of any breed become progenitors of the next generation. The best are chosen and the poorer rejected, and thus the average is raised each generation toward the ideal. There will be only a limited number of the very great among the dogs that are used as sires, and the ambition of every dog breeder is to own one of those few great dogs—great not only in themselves but great in their ability to transmit likeness close to the ideal.

We now know enough about genetics to realize that the selection of a sire for our future puppies is no simple matter, but we do know that there are principles which will help us. The chief one is this: Fix clearly in your mind the fact that the individual does not create the germ plasm which forms the next generation, but that the germ plasm created him and he is only the custodian of it. He exists for it.

If you keep that thought in mind it will help mightily either in getting started in the dog business, in selecting a sire in case you wish to breed a bitch, or in buying a dog which is to be the sire of future puppies. For the present let us consider what to keep in mind in the event that we are endeavoring to select a dog to which we shall breed a bitch which we know is a good one. Put the stud fee out of the question, and proceed along the line of heredity. In other words, in this case money is no object.

Would you choose the dog that had done the most winning? Perhaps you would, but we know that is a very poor indication of his value as a stud. It helps to get us a better price for our puppies because we can brag to the uninitiated about our puppies being from the great So-and-So. They will tumble all over themselves to buy. But that is another matter, and not necessarily real breed improvement.

Would you choose the dog that had cost the most money? That too is a value quite often based upon show wins and not too valuable an indication. It also may be only a publicized value, an agreement on the part of the seller and the buyer, when actually not nearly as much money changes hands as we are given to believe.

Would you choose the most renowned field trial dog? That is like selecting the best show dog.

Here is the way to choose. Look at the sire you are considering and say to yourself, "He is one dog out of a great many that were produced by the germ plasm of his parents. I shall inquire and see what kind of stock that germ plasm produced on the whole." In other words, the dog is only one exhibit, now it is time to see the whole show. If you do that you may find that there are some very poor specimens among the descendants of that germ plasm.

Instead of breeding to that dog, then you would try to find one which came from stock which produced uniformily excellent dogs. Then you would be reasonably sure that, if your bitch were a good one, the combination of these two strains of germ plasm would result in excellent offspring. But that is only one way of selecting a dog for a sire.

The surest way is the one which is used by the more

enlightened cattle breeders. In the case of dairy cattle where milk and butter yield count so greatly, the work of Dr. Gowan of Princeton University has given great impetus to selection of sires. As a result of his studies on measurable traits and of the work of others too, we know that you cannot tell by the looks of a toad how far he can hop. We know that there are bulls which produce large numbers of high testing offspring and others of apparently just as good stock, and as good appearance, which produce very much less capable offspring.

Applying this reasoning to dogs, we see that the same thing holds true. Where there are a large number of individual traits all to be thought of at the same time, whether we are considering intelligence, special aptitude, appearance, or what not, then the best way to choose a stud is on the basis of his record of excellence in his progeny. That is why an advertisement for a dog which has produced a large number of champions is the one to read with greatest interest. The untried sires may be able to produce as good dogs but one is sure and the other is still a speculation.

Put both ideas together and choose a dog which is from excellent stock which has also shown his worth by already producing excellent stock and you cannot go far wrong. That is, of course, if your bitch is a good one too.

The often total disregard of these principles is the reason for the deterioration of breeds. Serious experienced breeders often actually worry that the breed they fancy will become very popular. They know that once it does, demand for puppies brings into the picture the so-called puppy factories, which turn out as many pups as the demand calls for. Quality and prices go down. The average person has been educated to believe that only physical features of a dog (or of a human being) are inherited. If it looks like the popular breed, it will behave like the well-known specimens behave. So if Mrs. Jones has a vicious specimen, she blames it on the fact that it was mistreated while still a puppy. Mrs. Smith has a bitch of the same breed. It may be mentally unrepresentative of the breed but "that's only a matter of training," so they mate them and sell the inferior puppies to other unknowing persons who learn the hard way that training isn't everything. This has been the history of breed after breed, with the public finally deciding that here is a good breed to avoid. Then the hard core of knowledge breeders is glad to see the popularity diminish and they go on breeding sound typical dogs again with predictable behavior patterns.

Popularity too produces mongrels which are sold as purebreds. Good illustrations in a field trial breed is the Pointer which, as we have seen, often producess longhaired pups showing almost certain English Setter crosses in the ancestry of both parents. Another example is the Irish Terrier, which so often produces black-and-tan puppies showing part Airedale ancestry.

The wise stud dog owner is the man who refuses to breed his stud to any old bitch, because her hereditary qualities tend to drag down the record of excellent get from the dog. When he says, "I will breed my dog to approved bitches only," he would do very well to mean it, or before he knows it the owner of the poor bitch will be exhibiting poor puppies and bragging that they were from the great So-and-So. Sometimes, on this account, breeding to inferior stock is more costly than one imagines, and that is why if you have a poor bitch you should not feel disappointed or offended if the stud's owner politely informs you that he does not think that your bitch is good enough to breed to his dog. Maybe he will be doing you and the breed a good turn, and he is thinking also of his dog's best interests.

People have different ideas of the dog show or field trial. Some think of it as a social gathering, some as a place to educate the public, but down underneath is always the reason for its popularity, namely, that it gives the breeders a chance to display their dogs where they may be judged and if found best, to become likely progenitors of the next generation. Thus they will be more valuable. This helps give our pride, as well as our pocketbooks, a chance to swell. It is that basic reason that keeps shows going and increasing in popularity year after year. Basically, it is this constant opportunity of comparing one's dogs with those of others that is the chief basis for the interest in dogs.

344

In breeding for size, large or small, the stock is of greatest importance. Study the size of all the near kin, and you get a good idea of the potentialities of the stock.

When I say dog show, I mean the field trial as well, for after all, the field trial is a dog show, but instead of choosing the dog for a bench standard, he is chosen for a performance standard. The two standards are too often widely varied. What is now being done is that field trial men, those who compare their dogs for the work for which they have been selected, are admitting that in some cases the ideal has been wrong, and that it has proved impractical to be used in creating the working dog. If the English Setter standard calls for a dog with a massive head, and the field trial practically never is won by such a dog, then there must eventually be either two breeds or the standard must be altered to describe a dog of the type that does good work, and yet keep the standard far ahead of anything yet achieved. If the Pointer men want a dog for their southern trials that runs like a Greyhound, they should set a standard for a dog with Greyhound proportions in body and the head of the type of pointer that finds the birds. This would be far better than trying to breed for a medium chunky dog for the show bench, and then compete with dogs with as long legs as possible in the field.

Sometimes the bench standard and the field standard just coincide. In the case of Siberian Huskies the breeders have found that the standard which they created is adequate and that dogs which nearly approach it are splendid sled dogs. It did irk them to have a team composed of a litter which was half Doberman Pinscher and half Irish Setter win their field trials, so they excluded from their trials all but purebred sled dogs. They were right because the mongrels were bred only for speed and were not adapted to sleeping outside with only snow for a blanket.

We might consider many standards that are supposed to be dual standards, but I have mentioned enough to illustrate the point. It is that standards must be lowered and raised and changed constantly. They must be changed to produce dogs to fit new conditions, or when some breeder has bred a dog which is already up to the standard, or when time has shown they are false. But the dog show and the field trial are great agencies for breed improvement, and always will be, so long as judges are required to know the standard and not judge according to their own notions, but according to the will of the specialty clubs which originate the standards. In short, judges must realize that they are agents of the specialty club and who seek to carry out its wishes and not their own.

2

Improving Old Breeds; Creating New Ones

"THERE is nothing new under the sun." Don't be misled, for there is something new in dog lore every day of the year, if we will but watch for it. In this chapter we shall consider how the individual can take an already highly developed breed and from it create a strain on which he has all but stamped his name. There are such strains, you know. Secondly, I want to consider that much tabooed subject of creating a new breed.

The Mongrel Dog

Does the very word *mongrel* awaken in you a feeling of revulsion? If you are a worshiper of any one breed, it very likely does. Should it? Our ancestors set up taboos against mongrelization. As we have seen, they believed in telegony. A bitch bred to a dog of another breed was, to them, ruined for future breeding. Untrue, but that belief helped to keep the breeds of the day "pure."

And yet new breeds were evolving even when dog breeders

347

The author with "Spike", a Redbone x Farm Shepherd cross. Although lacking in the acute scenting ability of the pure hound, he compensated for it by his enormous energy.

felt a revulusion against mongrels. "Cur," "mutt" and other derogatory terms were applied to crossbred dogs. How could a new breed evolve without combining the characteristics of existing breeds into new combinations? Incorporating a mutation could do it and doubtless did account for some new breeds being established in the past. These mutations, which made the dog useful for a new kind of work or better at an old, would be set by inbreeding. The mutation might be in the brain or in the muscles.

Has the mongrel any uses today? Why aren't more used? Of course the mongrels have use today. They are not used for several reasons, chief of which is that their offspring usually are disappointing and unpredictable. Crosses of sled dogs with Arctic wolves produce powerful dogs better for hauling loads than the purebred sled dogs, or at least so we are told by those who have made the crosses.

The two greatest dogs in my life were both mongrels, but had an inherited drawback. One was Bill, the Bloodhound x Bull Terrier, a tremendous animal in every way except size and voice. His scream when he followed a trail was so disagreeable it was no fun to hunt with him, despite his wonderful ability. The other was Spike, a Redbone x American Farm Shepherd. He was larger than either parent, and had so powerful a voice he could be heard three miles away on a clear windless night, but his Achilles heel was that his scenting ability was that of the Shepherd. On dry nights a trail must be fresh if he was to be able to follow it. On damp nights he could run away from any dog he ever hunted with and was so adept at finding and treeing raccoons that everyone marvelled at his prowess.

New useful breeds could easily have been created from these two dogs, mongrels though they were.

Probably no one has produced more different kinds of mongrels than the author. The breed crosses were made to study genetics, with emphasis on inheritance of behavior patterns or aptitudes. Some showed such promise that four new breeds were started.

One was called the Upland bird dog, produced by combining Irish Setter, Pointer and Bloodhound.

Another was the Norman hound—a tricolor hound as large as a Bloodhound, tricolored and long eared.

A third was the Bullhound, mentioned several times earlier.

Fourth was the short-legged Cocker. Perhaps it was fortunate that no one besides the author saw enough promise in the usefulness of these four new breeds to cooperate. Or perhaps not enough persons knew about them. Certain it is that the Bullhounds would surpass any breed in the world for police or war work because they had excellent noses in the hound class, in contrast to the poor olfactory equipment of Alsatians and other breeds, and they had physical courage unlimited.

In England thousands of Lurchers were bred and used, often illegally. They were almost always crosses of breeds which carried their tails low. A Greyhound was frequently one of the parents. Perhaps a Border Collie or a Bull Terrier might be the other. These dogs were trained to be thieves. Some stole clothes drying on clotheslines, some stole boots. But mainly they caught rabbits and hares from the estates of the wealthy. The owner accompanied them on a bicycle. The dogs, trained to watch for rabbits, usually were so fast they caught them. Tales of the remarkable acuity of Lurchers are amazing. They would not retrieve to the owner if any other person was in sight. The war came, and all the Lurchers were conscripted and made the best of all British war dogs; these bad dogs made good.

No purebred dogs made good Lurchers, so an owner told me. They were cheap. For all their brilliance, they were so often shot by gamekeepers. Today they have all but disappeared. The Lurcher is the best evidence extant that mongrels can be useful, even though not beautiful according to breed standards.

I was sitting at the ringside of a prominent New England dog show and heard two men behind me talking. One of them said he had come all the way from Texas just to try to buy a good dog of a certain strain. The only kind of a dog he would buy would be one of that gentleman's because he felt that they were the first strain of the breed in the country. And they probably are, and the breed is among the most popular in America. It means something to have earned a reputation like that with one's dogs. How can a man come to that high

Cross of a Wirehaired Fox Terrier and Cocker
Spaniel.

Cross of a Bloodhound with Newfoundland. All of the
progeny were short- haired.

The varieties within each breed offers great possibilities for specialization. The breeders of this great Dachshund specialized in the Longhairs.

estate? Only by long and patient years of study and breeding.

Frankly, I have less patience than I should have with those who are eager only to win prizes, whether their dogs are bought or whether they are personally bred and raised. I do not see how anyone can get a lot of pleasure showing a dog he had bought, and knowing that all the time the breeder really deserved the credit. But some people do. I know many people who own some of the grandest specimens of their breeds, and who never raise more than a few litters of puppies a year. They very seldom breed anything outstanding, and rely almost wholly on bought dogs to win prizes. In contrast is the man whom I previously mentioned. He is so much on the other side, that side that most of us consider the right side, that he apologized to me once for showing a dog which had come about in this way: He had sold a woman a splendid bitch puppy. She had shipped her back to him to be bred to one of his dogs and he had taken the puppy he was showing as a stud fee. Somehow he didn't feel he was quite a good sport in showing this pup, when another person's name was on the registration papers as "Breeder." How I admire that spirit! Who doesn't?

Well, the real secret of any great breeder's fortune lies in breeding just as many puppies as he possibly can. If there is only one good pup in 10, even when the best are considered, then the man who raises 100 pups from good stock stands twenty times the chance of getting that one than the fellow who raises only five puppies a year. The greatest breeders are not those who raise a litter a year. They understand somehow that they have a better statistical chance of breeding great dogs, and they resort to numbers, for after all, heredity in dogs is what counts and the way you feed and groom does not greatly change the appearance of the dog, so long as both are well done.

Therefore, the way to fame in any breed is to breed and show plenty of dogs, and the more of both you do, the better are your chances to attain fame for your dogs and yourself.

In every breed there is sufficient variation so that there is nearly always something that appeals to any breeder. Here is a hound fancier who wants a strain with the longest ears he can possibly get, and the Cocker Spaniel breeder who specializes in reds and who takes pride in breeding dogs with beautiful shades of color. Then there is the Toy breeder who develops a strain of the smallest Toys in the breed and the breeder of Newfoundlands who specializes in Landseers. So it goes. Most breeders of renown have specialized in just this way and any newcomer to a breed of dogs can often find some such point to emphasize. The man who keeps a breed for the money there is in it does not make lasting fame as a breeder, because of his lack of devotion to the all-important ideal. He doesn't worry about these details that we are considering. Instead, we find him breeding Irish Terriers, then Fox Terriers, followed by Scotties and Bostons, or possibly several breeds at once. And tomorrow he may be breeding Poodles because there is where the most money is. And a few years hence he will be breeding some newly imported fad perhaps. Who can tell? He lacks imagination. Don't be like him.

Instead, remember the star and be guided by its light, always endeavoring to excel. Breed as many puppies as you can afford and always keep the best for yourself. That is not selfishness, but breeding toward an ideal. When you let your best go you are giving your best capital away, and it doesn't always come back as easily as people imagine.

Right here we must take account of a vexing problem to all breeders, namely that of the proper age at which to sell and to buy dogs. There is no person, no matter how experienced, who can always choose the best puppy from any given litter. The right time to buy a puppy from the other fellow is just as early in life as you are allowed to choose one, because the earlier you choose it, the better is your chance of getting the best pup in the litter. Of course one must make allowance for the development of the dog. Some pups in every litter develop faster than others which are smaller. When the smaller ones have reached a similar stage of development, they will often be better than those that developed rapidly.

The right time for the owner to sell a puppy is when it is as large as he thinks he can let it grow without reaching the awkward stage; that is, equivalent to that age in the adolescent

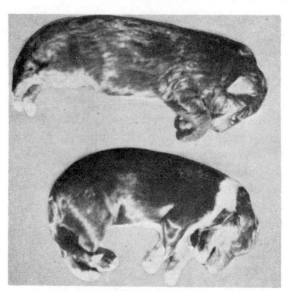

Bloodhound puppy at birth contrasted with a newborn Collie puppy. The younger they are, the greater the similarity, even between different breeds.

In every litter, some pups develop faster than others. Note the ears of these Norwegian Elkhounds.

child. There is a period between puppyhood and maturity when the owner can get no more than, if as much, for puppies as he could when they were just weaned. Every breeder likes to avoid keeping them that long, but he must keep them to as near that time as he can before making his own selection. This prevents his selling a puppy that may later develop into a show specimen, fine enough to defeat his brothers and sisters retained by the owner.

It is imperative that some puppies be sold as early as possible, since the appeal of the small puppy is the chief factor that sells certain breeds. There are other breeds, which are very homely at the stage when the puppies are neither one thing nor the other. But these very breeds when they are ready to wean are among the most attractive of all types of dogs. The time to sell them is at this period and that is why it is really so difficult to know what to do when one wants to keep the best and yet knows he must sell before the puppies are really large enough to make it possible for him to choose the right ones to keep.

If you will notice, you will see that when you send a bitch to be bred and have arranged for the owner of the sire to take a pup, always the pick of the litter, for the stud fee, he postpones coming to collect his pup until as late as it is possible for him to postpone the trip. He seldom tells you to send him the best pup. You couldn't anyway. But the wise owl knows that the longer you keep them, the less it will cost him to raise his pup, to be sure, but more important, the better pup he is going to get. You will be using the same strategy yourself some day after you have become an experienced breeder.

Creating a new breed of dogs is not so very different from improving an old one. In the case of the old one you collect all the best heredity into one strain and then hope for mutations which you capture. Thus, you improve because, as we have seen mutations are the stepping stones which allow a breed to overcome the natural barriers of the pure line.

But it takes time to create and perfect a new breed. I shall be vilified for saying that there are still places in dogdom where new breeds are needed. I sincerely believe there are. We have set our ideals very much higher than those of any breed have ever been set before. Each is decades distant from where we are today, but we know what we are striving for.

American Toy Fox Terriers, whose origin was the same as the English smooth Fox Terriers. The two breeds developed along different lines.

Full grown at 12 pounds. Their owner is developing a
new breed of Miniature Boxers.

Breed Crossing to Create New Breeds

The easiest way to create a new breed is by breed crossing.
First it is necessary to name the need, then find the dogs of
the breeds which most closely approximate it, mate these and
then through constant mating and selection, elimination of the
undesirable traits and accumulation and purification of the
traits which are in the right direction, the goal is approximated.

The next way in which it has been done is by the creation
of a different standard for an old breed and then breeding
toward that. Witness the Cocker Spaniel for example. The
American fanciers decided on a very different standard from
that which the English had established. Each went its way
merrily. Today they have virtually developed two different
breeds, surely as diverse one from the other, as are other breeds
of Spaniels.

A third way of creating a new breed is to watch for a mutation
and breed from the animal which possesses it. It is often possible
to create a new breed on this basis of a color alone. In my

357

laboratory we had a mutation in an albino rat. It had the same sort of coat which an Airedale dog has and it bred true. It would be very little trouble to originate a new strain of rats, which could be called a breed. Mutations accounted for the wire haired coat in one or more of our breeds of dogs, and new breeds were started on that basis. Certainly new breeds were started on the basis of mutations which produced very short legs.

How many generations will it take to produce a new breed? Not many. In three generations it is possible (but improbable) to produce a breed which will breed as true as most of the recognized breeds of today. There will be some variation, but not nearly as much as might be expected. But it cannot be done in a haphazard manner. It must be planned. The originator must understand what characters are dominant and what recessive and realize that when a dominant character has disappeared from a strain that it is gone for good, but that where recessives lurk, they are quite likely to be reappearing generation after generation. Because people were careless about matings we used to see white Irish Setters appearing in litters, longhaired Airedales, curly-coated Borzois, white Chows, and dozens of other recessives which are familiar phenomena to experienced breeders.

To thoroughly smoke out the recessives from a new breed requires great patience and many generations, but if a breed which is composed mostly of recessives is created, then it is possible to make it uniform in three generations. To create any new breed ought to be a ten-generation task at least and then a start will have been made, and with good planning, a very good start.

Beauty vs. Utility

It would hardly seem right if I were to conclude this book without a few words about a conviction which has been growing stronger and stronger as I come to be better and better acquainted with dogs. Since the advent of dog shows, at which the first dogs were judged comparatively, the breeds have been modified to conform to standards. That feature was the real

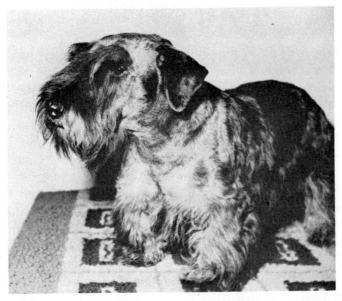

In the *New York Times* of July 1, 1971, Walter R. Fletcher reported the story of the Czech Terrier, a current example of breed crossing to create a new breed.

The Czech Terrier was developed by Frantisek Horak, of Czechoslovakia, a top-ranking geneticist with the Academy of Sciences there, an all-breed judge, and a Scottish Terrier breeder.

The Scottie is used for hunting in Czechoslovakia. However, once it has cornered its prey in a hole, its massive front and heavy coat make it uneffective underground. The fox is narrower and can safely wedge himself into the hole.

Horak decided to cross a Scottie and Sealyham to produce a terrier with better hunting qualities. He aimed for a dog with narrower chest, an ear that could give protection when working underground, longer legs than either of its progenitors, and a more practical color than the white of the Sealy.

He began in 1949 with cross of a Sealyham dog with a Scottie bitch. Four matings later, he had achieved what he had envisioned. By the fifth generation, no more crosses were necessary. The breed was accepted for registration by the International Federation of Cynology in 1963. Developing the breed had cost Horak about $4,500. But by the tenth generation there were some 150 Czech Terriers in Czechoslovakia, and 50 more in other countries.

foundation of dog breeds. That was what caused one breed to differ from the other.

In the early days certain groups of breeders had very indefinite standards. Some of these standards consisted in behavior standards. Certain mental and physical characteristics tend to be linked, but are not invariably linked. Let us take one breed as an example. The early owners of racing dogs raced them and the fastest dogs were those of a definite type. The fastest were the sires and dams most sought as progenitors. There is an association of bodily features which is conducive of great speed, so the type of dog which we know as the Greyhound began to become a breed. And finally, by the recognition of the fact that there is a definite association of physical characteristics, leaders found that they could also improve Greyhounds by inculcating beauty into the breed without sacrificing speed. Then they began to compare them in groups to see which most nearly approximated what they thought was the composite of beauty and usefulness.

In this way cliques were built up around all breeds which were interested not in the usefulness of the breeds but in the appearance. They gradually made their idea of beauty the goal and forgot usefulness. In fact they did the most absurd things and they are still doing them. They bred dogs more and more unnatural until they had developed monstrosities and then they glorified them. They developed characteristics in dogs which were decidedly inimical to the good of the dogs, all to satisfy a very ill-considered and foolish idea.

One group copied another until breeds which started out to be one thing ended up by being something altogether different. If a terrier fancier of many years became interested in the English Setter as a breed, he naturally chose Setters which had the best terrier characteristics. And if a Borzoi breeder became interested in Collies, he would try to develop Collies with extra long heads. If a St. Bernard breeder took up Newfoundlands, he tended to develop the breed away from the alert active dog he once was, and instead, make him of a phlegmatic type. So few people realize the grip which long association with a breed has on one!

So few are able to forget what they once knew about the standard of one breed when they are managing another!

This is bad but it can be overcome. It is not nearly as bad as is that about which I wish to appeal to every reader of this book. I have in mind principally what I mentioned previously, namely the mistake of incorporating into the breeds points which are useless and often detrimental. Why should Boston Terriers be bred with pelvises so small that they cannot whelp naturally? Why should an Irish Wolfhound be bred with legs which look like clubs instead of being bred with beautiful trim legs? Why is every fancier today talking about "building bone" in dogs? Why are Bulldogs bred with noses so pushed in that they cannot breathe naturally? Why are dogs almost universally selected for shorter and shorter backs and loins? Why is disposition so often completely overlooked in the mad scramble for "show points"? Why are Basset Hounds bred with legs so short as to make them foolish when they go into the field? Why has the public tolerated the dispositions of recently imported dogs, to say nothing of breeding them with dogs of the same breed at home with fine dispositions and thus often ruining breeds? These are just a very few of the many, many questions which occur to me. But in order to show every reader that I mean no offense toward his breed I shall take the breed of my own fancy and show just what has happened to it. Then surely no one can take offense except those who recognize their own attitudes and they will possibly disagree with me.

The Bloodhound is primarily a useful dog. Once he was used as a hunting dog and found great usefulness. Then some breeders organized and decided to develop a standard. That was before the rage for "bone." They gradually selected mutations until they had developed a large dog with a powerful body and legs, which was slow on the trail, had a deep melodious voice, probably crossed it with the St. Bernard and developed extremely deep lips, and loose skin, and eyes over which the skin was pulled from the weight of the facial skin, and below which the red haw showed in conspicuous contrast. They were sad looking specimens. But there was one characteristic about them, and that was their unusual gentleness. It took a very great

361

A 1932 photo of the author with the Bloodhounds, Toughy and Jack, after a successful hunt for a lost child.

deal of irritation to rouse one up sufficiently to make him growl at a man to say nothing of biting.

I can recall seeing some of these dogs when I was a little boy, and going to the Madison Square Garden on several occasions where I watched them with the greatest of interest. My mind picture of them has remained. I grew up and bought some of my own. But during the interim a change had come over the breed so that what I got were unlike the dogs I had watched with such awe twenty years before. What I bought were more like the useful dogs before the show people began to tinker with them. They had short lips, they were agile instead of phlegmatic, they were extremely alert instead of depressed. But most important of all, they were mightily better suited to their jobs. Now how did such a transformation come about in America?

It came about by the dogs being used, and selected on the basis of their usefulness. And the men who used them in trailing lost people and criminals, found that the show type had meagre vitality, was too slow for the purposes, were no earthly use for hunting game because of their ponderous size, were no good for pets because of their drooling lips, often made people exclaim when they saw the big patch of red skin under the eyes, "disgusting." So these men who found the dogs useful bred for utility until within ten years the breed reached the greatest usefulness the world has ever known.

But then along came the show enthusiasts again. Instead of realizing the marvelous opportunity at their feet, in studying the features which the best and most useful specimens had developed, they went back to the old standards and because their dogs won in shows, and because the breeders of the vastly better type hid their lights under bushels, because they didn't care who knew they owned Bloodhounds, the show people succeeded again in harming the breed, but now instead of trim legged dogs they breed for club legs. For in England, where Bloodhounds are practically never used, the old standards had, with a few exceptions, persisted. Ignoring the American dogs which were going their separate ways the show people began importing in a big way, and since the year 1900 have imported over $100,000 worth of Bloodhounds. There may be a few dozen of them and their descendants alive but few there were which lived to leave descendants.

Go to the shows and see the dogs which win; go to the small kennels of man trailers and then compare the two types and it becomes increasingly obvious that the show standard and the type which has survived are widely apart. It makes such a grand lesson that it behooves us to consider some of the points of difference.

The first look, the general appearance, shows us two dogs, one of which is ponderous and the other light. Closer examination reveals differences all the way from the feet to the tip of the nose. The great trailers more than likely have trim forearms. Now the forearm of the dog corresponds to the ankle in man.

363

The ideal of beauty in a human ankle is trimness. While research has revealed that the size of the ankle is no indication of the degree of human emotions or intellect—a misconception which some people still hold—nevertheless, even the woman or man with heavy ankles wishes that her or his children might have trim ones. No one denies that trim ankles are more beautiful than heavy ones. And yet the show people have deliberately developed great coarse ponderous ankles in their dogs which are by test no better for the dog than trim ankles. At any rate the useful dogs in general have been those which had heavy calves, a it were, tapering to clean trim ankles, and so had some of the best of the breed long ago.

But somebody set up a hue and cry for "great bone" in almost all breeds, and so, thoughtlessly, the Bloodhound breeders who were interested in shows, had to breed for heavy ankles. Now actually there is no study which shows that heavy club-like ankles are stronger or permit greater endurance than trim ankles. The English Foxhounds which were brought to America for the hunt clubs all had great heavy ankles and pasterns which were so straight they had no spring. The hunt clubs, after patient experiment are now replacing them with trim legged American hounds because actual results prove they cannot stand the test and the heavy club-like legs are actually less capable of endurance than the trim legs.

Or consider the head. The useful type was not ponderously headed. They had extremely long ears which seemed to be hung on the head almost by a point. The show head has ears which fit against the head closely and are nothing in contrast to the heavy wrinkles. The men who were breeding the useful type thought a great deal of the ear length, although they had no proof that the longer the dogs' ears were, the greater were their trailing abilities. They evolved a type of as great beauty as did the show type lovers. Now neither group was antagonistic to the other, but one group developed a hound that could live and was useful and beautiful, while the other developed a type that was fragile and beautiful according to the breeders' type of beauty. The point I am trying to drive home is this: Why should the proper type not be that which is best for the purposes for which the breed is intended? And is it not so in the case of every breed?

It is almost axiomatic that the more popular a breed is, the sloppier the breeding will be. The easier it is to sell puppies the greater is the number of people breeding them and the greater the temptation to mate any two dogs of the breed regardless of their quality. Thus, the more popular a breed is the greater is the necessity of choosing a puppy with care.

This applies to the disposition and mental aptitudes even more than it does to appearance. Selecting a puppy for a pet or to be a sire must be done with great care. In my humble estimation a dog should be chosen 90 percent on his mental side and 10 percent on the physical. Since most of our breeds were evolved to be useful mentally first, the emphasis should be on the mental side. But so many dogs are kept for pets and not to be useful in any particular way that disposition then becomes our prime thought in choosing any dog.

Now, as every breeder knows, most dogs are bought on the basis of what cute puppies they are. The buyer hardly stops to ask, "will it have a calm even disposition when it is grown?" Nor does the breeder usually stress disposition. Instead he usually brags about the wonderful champion show dogs in the pedigree—anything to sell the pup.

Why can't breeders all realize that what makes dogs lastingly popular is first, disposition? Can't they see all the cute, smart animated window mops or bristly atrocities which people have come to love because of their dispositions, and realize that to keep their breed popular it is vastly more important to breed from lovable dogs than from champions? Or better still why not always combine the disposition and the looks?

Should not the aim of every breeder be to develop a dog which has every physical and mental feature to make him a better dog for his work? If you agree that it should then use your influence to see that this yardstick is applied to the breed of your choice. If your breed is useful only as an ornament or as something to look at and to feel of, then at least you have disposition to consider and surely there is no need to breed sickliness into any breed.

So I leave with you the thought that, as you apply the practical dog breeding principles which I have presented in this book, you give some thought to developing dogs which are constituted so they are better dogs, better for you because they are constitutionally better in themselves. If you do that, perchance you won't want to develop dogs with shorter bodies, because you may find that a long body is not necessarily weaker than a short and has more space for vital organs. Perchance you will forget to mention that "the dog has great bone" when you learn that what you see is only partially bone and that bone constitutes one twentieth of the actual weight of the dog. Or again that you will insist that the dog, every dog, be of mental make-up such that he is fitted for human companionship and best adapted for this job.

Breeding for Intelligence

If by intelligence we accept the definition "the ability to cope with the environment," it should be a rather easy matter to create families of dogs which are vastly more intelligent than the best dogs we have today. When we investigate families of Pointers and Setters, we find a very high percentage whose hunting intelligence is excellent. They have been bred by selection to conform to a definite form of behavior. They supply one of the finest illustrations of what can be done.

Only two human generations ago the Pointer or Setter were expert personal hunting breeds. Taken to the bird field, they quartered back and forth and were seldom out of sight of the hunter. The field trials demanded dogs which ran fast, so fast and so far that they were practically useless as personal hunters; they had to be followed on horseback. Owners of dogs which were most efficient at the field trial kind of hunting reaped a harvest in stud fees. To sell puppies, one needed bitches of the field trial type and studs which were winners or sires of winners. When a litter was advertised as sired by the winner of the Grand National Field Trials, the pups brought the highest prices. Those who bought the pups to use as personal hunters were

The English Springer Spaniel is a heavy favorite of hunters. Because of selective breeding, retrieving is as natural for the English Springer as trailing is for a hound.

disappointed, but found they could sell the wide hunters to field trial men who wanted just that kind of dog.

And so the Pointers and Setters of the old type all but disappeared. Nothing better illustrates the inheritance of behavior patterns than this great change. As of 1971 it is very difficult to find Pointers and Setters useful for personal hunting where the hunters want to walk. That is why so many hunters have turned to Springer Spaniels and Brittany Spaniels, which will hunt close.

This is only an illustration of what can be done. To breed dogs for more intelligence is a long-term, expensive process, far beyond the financial capacity of most dog breeders.

Breeding for Charm

The vast majority of American dogs are kept as pets. This proportion will increase and the size of dogs will decrease, the smaller dogs being more compatible with apartment living. This

Betty White, star of the television show "Pet Set", finds the charm of these 6-weeks-old Samoyeds irresistible.

means that the principal attribute of city dogs, the one most sought after, will be charm. A good example of charm is some little shaggy mongrel; despite its looks, it has won its way into the hearts of the family by its adaptability, the delight it shows in human companionship, alertness, friendliness, selfless confidence in its master, expressions of enjoyment from human caresses and attitude of seemingly always trying to please.

Charm was especially typified in the old-fashioned Cocker Spaniel and is today in many Toy breeds, yes, and even larger breeds. The Poodle's rapid rise in popularity was due to charm. How do we go about breeding for this intangible quality? To begin with, most persons would prefer having a dog of a definite breed to having a mongrel. The constructive breeder of pet dogs must keep charm in mind if he hopes to popularize his family of dogs. Since charm is a composite of many qualities, it comes down to the use of special care in breeding to stud dogs which exhibit it most among all the possible selections of available studs.

The neglect of special care is what brings undesirable qualities into the breeds. Popularity is a special temptation to breed dogs which sell easily without regard to their temperaments or charm.

Any one of the qualities which go to produce charm may be missing. Handling and training contribute their parts. The constructive breeder will take these facts into consideration in choosing sires and dams, along with the information he or she has gained in knowledge of genetics and the general principles of breeding better dogs.

Bibliography

ALLEN, G. M. "Dogs of the American Aborigines." *Bull. Mus. Compar. Zool.* (Harvard Univ.) *63:431–517,* illus., 1920.

AMERICAN KENNEL CLUB. *Pure-Bred Dogs; The Breeds and Standards as Recognized by The American Kennel Club.* 640 pp., illus., New York, 1935.

ANDERSON, H. D., JOHNSON, B. C., and ARNOLD, A. "The Composition of Dog's Milk." *Amer. Jour. of Physio. 129:631,* 1940.

ANDERSON, O. D. "The Role of the Glands Internal Secretion in the Production of Behavioral Types in the Dog." *Amer. Anat. Mem. No. 19, Wist. Inst. of Anat. and Biol.,* 1941.

ANKER, J. "Die Vererbung der Haarfarbe Beim Dachshunde Nebst Bemerkungen Uber Die Vererbung Der Haarform." *K. Dankse Vidensk. Selsk. Biol. Meddel. 4, No. 6,* 72 pp., 1925.

ANONYMOUS. "The Hairless Dog." *Jour. Hered. 8:519–520,* illus., 1917.

ARENAS, N., and SAMMARTINO, R. "Estudio Experimental Sobre los Organos Genitales de la Perra." *Aviceto Lopez,* Buenos Aires, 1938.

———. "Le Cycle Sexuel de la Chienne. Etud. Histol." *Bull. Histol. Appl. Physiol. et Path. 16:229,* 1939.

ASH, E. C. *Dogs: Their History and Development.* 2 v., illus., London, 1927.

BARROWS, W. M., and PHILLIPS, J. N. "Color in Cocker Spaniels." *Jour. Hered. 6:387–397,* 1915.

BISSONNETTE, T. H. "Modification of Mammalian Sexual Cycles." II. Effects Upon Young Male Ferrets (Putoris vulgaris) of Constant Eight and One-Half Hour Days and of Six Hours of Illumination After Dark, Between November and June. *Biol. Bull.*, Vol. LXVIII, No. 2:300–313, April 1935.

———— "Modification of Mammalian Sexual Cycles." III. Reversal of the Cycle in Male Ferrets (Putoris vulgaris) by Increasing Periods of Exposure to Light Between October second and March thirtieth. *J. Exp. Zool.*, Vol. 71, No. 2:341–367, August 1935.

———— "Modification of Mammalian Sexual Cycles." IV. Delay of Oestrus and Induction of Anoestrus in Female Ferrets by Reduction of Intensity and Duration of Daily Light Periods in the Normal Oestrous Season. *Jour. Exper. Biol.*, Vol. XII, No. 4:315–320, October 1935.

————"Relations of Hair Cycles in Ferrets to Changes in the Anterior Hypophysis and to Light Cycles." *Anat. Rec.*, Vol. 63, No. 2:159–168, September 1935.

BISSONNETTE, T. H., and CZECH, A. G. "Fertile Matings of Raccoons in December Instead of February Induced by Increasing Daily Periods of Light." *Proc. Roy. Soc. of London, Series B, No. 827, Vol. 122*, p. 246, April 1937.

BJORK, G., DYRENDAHL, S., and OLSSON, S. E. "Hereditary Ataxia in Smooth-haired Fox Terriers." *Vet. Record*, September 14, 1957.

BREUIL, ABBE H. "Les Subdivisions du Paleolithique Superieur et Leur Signification." *Cong. Internatl. Anthropol. et Archéol. Prehist. 14th sess., Genéve, Compt. Rend.*, pp. 165–238, 1912.

BREIUL, GOMEZ, SERRANO, P., and AGUILO, CABRE J. "Les Peintures Rupestres D'Espagne. IV. Les Abris del Bosque a Alpéra (Albacte)." *Anthropologie 23:529–562*, illus., 1912.

BRIGGS, L. C. "Some Experimental Matings of Color-Bred White Bull Terriers." *Jour. Hered. 31:236*, 1940.

BRIGGS, L. C., and KALISS, N. "Coat Color Inheritance in Bull Terriers." *Jour. Hered. 33:223–228*, 1942.

BURNS, M. *The Genetics of the Dog.* R. Cunningham & Sons, Alva, Eng., 1952.

CASTLE, W. E. *Genetics and Eugenics.* Harvard University Press, Cambridge, Mass., 1930.

————. *American Naturalist, Vol. 46*, 1912.

The Complete Dog Book. (Official publication of the American Kennel Club). Garden City Books, Garden City, New York, 1951.

DAHL, L. E., and QUELPRUD, T. "Die Vererbung der Haarfarbe Beim Deutschen Boxer." *Zeitsch. Zucht. Reihe B: Tierzucht v. Zuchtungsbiol. 37:159,* 1937.

DARLING, F. F. *Colour Inheritance in Bull Terriers, Coloured and Colour Breeding.* A. Walker & Sons, Dalashiels, Scotland, 1932.

DARLING, F. F., and GARDNER, P. "A Note on the Inheritance of the Brindle Character in the Coloration of Irish Wolfhounds." *Jour. Genetics 27:377–378,* 1933.

DARWIN, C. *The Variation of Plants and Animals Under Domestication.* 2nd edit., D. Appleton & Co., N.Y., 1896.

————. *Voyage of the Beagle.* 1845.

DAVIS, H. P. *The Modern Dog Encyclopedia.* Stackpole and Heck, Harrisburg, Penn., 1949.

DAWSON, W. M. "Heredity in the Dog." *Yearbook of Agriculture,* U.S. Dept. of Agriculture, Washington, D. C., 1937.

de BOOM, H. P. A. personal correspondence, January 1969.

DE BYLANDT, H. *Dogs of All Nations.* 2 vols. Kegan Paul, Trench, Trübner & Co., London, 1905.

DE VRIES, H. *Die Mutationstheorie* (Leipzig), 1901.

DIGHTON, A. "The Sex Ratio." *Sporting Chronicle, Sept. 23rd issue,* 1922.

————. "Coat Colour in Greyhounds." *Zool. Soc. London, Proc. 1923:1–9,* 1923.

DONCASTER, L. *Proc. Camb. Philos. Soc. 13:215,* 1905.

DuBUIS, E. M. "A Rose by Any Other Name." *New England Dog,* July 1948.

ENGELMANN, F. *Der Dachshund.* Carl Schmitt, Jena, 1925.

EVANS, H. M., and COLE, H. H. "An Introduction to the Study of the Oestrus Cycle in the Dog." *Mem. Univ. Cal., Vol. 9, No. 2.*

GAIR, R. "Die Werchsformen des Haarlcleides bei Huastieren nach Untersuchungen Beim Hunde." *Zeitsch. Tiersucht u. Zuchtungsbiol. 11 (1) : 57,* 1928.

GALTON, F. *Proc. Roy. Soc. of London, Vol. 61, Part II,* pp. 460–512, 1897.

———— *Proc. Roy. Soc. of London, Vol. 91,* 1914.

GATES, R. R. "A Litter of Hybrid Dogs." *Science (n.s.) 29:744–747,* 1909.

GAYOT, E. *Le Chien.* Firman Didot Frères, Paris, 1867.

GRAY, D. J. T. *The Dogs of Scotland.* J. P. Mathew & Co., Dundee, Scotland, 1891.

GRIFFITHS, W. F. B., and ANOROSOL, E. C. "Proestrus, Estrus, Ovulation and Mating in Greyhound Bitch." *Vet. Rec. 51:1279,* 1939.

GRUENBERG, H., and LEA, A. J. "An Inherited Jaw Anomaly in Long-Haired Dachshunds." *Jour. Genetics 39:285,* 1940.

HACHLOV, V. *Uber Die Genetic Der Hunde.* Zuchter 2:261.

HAGEDOORN, A. L. "On Tri-color Coat in Dogs and Guinea-Pigs." *Am. Nat., Vol. 46,* pp. 682–683, 1912.

HALDANE, J. B. S. "The Comparative Genetics of Colour in Rodents and Carnivora." *Biol. Rev. 2:199–212,* 1927.

HARBERT, J. P. "Collies and Mendel's Law." *Dog Fancier 42:I–IV,* 1933.

HARE, T. "A Congenital Abnormality of Hair Follicles in Dogs." *Jour. Path. and Bact. 35:569,* 1932.

HEAPE, W. "Notes on the Proportion of the Sexes in Dogs." *Proc. Cambridge Phil. Soc. 14,* 1908.

HENRICSON, B., NORBERG, I., and OLSON, S. E. "On the Etiology and Pathogenesis of Hip Dysplasia: a Comparative Review." *J. Small Animal Pract., Vol. 7, p. 673,* 1966.

HERMANN, G. R. "The Heart of the Racing Greyhound." *Proc. Soc. Exp. Biol. and Med. 23 (8) :856,* 1926.

HERMANSSON, K. A. "Artificial Impregnation of the Dog." *Svensk. Vet. Tidshr. 39:382,* 1934.

HILL, A. B. "The Inheritance of Resistance to Bacterial Infection in Animal Species. A Review of the Published Experimental Data." (Gt. Brit.) *Med. Research Council, Spec. Rept. Ser. 196,* 71 pp., 1934.

HIPPEL, E. "Inheritance of Cataracts in Dogs." *Graefe's Arch. Opthal. 124:300,* 1930.

HIRSCHFELD, W. K. "Haarfarbenvererbung bei Hockbeinigen Terriern." *Züchter 5:141–144,* 1933.

HOGARTH, T. W. *The Coloured and Colour Breeding.* A. Walker & Sons Ltd., Galashiels, England, 1932.

HOGE, M. A. "The Influence of Temperature on the Development of a Mendelian Character." *Jour. Exp. Zool., Vol. 18,* 1915.

HUBBARD, C. L. B., *The Observer's Book of Dogs.* Frederick Warne & Co., London, 1952.

HUMPHREY, E. S. "Mental Tests for Shepherd Dogs." *Jour. Hered. 25:129,* 1934.

HUMPHREY, E., and WARNER, L. *Working Dogs; An Attempt to Produce a Strain of German Shepherds Which Combine Working Ability and Beauty of Conformation.* 253 pp., illus., Baltimore, 1934.

373

IBSEN, HERMAN L. "Tricolor Inheritance. II. The Basset Hound." *Genetics 1:367–376,* 1916.

"Idstone." *The Dog.* Cassell, Petter and Galpin & Co., London, 1872.

ILJIN, N. A. *Genetics and Breeding of the Dog.* (In Russian), 162 pp., illus., Moscow and Leningrad, 1932.

—— "Ruby Eye in Dogs and Its Inheritance." *Trans. Lab. Exp. Biol. Zoopark., (1) :107,* Moscow, 1926.

—— "Segregation in Crosses Between a Wolf and a Dog and Material on the Genetics of the Dog." *Trudy Din. (Moskva) Razvitia (Trans. Dynamics of Devlpmt.) 8:105–166,* illus. (In Russian, English summary, pp. 165–166), 1934.

ILJIN, N. A. (ILIIN, N. A.). "Uber Die Vererbung Der Färbung Beim Dobermann Pinscher." *Züchter 3:370–376,* illus., 1931.

ISEKI, N., and TIRASHIMA, S. "Blood Types D_1 and D_2 of the Dog." *Tokyoer Med. Wochenschr. 3192,* 7–8, 1940.

JAMES, W. T. "Morphological Form and Its Relation to Behavior." *Amer. Anat. Mem., No. 19, Wist. Inst. of Anat. and Biol.,* 1941.

KEELER, C. E. "The Inheritance of Predisposition to Renal Calculi in the Dalmatian." *Jour. A.V.M.A. 96:507,* 1940.

KEELER, C. E., and TRIMBLE, H. C. "The Inheritance of Dewclaws in the Dog." *Jour. Hered. 29:145,* 1938.

—— "Inheritance of Position Preference in Coach Dogs." *Jour. Hered. 31:51,* 1940.

KELLY, G. L., and WHITNEY, L. F. "Prevention of Conception in Bitches by Injections of Estrone." *J. Ga. Med. Assoc. 29:7,* 1940.

KLATT, B. "Erbliche Missbildungen den Warbelsaule Beim Hunde." *Zool. Auz. 128:225,* 1939.

KLODNITSKY, I., and SPETT, G. "Kurzschwanzige und Schwanzlose Varianten bei Hunden." *Ztschr. Induktive Abstam. u. Vererbungslehre 38:72–74,* 1925.

KOCH, W. "Neue Pathogene Erbfaktoren bei Hunden." *Ztzchr. Induktive Abstam. u. Vererbungslehre 70:503–506,* illus., 1935.

KRALLINGER, H. F. "Die Chromosomen der Haustiere." *Züchtungskunde 2:441–466,* 1927.

KRAUS, C. "Beitrog zum Prostatakrebs und Kryptorchismus des Hundes." *Frankfurter Zeitsch. Path. 41:405,* 1931.

KREPS, E. M. "Conditioned Reflexes of a Dog in Heat." *Report Fiziol. Bes.,* 1923.

374

KRUSHINSKY, L. V. "Hereditary 'Fixation' of an Individually Acquired Behavior of Animals and the Origin of Instincts." *Jour. Gen. Biol. T. V. 5*, 1944.

―――― "Interrelation Between the Active and Passive Defence Reactions in Dogs." *Bull. Russian Acad. Sci. No. 1,* 1945.

―――― "A Study of the Phenogenetics of Behavior Characters in Dogs." *Biol. Jour. T. VII, No. 4, Inst. Zool. Moscow State Univ.,* 1938.

KUNDE, D'AMOUR, GUSTAVSON, and CARLSON. "Effect of Estrin Injections on the Basic Metabolism, Uterine Endometrium, Lactation, Mating and Maternal Instincts in the Adult Dog." *Am. Jour. Physiol. 95:630,* 1930.

LANG, A. "Über Alternative Vererbung bei Hunden. Ztchr." *Induktive Abstam. u. Vererbungslehre 3:1–33,* illus., 1910.

LEIGHTON, R. *The New Book of the Dog.* 624 pp., illus., London, Paris (etc.) , 1907.

LETARD, E. "Les Applications de la Génétique a L'Élevage des Animaux Domestiques." *12th Internatl. Vet. Cong.,* New York, *3:437–499,* 1934.

LILLIE, F. R. "The Free-martin: a Study of the Action of Sex Hormones in the Foetal Life of Cattle." *Jour. Exp. Zool., Vol. 23, No. 2,* 1917.

LITTLE, C. C. "Genetics in Cocker Spaniels." *Jour. Hered. 39:181–185,* 1948.

―――― "Inheritance of Coat Color in Pointer Dogs." *Jour. Hered. 5:244–248,* 1914.

―――― "Inheritance in Toy Griffons." *Jour. Hered. 25:198–200,* 1934.

―――― "A Note on the Origin of Pie-Bald Spotting in Dogs." *Jour. Hered. 11:12–15,* 1920.

LITTLE, C. C., and JONES, E. E. "The Inheritance of Coat Color in Great Danes." *Jour. Hered. 10:309–320,* 1919.

McCLUNG, C. E. "The Accessory Chromosome—Sex-Determinant?" *Biol. Bull., Vol. 3,* 1902.

MALONE, J. Y. "Spermatogenesis in the Dog." *Trans., Amer. Micr. Soc. 37:97–100,* 2 plates, 1918.

MARCHLEWSKI, T. "Genetic Studies on the Domestic Dog." *Akad. Umiejetnosci Krakow (Acad. Sci. Cracovie) Bull. Internatl. (B) 2:117–145,* illus., 1930.

MARSHALL, F. H. A. *The Physiology of Reproduction.* 2nd edition, London, 1922.

MENDEL, G. "Versuche über Pflanzen-hybriden." *Verh. d. Naturf. Vereins in Brünn, Vol. 4,* 1865.

375

MEYER, ARTHUR W. "Uterine, Tubal and Ovarian Lysis and Resorption of Conceptuses." *Biol. Bull., Vol. 36*, 1919.

MILLAIS, E. *Two Problems of Reproduction.* Our Dogs Publ. Co., Manchester, Eng., 1930.

MITCHELL, A. L. "Dominant Dilution and Other Color Factors in Collie Dogs." *Jour. Hered., Vol. XXVI, No. 10*, 1935.

—— "Mendelian Color Factors in Collies." *Dog Fancier 43:IX*, 1934.

MORGAN, T. H. "Chromosomes and Heredity." *Am. Nat., Vol. 44*, 1910.

MORGAN, T. H. *The Physical Basis of Heredity.* Lippincott, Philadelphia, Pa., 1919.

—— "The Theory of the Gene." *Am. Nat., Vol. 51*, 1917.

NEWMAN, H. H. *The Biology of Twins.* The University of Chicago Science Series (Chicago), 1917.

OGUMA, K., and KAKINO, S. "A Revised Check List of the Chromosome Number in Vertebrata." *Jour. Genetics 26:239–254*, 1932.

ONSLOW, H. "The Relation Between Uric Acid and Allantoin Excretion in Hybrids of the Dalmatian Hound." *Biochem. Jour. 17:334–340*, illus., 1923.

ONSTOTT, K. *The Art of Breeding Better Dogs.* Howell Book House, Inc., New York, N.Y. 1946.

PAINTER, T. S. "A Comparative Study of the Chromosomes of Mammals." *Amer. Nat. 59:385–409*, illus., 1925.

PAVLOV, I. P. *Lectures on Conditioned Reflexes; Twenty-five Years of Objective Study of the Higher Nervous Activities (Behaviour) of Animals.* Transl. by W. H. Gantt, and G. Volbroth. 414 pp., illus., New York, 1928.

PEARSON, K., NETTLESHIP, E., and USHER, C. H. *A Monograph of Albinism in Man*, 1913.

PEARSON, K., and USHER, C. H. "Albinism in Dogs." *Biometrika 21:144–163*, illus., 1929.

PEARSON, M., and PEARSON, K. "The Relation of the Duration of Pregnancy to the Size of Litter and Other Characters in the Bitch." *Biometrika 22:309*, 1931.

PEARSON, O. P., and ENDERS, R. K. "Ovulation, Maturation, and Fertilization in the Fox." *Anat. Record 85:69*, 1943.

PHILLIPS, J. McI. "Albinism in a Cocker Spaniel." *Jour. Hered. 28:103*, 1937.

—— "Pig Jaw in Cocker Spaniels." *Jour. Hered. 36 (6):177*, 1945.

—— "Recessive Sable Color in Cocker Spaniels." *Jour. Hered. 29:67–69*, 1938.

PHILLIPS, J. McI., and FELTON, T. M. "Hereditary Umbilical Hernia in Dogs." *Jour. Hered. 30:433,* 1939.

PHILLIPS, J. McI., and KNIGHT, E. D. "Merle or Calico Fox-hounds." *Jour. Hered. 29:365,* 1938.

PHODKE, V. R. "Rejuvenation by Grafting Sections of Testicles on an Old Great Dane." *Indian Vet. Jour. 6 (3) :208,* 1930.

PICKHARDT, E. L. *The Collie in America.* Field and Fancy Pub. Co., New York, 1924.

PLATE, L. "Über Hunderkreuzungen." *Verhandl. Deut. Zool. Gesell. 30:89–91,* 1925.

———— "Über Nackthunde und Kreuzungen von Ceylon-Nack-thund und Dachel. Jenaische Ztschr." *Naturwiss. 64 (N.F. 57) :227–282,* illus., 1930.

POCOCK, R. I. "On the Black and Tan Pattern in Domestic Dogs." *Am. Mag. Nat. Hist., Sec. 7, 19:192–194,* 1907.

POTTER, CORINNE C. "The White Toy Poodle." *Poodle Review,* December 1957.

QUISENBERRY, J. H. "Additional Data on Sex Control in Rabbits." *Jour. Hered. 36 (5) :160,* 1945.

RCHEULISHVILI, M. "Shorttailedness in Georgia Dogs and Its Inheritance." *Compt. Red. Acad. Sci. 19:535,* U.S.S.R., 1937.

RIDDLE, OSCAR. "Internal Secretions in Evolution and Reproduction." *Sci. Monthly, Vol. 26,* 1928.

ROBSON and HENDERSON. "The Action of Estrus on the Bitch." *Proc. Roy. Soc. of London, S.B. 120.1,* 1936.

ROSENTHAL, I. S. "The Effect of Pregnancy and Lactation on Conditioned Reflexes." *Rus. J. of Physiol., Vol. V,* 1922.

Schmid, B. "Zur Psychologie der Caniden. Zentbl. Kleintierk. u. Pelztierk." *Kleintier u. Pelztier 12 (6) 6:76–77,* 1936.

SCHOTTERER, A. "Confirmation of the Number of Eggs at Different Age Periods in Bitches." *Anat. Auzeiger 65:117,* 1928.

SCORGIE, N. J. "The Treatment of Sterility in the Bitch by the Use of Gonadotropic Hormones." *Vet. Record 51:265,* 1939.

SCOTT, J. P., BRONSON, FRANK, and TRATTNER, ALICE. "Differential Human Handling and the Development of Agonistic Behavior in Basenji and Shetland Sheepdogs." *Developmental Psychobiology 1 (2) :133–140,* 1968.

SCOTT, J. P., SHEPARD, JANE H., and WERBOFF, JACK. "Inhibitory Training of Dogs: Effects of Age at Training in Basenjis and Shetland Sheepdogs." *Jour. of Psychology 66:237–252,* 1967.

377

SHAW, VERO. *Book of the Dog.* Cassell, Petter and Galpin & Co., London, 1881.

SHIELDS, G. O. *The American Book of the Dog.* Rand, McNally & Co., New York, 1891.

STEPHANITZ, M. VON. *The German Shepherd Dog in Word and Picture.* Amer. ed. rev. from original German by J. Schwabaher. 712 pp., illus., Jena, 1923.

STEPHENSON, H. C. "A Discussion of the Spaying Operation in the Dog and Cat." *Cornell Vet. 29:125,* 1939.

"STONEHENGE" *The Dog in Health and Disease.* Longmans, Green, Reader & Dyer, London, 1872.

STOCKARD, CHARLES R. *The Genetic and Endocrine Basis for Differences in Form and Behavior.* Wist. Inst. of Anat. and Biol., Philadelphia, Pa., 1941.

——— "The Genetics of Body Form and Type in Breed Crosses Among Dogs." *Proc. 6th Internatl. Cong. Genetics, Vol. 2,* p. 244, 1932.

———"The Genetics of Modified Endocrine Secretions and Associated Form and Pattern Among Dog Breeds." *Proc. 6th Internatl. Cong. Genetics, Vol. 2,* pp. 193–195, 1932.

——— "An Hereditary Lethal for Localized Motor and Preganglionic Neurones with a Resulting Paralysis in the Dog." *Amer. Jour. Anat. 59:1–53,* illus., 1936.

——— "Inheritance of Localized Dwarfism and Achondroplasia in Dogs." *Anat. Rec., Vol. 38,* p. 29, 1928.

——— *The Physical Basis of Personality.* W. W. Norton and Co., New York, 1931.

——— "The Presence of a Factorial Basis for Characters Lost in Evolution: the Atavistic Reappearance of Digits in Mammals." *Am. Jour. Anat., Vol. 45,* 1930.

——— "Rickets in Dogs as Probably Related to Sex." *Am. Jour. of Diseases of Children, Vol. 36,* 1928.

STOCKARD, CHARLES R., and PAPANICALAOU, G. N. "The Existence of a Typical Oestrous Cycle in the Guinea-pig, with a Study of Its Histological and Physiological Changes." *Am. Jour. Anat., Vol. 22,* 1917.

STUDER, T. "Die Prähistorischen Hunde in Ihrer Beziehung zu den Gegenwartig Lebenden Rasses." *Abhandl. Schweiz. Palaontol. Gesell 28:1–137,* 1901.

STUDER, T. "Etude sur un Nouveau Chien Prehistorique de la Russe." *Anthropoplogie 16:269–285,* 1905.

TEHVER, J. "When Is the Heat Period of the Dog?" *Eesti. Loomaarstl. Ringv. 10:233,* 1934.

TJEBBES, K., and WRIEDT, C. "The Albino Factor in the Samoyede Dog." *Hereditas 10:165–168,* 1927.

TRIMBLE, H. C., and KEELER, C. E. "The Inheritance of 'High Uric Acid Secretion' in Dogs." *Jour. Hered. 29:28,* 1938.

VICARI, E. M. "Inheritance of Thyroid-Size and Thyroid-Structure in Six Crosses of Pure-Bred Dogs." *Proc. 6th Internatl. Cong. Genetics 2:200–201,* Ithaca, 1932.

WARREN, D. C. "Coat Color Inheritance in Greyhounds." *Jour. Hered. 18:513–522,* illus., 1927.

WEATHERFORD, H. L., and TRIMBLE, H. C. "A Further Morphological and Biochemical Study of the Intraneuclear Crystals in the Hepatic Cells of the Dog—the Pure Breed and Hybrid Dalmatian." *Anat. Rec. 77:487,* 1940.

WHITNEY, D. D. "Breeding Blue Coats in Hybrids of Black and Silver Poodles." *Popular Dogs,* August 1958.

———— "Color Inheritance in Poodles." *Jour. Canine Genetics,* April 1955.

———— "The Inheritance of Coat Color in Dogs." *Jour. Hered. Vol. XLVIII, No. 5,* Sept.–Oct. 1957.

WHITNEY, L. F. *The Basis of Breeding.* New Haven, Conn., 1928.

———— "Canine Mental Genetics." *Nordisk Vet. Med. 17:103–110,* 1965.

———— "Color Inheritance in the Doberman Pinscher." *The Dog News,* Aug. and Sept. 1934.

———— "The Diagnosis of Pregnancy in the Bitch by Palpation." *Vet. Med., Vol. XXXI, No. 5,* 1936.

———— "The Effect of Malucidin on Canine Pregnancy." *Vet. Med., Vol. 52,* p. 25, January 1959.

———— "Encephalitis Following Carre Distemper." *Vet. Med., Vol. XLIII, No. 9,* September 1948.

———— "Further Studies on the Effect of Malucidin on Pregnancy." *Vet. Med., Vol. 53,* p. 57, November 1960.

———— "The Gestation Period in the Bitch." *Vet. Med., Vol. 35, No. 1,* 1940.

———— "Heredity of the Trail Barking Propensity in Dogs." *Jour. Hered. 20:561–562,* illus., 1929.

———— *How to Breed Dogs.* Orange Judd Co., New York, 1947.

———— "Inheritance of Mental Aptitudes in Dogs." *Proc. 6th Internatl. Cong. Genetics 2:211–212,* Ithaca, 1932.

———— "The Inheritance of a Ticking Factor in Hounds." *Jour. Hered. 19:499–502,* illus., 1928.

———— "The Mating Cycle of the Dog." *Chase Mag.,* 1927.

———— "Ovarian Transplantation in Dogs." *Vet. Med., Vol. XLII, No. 1,* January 1947.

———— "Resistance to Distemper in the Pregnant Bitch." *Vet. Med., Vol. XXXI, No. 6,* 1936.

———— "The Sex Ratio in Dogs Maintained under Similar Conditions." *Jour. Hered., Vol. 30, No. 9,* 1939.

———— "Tetrachlorethylene as an Anthelmintic for Small Puppies." *Vet. Med., Vol. 34, No. 11,* 1939.

———— "The Time of Ovulation in the Bitch," *Vet. Med., Vol. 35,* No. 3, 1940.

WILSON, E. B. "The Sex-Chromosomes." *Arch. Mikr. Anat., Vol. 77,* 1911.

WINGE, Ö. *Inheritance in Dogs.* Comstock Publishing Co., Ithaca, New York, 1950.

WINZENBURGER, W. "Die Haufegkeits Verteilung der Geschlechtskombination Beim Hunde." *Zeit. Aucht. Reike B, Treizucht. u. Zuchtungsbiol. 36:227,* 1936.

WREIDT, C. "Hvite Farver Hos Pattedyr." *Naturen 47:77–78,* illus., 1923.

———— "Letale Faktoren (Todbringende Vererbungsfaktoren)." *Ztschr. Tierzüchtung u. Züchtungsbiol. 3:223– 230,* illus., 1925.

———— "Aufpaltung der Schädelform des Pekingesers." *Züchter 1:203–204,* illus., 1929.

WRIGHT, S. "Color Inheritance in Mammals. IX. The Dog." *Jour. Hered. 9:87–90,* 1918.

YOUATT, W. *The Dog.* Longmans, Green & Co., London, 1886.

Index

382

Reproduce period, prolongation of with stilbestrol, 78
Reproductive tract of bitch, 36
Reproductive tract, location in abdomen, 65
Resorption of fetuses, 93
Riboflavin, 84
Rickets and Vitamin D deficiency, 84
Rhodesian Ridgeback, 317
Rutting season, none in dogs, 90

Scotch itch, 325
Selectivity on part of bitch, 103
Semen, alkilinity of, 92
Semen, in female reproductive tract, 46
Sex 17, 28
Sex cells, 28, 38
Sex characteristics, secondary, 75
Sex hormones, 75ff.
Sex linkage, 149
Sex organs, 10
Sex ratios, 145
Sex theories, 142
Sexual drive, 75
Skin disease, susceptibility to, 325
Spaying and castration, 104
Spaying and obesity, 105
Spaying, effect on racing ability, 105
Sperm, 30ff.
Sperm, effect of heat and cold on, 32
Sperm, migration in female reproductive tract, 58
Sperm, number in satisfactory service, 89
Sperm, size of, 30
Sperm, storage of, 30
Spermatozoa, 30
Sport, 113
Sterility, 32, 87
Stilbesterol, 77f.

Sugar theory of sex determination, 142
Surgery for cryptorchids, 33

Telegony, 126
Temperatures, effect on conception, 52
Testosterone, 75ff.
Testicle, influence on behavior and youthfulness of dog, 34
Testicle, undescended, 32
Tests for pregnancy, 78
Theelin, 78
Thiamin requirement, 83
Tract, reproductive, 58
Tubules, 28
Twinning, 153
Twins, identical, 155

Uterus, 30

Vaccination, reaction to, 256
Vaginal smear, 48
Variations, 174
Vitamin A, 82
Vitamin B1 (Thiamin Chloride), 83
Vitamin B2 (Riboflavin), 84
Vitamin B6 (Pyridoxine Hydrochloride), 84
Vitamin C (Ascorbic Acid), 84
Vitamin D, 84
Vitamin E (Tocopherol), 85
Vitamin F, 85
Vitamins, effect on reproduction, 81ff.
Voice differences, 243

Whelping bed, 66
Wirehaired Fox Terriers and glaucoma, 332

Yeast, irradiated, 86
Yellow eyes, 152